# MANAGED CARE AND MONOPOLY POWER

# Managed Care and Monopoly Power

## THE ANTITRUST CHALLENGE

Deborah Haas-Wilson

HARVARD UNIVERSITY PRESS

*Cambridge, Massachusetts*
*London, England   2003*

*Library of Congress Cataloging-in-Publication Data*

Managed care and monopoly power : the antitrust challenge /
Deborah Haas-Wilson.
   p.  cm.
  Includes bibliographical references and index.
  ISBN 0-674-01052-3 (alk. paper)
  1. Medical care—United States.  2. Medical economies—United States.
3. Managed care plans (Medical care)—United States.  4. Monopolies.

RA395.A3M3555 2003
362.1'.0973—dc21     2003041694

To my father, Walter M. Haas Jr.,
and in memory of my mother, Carol Ann Haas

# Acknowledgments

I wish to acknowledge with gratitude the financial support of the Robert Wood Johnson Foundation through its Investigator Awards in Health Policy Research Program and the personal encouragement and support of Barbara Kivimae Krimgold, the former Deputy Director of the program.

I am especially grateful to two anonymous reviewers who generously shared their expertise with me and thus greatly improved the manuscript. In addition, Randy Bartlett and Roger Kaufman, friends and colleagues at Smith College, read an earlier version of the manuscript, gave helpful comments, and asked thought-provoking questions.

Discussions and conversations with attorneys practicing in health care markets were also extremely productive. I am grateful to Bob Bloch, Jesse Caplan, Pam Cole, Eugene Crew, Mark Jansen, Chris Kellner, Bob Leibenluft, Tom Reilly, and Jerre Swann. I also wish to acknowledge Martin Gaynor for many extensive discussions that helped to frame much of the material in Chapters 6 and 7. In addition, I gained valuable information and important leads in conversations with Bob Berenson, Mark Butti, Kenneth Danger, David Dranove, Roger Feldman, Ted Frech, Ruth Given, Lee Mobley, Michael Morrisey, Paul Paulter, Jamie Robinson, Bill Sage, Richard Scheffler, Sara Thran, Greg Vistnes, and Kathryn Wilber. The reference librarians at Neilson Library, especially Sika Berger, were also very helpful in locating information and the most up-to-date statistics.

The editors at Harvard University Press have been extremely helpful. Michael Aronson was a patient and perceptive editor throughout the six-year process of writing this book. Mary Ellen Geer's editorial work greatly improved the readability of the manuscript.

Without my family and friends, this book would have never seen the light of day. I will be forever thankful for their love, understanding, perspective, generosity, and encouragement. The example my mother set in her lifetime gave me the courage to start this book, and then after her death to finish it. My husband's love, encouragement, and generosity gave me strength, especially when the going got rough. My children, Carrie and Matthew, were extraordinarily understanding about the hours I spent writing. Matthew's questions (How many pages have you written? Isn't the book long enough yet?) helped to keep me focused on what is most important. The many times Carrie volunteered to cook dinner made me realize she truly understands the meaning of family. My father carefully read many chapters, offered valuable suggestions, and spent a day thinking of possible titles, including the one on the front cover. My mother-in-law even got involved with formatting the notes.

I think Paul McCartney and John Lennon said it best, albeit with one needed addition: "I get by with a little help from my friends"—and family.

# Contents

# MANAGED CARE AND
# MONOPOLY POWER

# Introduction

IN RESPONSE TO powerful market forces, changing government policies, and technological innovations, the U.S. health care industry is undergoing a kaleidoscopic transformation. As part of this transformation, physicians and hospitals, previously insulated from the kinds of economic dynamics existing in markets for most other goods and services, have been introduced to the realities of competitive markets. These realities include greater pressures to offer care at the lowest possible prices, at least relative to rival physicians and hospitals. In addition, rapid consolidation—in the form of mergers, acquisitions, and joint ventures—among hospitals, physicians, and insurers is decreasing the number of competitors.

While no one knows what health care markets will look like when the dust settles, it is certain that this transformation is having (and will continue to have) a dramatic impact on health care prices, costs, quality, and technological innovation. It is hoped that at the end of this transition what was meritorious about the old system (for example, the availability of the highest-quality hospitals and physicians; technological advances that have allowed medical interventions such as organ transplants, hip replacements, and bypass surgeries, and noninvasive diagnostic tests such as magnetic resonance imaging, to become commonplace) will have been preserved, while the ills associated with the old health care system (for instance, the well-documented excesses in the form of unnecessary medical treatments)[1] will have been cured.

1

Usually competition is good for consumers. In most cases competitive markets motivate sellers to keep their costs and prices low. Further, in most cases competitive markets are the best vehicles for allocating scarce resources.[2] Resources are scarce relative to human wants, in the sense that resources used to produce health care services are not available to produce food, housing, clothing, and the millions of other goods and services that individuals want.

Competitive markets, however, do not always work well, and some fear that competitive health care markets, in particular, will not work well. For example, there may be too few physician organizations, hospitals, or insurers competing with each other in certain geographic areas for competition to achieve its benefits. When there are just a few incumbent competitors and when barriers exist to the entry of new competitors (factors that prevent the entry of new competitors in markets where incumbent firms are earning excess profits), market forces may not be sufficient to prevent the small number of physician organizations, hospitals, or insurers from conspiring to exercise monopoly power (the power to raise prices above costs or raise prices above competitive levels).[3] Richard Posner, Chief Judge of the U.S. Court of Appeals for the Seventh Circuit, has defined monopoly or market power as "the ability of a firm (or group of firms acting together) to raise price above the competitive level without losing so many sales so rapidly that the price increase is unprofitable and must be rescinded."[4] Markets with few incumbent competitors and with entry barriers may provide physicians, hospitals, or insurers with opportunities to charge excessively high prices.

## Physicians, Hospitals, and the Exercise of Monopoly Power

Even before the consolidation of the 1990s, physicians and hospitals had a poor track record with respect to conspiracies to exercise monopoly power. Physicians have been found guilty of illegal conspiracies to squash the growth of prepaid insurance programs. Some viewed such insurance plans as a potential threat to physicians' incomes. As early as 1943 the U.S. Supreme Court ruled that the American Medical Association (AMA) and the District Medical Society (the medical society in the District of Columbia) had illegally conspired to destroy the Group Health Association (GHA, a nonprofit, prepayment insurance program in which enrollees received their medical care only from the physicians employed by this insurance program).[5] Their conspiracy included enlisting almost all of the hospitals in the District to deny GHA physicians staff privileges and bed space for their patients and circulating a "white list" of approved organizations and individuals, from which GHA was excluded, thereby making it impossible for the physicians employed by the GHA to obtain consultations with physicians outside the GHA.[6]

Likewise, in 1951 the Washington Supreme Court ruled that the physicians of the Washington state medical society illegally conspired to eliminate the Group Health Cooperative of Puget Sound (a prepaid insurance program that employed twenty physicians).[7] As with the District Medical Society, the local medical society's intervention resulted in hospitals throughout Washington refusing to grant staff privileges to these twenty physicians.[8] Moreover, the society's characterization of these twenty physicians as "unethical" resulted in its withholding or withdrawing membership from several physicians, who consequently lost certification by those specialty boards requiring society membership.[9]

The AMA has also been found guilty of using its authority to deny hospital admitting privileges to a whole class of potential nonphysician competitors—an unreasonable restraint of trade. In *Wilk et al. v. American Medical Association*,[10] the Court of Appeals upheld the District Court's ruling that the AMA's Principles of Medical Ethics, which prohibited physicians from associating professionally with "unscientific practitioners," prevented chiropractors from obtaining hospital admitting privileges and resulted in a group boycott of chiropractors by physicians (effectively preventing physicians from referring patients to chiropractors and accepting referrals from chiropractors).

In addition, physicians have been found guilty of illegal price-fixing agreements. For example, in 1982 the Supreme Court ruled that the maximum schedule of fees agreed upon by the physicians of two medical foundations constituted illegal price-fixing by those physicians.[11]

More recently, the Federal Trade Commission (FTC) charged twenty-three obstetrician/gynecologists in Jacksonville, Florida, with illegally conspiring to fix the fees they charged to third-party payers and boycotting or threatening to boycott third-party payers.[12] The physicians' independent practice association (IPA) was alleged to be a sham IPA formed to facilitate price agreements among its members, who constituted nearly the entire medical staff of OB/GYNs at one of the most highly regarded hospitals in Jacksonville. The physicians signed a consent order in which they agreed (1) to dissolve the IPA, (2) not to deal collectively with third-party payers, and (3) not to fix prices.

Likewise, the FTC charged ten surgeons in Broward County, Florida, with conspiring through their corporation (the Trauma Associates of North Broward) to fix fees at the trauma centers at two hospitals and threatening and carrying out a concerted refusal to deal.[13] The physicians agreed in the consent order to dissolve their corporation and not to deal with any other provider on collectively determined terms. In 2002 the FTC successfully stopped illegal price-fixing by physician organizations in California, Texas, and Colorado.[14] In April the FTC charged the physician members of an IPA that included nearly every OB/GYN with active medical staff privileges at the two acute care hospitals in Napa County, California, with fixing prices and refusing to deal with payers except on collectively determined terms. The OB/GYNs signed a consent order in which they agreed to disband their IPA and refrain from engaging in similar anticompetitive conduct in the future. In May of 2002 the FTC charged two Denver-area physician organizations comprised of approximately 86 primary care physicians with fixing prices and refusing to deal with payers except on collectively determined terms. Again the case was settled by a consent order in which the internists, pediatricians, family physicians, and general practitioners agreed to stop these illegal concerted actions. Although these more recent cases never went to trial and, therefore, set no formal precedent, they still provide interesting evidence of physicians' ability and willingness to exercise monopoly power.

Hospitals' track records have not been perfect either. There are examples of hospitals acquiring or merging with other hospitals in order to increase their monopoly power. In 1985 the FTC ordered the divestiture of several hospitals in the Chattanooga, Tennessee, area because the acquisition of those hospitals by a for-profit chain of hospitals lessened competition.[15] In 1989 a proposed hospital merger in Rockford, Illinois, was not allowed because the court found the proposed merger would increase the merged hospital's ability to charge higher prices and thus would harm consumers.[16]

## Policy Alternatives to Deal with Monopoly Power

Basically, there are two policy approaches to address the very relevant concern that consolidation among health care firms will increase the opportunities for hospitals, physicians, and insurers to exercise monopoly power: government regulation of prices, and facilitation of competition through enforcement of the antitrust laws. Some health policy experts view direct government regulation of health care prices as the best solution to the problem of health care firms charging excessively high prices. In recent years, however, this view has fallen out of favor for good reason—the abandonment of previously implemented state programs for regulating hospital prices.[17] State programs in Wisconsin, Washington, Massachusetts, New Jersey, Connecticut, Maine, Minnesota, and New York have been abandoned and hospital prices deregulated.[18] Under these mandatory rate-setting programs (where a state authority established the payment rates to be paid by public and private insurers), "the hospital community demonstrated an ability to learn the rules of the regulatory system better than any other affected interests, and use their knowledge and political skills to win substantial concessions from regulators, legislators, or both."[19]

Fortunately, there is a better, although not perfect, policy alternative to direct government regulation of health care prices. Enforcement of the antitrust laws—laws that have been successfully enforced in other markets since the late 1890s and sporadically enforced in health care markets since the 1970s—is a potent weapon against anticompetitive behavior (collusion or consolidation in order to raise prices) on the part of hospitals, physician organizations, and insurers.

Further, the antitrust laws can be thought of as a system of deterrence that sends a loud and clear message to all players—physicians, hospitals, and insurers—that anticompetitive behavior will not be tolerated. The antitrust laws influence the economic behaviors of physicians, hospitals, and insurers by attaching a legal risk to certain forms of conduct under certain conditions.

Relying on the antitrust laws and their enforcement, however, is not without its potential pitfalls. Antitrust enforcement must be neither too vigorous nor too lenient. If pursued too vigorously, antitrust enforcement activity could discourage the growth of new and better (more efficient) forms of health care organization. If antitrust enforcement is pursued too leniently, anticompetitive behavior could flourish and harm consumers.

There is ongoing debate on whether the antitrust laws have been enforced too vigorously in health care markets. Interestingly, the record of the federal enforcement agencies suggests caution. In particular, the number of challenges by the FTC and the Department of Justice (DOJ) to health care consolidations seems small relative to the large number of hospital, physician, and insurer mergers and acquisitions. For example, the FTC and DOJ have challenged in federal court only one proposed merger/acquisition between health care insurers, despite the commonly held belief that "the health insurance industry is rapidly whittling itself down to a few giant companies that dominate the health systems of some of the country's biggest cities."[20] Further, they challenged only about 2 percent of the 956 hospital premerger filings received between 1981 and 1997.[21] Similarly, between 1991 and 1996 the FTC and DOJ approved the formation and activities of 31 out of the 34 health care provider networks that they reviewed.[22]

Despite this record, organized medicine argues that physicians need relief from the antitrust laws and has convinced many legislators and governors that consistent enforcement of the antitrust laws (defined as enforcement applied uniformly to all parties) may not be in the public interest. In June 2000 the House passed legislation (the Quality Health Care Coalition Act of 2000, H.R. 1304) that if enacted would have established an exemption to the antitrust laws for physicians, thereby enabling physicians in independent practices to bargain collectively and jointly raise their fees. Since 1999 legislation quite similar to this has been enacted in Texas, Washington, and New Jersey. Moreover, under the state action immunity doctrine at least 22 states have enacted laws exempting a wide range of collaborative activities among health care firms from federal antitrust laws.[23]

Likewise, defense lawyers have convinced the courts to allow challenged hospital consolidations to proceed. The courts rejected the federal agencies' last five challenges to hospital consolidations—allowing all five of the challenged hospital mergers/acquisitions decided between 1995 and 1999 to proceed.[24]

One possible explanation for these court decisions against the federal antitrust agencies is over-zealousness on the part of the federal agencies. An alternative explanation, and one that may also explain three states' decisions to exempt physicians from the antitrust laws, is that a large number of people, including many judges, legislators, and governors, have the naïve view that physicians are too ethical to collude for their own financial benefit and that nonprofit hospitals will not exercise monopoly power after a merger.[25] Still another explanation is that the individuals in a position to make health care policy do not fully understand the economic issues on which antitrust enforcement activity is predicated, and thus make erroneous decisions concerning which proposed bills to support or which antitrust challenges to reject.

In support of the last explanation, the legal scholar Thomas Greaney noted that "those concerned about the drift in antitrust law toward standardless inquiries in merger cases may find their worst fears realized in the hospital merger cases. Left to ramble through the wilds of economic theory, some courts have exhibited an alarming tendency to reach results that a legal realist may conclude reflects their political or social preferences more than a reasoned parsing of the economic facts before them."[26] In addition, he wrote: "Courts have followed a pattern of symmetry between their findings on the merits of the government's (hospital) merger case and their treatment of efficiencies. That is, courts siding with defendants on other grounds uphold their efficiency claims as well while those concluding that the merger will lessen competition reject efficiencies claims. . . . In short, courts may be taking the easy way out on this complex [economic] issue."[27]

## Focus of This Book

If the problem is incomplete understanding of the economic issues on which antitrust enforcement activity is based, we have a serious problem indeed—health care legislation that is not in the public interest will be enacted, and health care consolidation that is not in the public interest will be allowed to happen. Accordingly, this book focuses on understanding the economic concepts essential to enforcement of the antitrust laws in health care markets.

In health care markets, just as in other markets, the key issue in most antitrust cases is to what extent the challenged business conduct facilitates or the proposed merger, acquisition, or joint venture will facilitate the growth of more efficient organizations, and to what extent the business conduct facilitates or these proposed consolidations will facilitate the exercise of monopoly power. The antitrust enforcement challenge is to determine which challenged business practices are and which proposed consolidations will be procompetitive—that is, will have net positive impacts on consumers because the efficiency gains (for example, lower costs and higher qualities) are greater than the associated costs— and which challenged business practices are and which proposed consolidations will be anticompetitive—that is, will have net negative impacts on consumers because the resultant gain in monopoly power is greater than the associated benefits. In this book I will examine the theoretical and empirical evidence from the economics and health services research literatures that help to draw the line between health care conduct and consolidations that should be allowed because consumers will be made better off, and those that should be disallowed because consumers will be made worse off.

The science of drawing the line that distinguishes procompetitive from anticompetitive consolidations or conduct is the science of economics.[28] Robert Bork summed up the importance of economics in antitrust analysis when he wrote, "Antitrust is about the effects of business behavior on consumers. An understanding of the relationship of that behavior to consumer well-being can be gained only through basic economic theory."[29]

Using economic analyses to decide when to challenge potentially anticompetitive conduct and consolidation increases the probability that scarce enforcement resources will be focused on those antitrust cases involving the greatest potential to decrease competition, and thus those cases with the greatest potential to harm consumers. Likewise, basing decisions about when to challenge potentially anticompetitive conduct and consolidation on economic analyses decreases the probability that resources will be wasted on groundless, self-interested private lawsuits aimed at protecting individual competitors, rather than competition. And most important, for ongoing antitrust cases basing antitrust enforcement decisions on economic analyses increases the probability that antitrust enforcers will make decisions that are in the public interest.

In the heath care industry, as in any other industry experiencing rapid transition, the use of economic analyses to address complicated questions concerning the likely efficiency gains and monopoly power enhancements is especially important. In industries undergoing rapid transition, each firm's potential to realize efficiencies and each firm's potential to exercise monopoly power is changing, and thus the line that distinguishes between anticompetitive and procompetitive consolidations and conduct is changing over time. In the health care industry the growth of managed care (a variety of organizational arrangements for financing and providing medical care that involve management or intervention into patients' and physicians' choices of providers and treatments) has simultaneously (1) increased competition and consolidation in existing markets for health care financing, hospital services, and physician services; (2) increased the growth of markets for new products and support services, such as risk-adjustment software, development and dissemination of clinical guidelines, formation and management of provider networks, and profiles of physician practices;[30] and (3) increased the controversies surrounding the enforcement of the antitrust laws in health care markets. Greaney wrote that courts deciding hospital merger cases today "require factual judgments regarding what the future may hold in an industry undergoing revolutionary change. Like pilots landing at night aboard an aircraft carrier, courts are aiming for a target that is small, shifting and poorly illuminated."[31]

Given the increasing reliance on markets to allocate health care resources, to constrain health care costs, and to promote both low health care prices and high health care quality, it is essential that health policymakers seek to ensure that these markets work well. I hope that the synthesis of the economic, legal, and health services literature included in this book can be used to facilitate both private and public policies to encourage those organizational structures and market practices that enhance efficiency and discourage those that mainly serve to increase hospitals', physicians', and insurers' monopoly power. I have tried to present this synthesis in ways that will be of interest both to concerned health care consumers and to professionals of various backgrounds—economists (including those with little previous knowledge of the antitrust laws or the special characteristics of health care markets), lawyers (including those with little previous knowledge of health care markets or economics), and health care providers, administrators, and policymakers (including those with little previous knowledge of economics and the antitrust laws).

# 1

## The Transformation of the Health Care System

Private market economics and the antitrust laws are to the health professions
what Copernicus' ideas were to the western world of the 16th century: a
fundamentally new way of thinking about reality.
~ Charles D. Weller, 1982[1]

Health care in the mid-nineties is best characterized as an enterprise caught in
the violent cross winds of a tropical storm known as managed care.
~ John D. Blum, 1996[2]

THE UNDERLYING MOTIVATION for the transformation of the health care
system is economic. Total expenditures on health care in the United
States have been increasing at an extremely rapid rate for many years.
As a result, we went from spending 5.1 percent of gross domestic product on health care in 1960 to spending 13 percent on health care by
2000.[3] Switzerland, Germany, and France, the OECD countries with
the next highest percentages of gross domestic product spent on health
care in 2000, spent only 10.7, 10.6, and 9.5 percent, respectively.[4]

### What Was Broken and Needed Fixing?

The old health care financing and delivery system (sometimes described as a cottage industry) was characterized by (1) physicians practicing in their own solo or small group practices; (2) generous public
insurance programs, such as Medicare; (3) generous private insurance
plans, such as those sponsored by employers and unions; (4) cost-based
reimbursement of hospitals; (5) fee-for-service reimbursement of physicians; (6) public subsidies for hospital construction and physician education; and (7) little formal accountability to external parties for quality of care delivered outside of hospitals.[5] It is widely recognized that
this system led to at least two major problems—first, excessive costs as-

sociated with the excess supply of hospital beds and specialists, the overuse of medical care services, and the inadequate evaluation of new technologies, and second, excessive variation in medical practice and quality. Physicians varied greatly in how often and for how long they hospitalized patients with the same kind of medical problem, even after controlling for the many factors that might explain these differences in hospitalization rates and lengths of stay.[6]

The excessive costs of the old system are blamed on the financial incentives inherent in that system. The old health care system created financial incentives for consumers and providers to use/produce too many health care services and for the development and adoption of new technologies, independent of their costs and benefits. The economist Jamie Robinson wrote: "The Achilles heel of the professional system was the lack of financial controls. Physicians and hospitals were motivated to provide ever more and better services, since higher costs generated higher revenues. Patients were motivated to demand more and better services since the costs were shifted onto insurers and thence to employers and taxpayers. Everyone was saying yes and no one was saying no to the expansion of utilization, specialization, and expenditure."[7] Similarly, the economist Uwe Reinhardt wrote: "For four decades following World War II, the health insurance industry granted the individual physician not only complete therapeutic freedom, but also the economic freedom to bill the insurer at the physician's 'usual, customary and reasonable' fees."[8]

The excessive variation in medical practice and quality, especially across geographic markets, is blamed on the severe informational problems that characterized the old system. Even physicians lacked the means to gather systematic evidence regarding the outcomes of various medical treatments and thus the effectiveness and cost-effectiveness of various treatments.

The "solution," therefore, must both change the financial incentives facing consumers and providers and increase the availability of information on treatment efficacy and quality of care.

## The History of Health Care Regulation

Regulation in health care has been pervasive. Health care industry-specific government regulation includes (1) regulation of prices (federal regulation of hospital and physician charges under the Medicare program and state regulation of hospital charges); (2) regulation of hospital capacity and investment (Section 1122 of the 1972 Social Security Act Amendments,[9] the 1974 National Health Planning Act, and state certificate of need regulations [CON]); (3) regulation of access (mandated insurance benefits, any-willing-provider laws, and anti-dumping laws[10] that make it illegal for hospitals with emergency rooms to refuse to treat emergency patients who lack health insurance or who are otherwise unable to pay for their care); and (4) regulation of information (such as mandatory disclosure laws).

Despite this extensive government regulation of health care prices, capacity, access, and information, historically self-regulation, rather than government regulation, has been relied on to ensure clinical quality by health care professionals and organizations. Regulation of the clinical quality of care provided by physicians (licensure and certification) has been left to private organizations, such as state medical societies and national specialty boards. Likewise, accreditation of hospitals and other health care facilities has been left to an industry-based entity, the Joint Commission on Accreditation of Healthcare Organizations (JCAHO).

The myriad of health care industry–specific government regulations and private self-regulations are based on the belief that unregulated health care markets do not work well. More specifically, these policies are based on the belief that, in the absence of government and private interventions, health care markets will result in excess supplies of hospital beds and technologies and excessively high hospital costs (thus the need to regulate hospital capacity), excessively high health care prices (thus the need to set maximum prices), dangerously low levels of health care quality (thus the need to self-regulate minimum levels of education and experience for professionals), and patients being denied care for the wrong reasons, such as their lack of ability to pay for care (thus the need for hospital antidumping laws, mandated insurance benefits, government standards for consumer grievance procedures and remedies for wrongfully denied benefits, and government-provided insurance programs).

Even market proponents agree that markets are not the best way to achieve an equitable or "fair" allocation of health care resources. In a market system, consumers' abilities to pay for goods and services determine, at least in part, the answer to the question: "Who consumes those goods and services?" Many people believe that an individual's access to health care goods and services should not be limited by his/her ability to pay for those services. This is one of the major justifications for government programs that directly provide health insurance and health care goods and services to persons with low incomes or special needs.

Industry-specific government regulations are also based on the belief that these sorts of regulations work well; however, this is not always the case. Sometimes government regulations improve market outcomes, but it is also true that these regulations can have unintended, negative consequences.[11] For example, in the trucking and airline industries, government regulation "effectively cartelized both fields by restricting entry, by suppressing competition, by promoting consolidation and concentration, and by permitting—nay, indeed, by actively encouraging—collusion and price fixing. The results were scarcely in the public interest: inefficiency, waste, lack of technological progress, and artificially inflated fares of 30 to 50 percent in airlines, and 20 to 40 percent in trucking."[12]

History suggests that certain health care industry–specific government interventions have been more successful than others. Government interventions designed to ensure access to medical care have been somewhat successful. Specifically, federal and state governments have proved to be relatively effective in establishing standards for private insurers in the areas of benefit determination and consumer grievance processes.[13] However, other health care industry–specific government interventions and private self-regulations have been less successful. For example, in a review of the evidence from the United States, Japan, Korea, and Canada, the economist Ted Frech concluded that government price controls in medical markets "create major problems and impose large hidden costs, mostly on consumers, through subtle nonprice rationing and changes in quality."[14] In the United States, government interventions designed to contain health care costs, such as federal health planning programs, state CON programs, and state programs to regulate hospital prices, have records of failure or unintended consequences. An empirical study using national data for the years between 1968 and 1990 found that hospital rate regulation and state CON programs had no effect on per capita hospital costs, and the current Medicare prospective payment system is associated with higher, rather than lower, per capita hospital costs.[15] In markets for physician services there is empirical evidence suggesting that public regulation of physician fees under the Medicare program (a regulated fee schedule based on the Resource Based Relative Value Scale) has resulted in physicians performing more services (and presumably less necessary services) for both Medicare patients and privately insured individuals.[16] Finally, self-regulation of physicians, in particular the licensing laws, has been shown to serve the self-interest of physicians.[17]

Many of these federal regulations have been repealed or allowed to expire. The National Health Planning Act was repealed, and the Section 1122 regulation was allowed to expire in 1984 with the implementation of the Medicare prospective payment system. In addition, many state CON and hospital rate regulation programs have been abandoned.

There are multiple reasons why these sorts of industry-specific regulations failed or had unintended consequences. The chief drawback of regulation, as pointed out by Kenneth Arrow, is that "it is hard to make regulations flexible enough to meet a wide variety of situations and yet simple enough to be enforceable."[18] Flexibility is an especially important characteristic in rapidly changing industries such as health care. Moreover, regulations mandate change, and mandated changes often are not in the regulated party's financial interest. Accordingly, rather than complying with the mandated change, regulated firms tend to pursue methods of avoiding or minimizing the impact of the mandate. For example, in response to rate regulation programs that set maximum charges per inpatient day, hospitals may provide fewer services per day but extend patients' length of stay. Or hospitals may discharge and then re-admit patients in response to rate regulation programs that set maximum charges per inpatient admission.

In addition, industry-specific regulatory entities may regulate poorly because the regulators are (1) "captured" by the regulated, special-interest groups (such as physicians, hospitals, or insurers) and, as a result, regulate to protect special interests rather than the public interest, or (2) forced to set regulated prices and quantities with limited information on continuously changing demand and cost conditions. Regulators may be captured for three reasons: first, regulatory agencies tend to be staffed by experts on the regulated industry who have worked in the industry and are sympathetic to the interests of firms in that industry;

second, regulatory staff members may hope to receive attractive job opportunities in the regulated industry after leaving the regulatory agency; and third, the regulated firms may cover some of the costs of a regulatory agency that operates on a fixed budget.[19] With respect to the second reason why regulators may regulate poorly, regulators often are forced to rely on the regulated firms to supply the necessary information to set regulated prices and quantities. The experience of hospitals with CON regulation is consistent with the story that large hospitals gained substantial influence over the CON approval process (captured the regulators) and used their influence to limit competition from new competitors.[20]

Antitrust enforcement "can be viewed as government regulation of the ground rules for competition."[21] Accordingly, one must address the question of whether antitrust enforcement will suffer from these same sorts of problems. Are the antitrust laws flexible enough to meet a wide variety of situations and yet simple enough to be enforceable? Will special interest groups capture antitrust enforcers?

Unlike health care industry-specific regulations, the hallmark of the U.S. antitrust laws is their flexibility and simplicity. John J. Miles, an antitrust attorney, wrote: "The federal antitrust statutes are few in number but broad and ambiguous in language, scope, and interpretation. . . . antitrust cases frequently turn on whether particular business conduct had an 'unreasonable' effect on competition. Reasonableness, like beauty, however, frequently is in the eye of the beholder."[22]

Further, unlike health care industry–specific regulatory agencies, the federal and state antitrust enforcement agencies "regulate" in multiple industries. Accordingly, relative to industry-specific regulators, "antitrust regulators" are likely to have less regular and less close contact with the special interest groups of a particular industry. This suggests that antitrust regulators may be less at risk for capture. Moreover, agencies at both the federal and state levels often have responsibility for enforcing the antitrust laws. The involvement of multiple agencies makes capture more difficult.

Nevertheless, the potential for political, community, and competitor involvement in the merger review and litigation processes creates the possibility for capture of the antitrust regulators by special interests. Politicians may attempt to influence the antitrust enforcement process when proposed mergers will create losers among the firms and constituents in their districts, and thus result in the exit of resources and votes from their districts. The results of one empirical study suggest that political pressure is positively associated with the number of mergers challenged by the FTC.[23]

Barbara Ryan, an economist, argues that "just as the regulatory process is used by self-interested parties in their rent-seeking endeavors, antitrust authorities may be subverted by less efficient competitors who seek to prevent efficiency-enhancing mergers," and that in the market for hospital services the Horizontal Merger Guidelines have been "asymmetrically enforced, with the likelihood of challenge enhanced in instances in which mergers incite community involvement."[24]

Despite these concerns, capture of the antitrust enforcement process is highly unlikely because ultimately, it is not federal or state antitrust regulators but the courts that enforce antitrust policy. Federal and state antitrust agencies can initiate suits to enforce the antitrust laws, but the views of these agencies do not bind the courts.

## The Future of Health Care Regulation

Despite the failure and discontinuation of certain health care regulations, health care industry–specific regulation will continue to be pervasive. Increasing public anxiety about the impact of managed care on quality and accessibility has led to an explosion of new managed care regulations. As of 1999, 41 states had passed minimum maternity length-of-stay laws, 13 states had enacted similar mandates for mastectomy, and 17 states had enacted length-of-stay laws for reconstructive breast surgery.[25] In addition, 33 states had enacted laws allowing women direct access (without referral from a gatekeeper) to women's health specialists, and 37 states had enacted laws increasing access to emergency care services.[26]

By 1998 12 states had also begun to stipulate that managed care plans must disclose information about their financial arrangements with physicians, and 11 states had begun to regulate the methods used by managed care plans to compensate physicians.[27] Likewise, many states have enacted "any willing provider" (AWP) and "freedom of choice" (FOC) laws requiring managed care plans to include any health care provider willing to accept the terms and conditions of the plans' standard contracts or allowing insured enrollees to obtain health care services from non-network providers, respectively. By 1996 13 states had enacted AWP or FOC laws relating to hospitals, and 17 states had enacted these sorts of laws covering physicians.[28]

Even the staunchest market proponents agree that regulation of certain aspects of health care markets, in particular quality, information, and accessibility, is essential. Mark Pauly, an economist, and Marc Berger, director of Outcomes Research at Merck, wrote: "Does managed care need some regulation? Our answer is a resounding yes."[29]

Fortunately, regulations to ensure quality, accessibility, and adequate information in health care markets are consistent with active enforcement of the antitrust laws in health care markets. In fact, antitrust enforcement and some government regulations share similar goals—enhancing market competition, empowering consumers, and facilitating the provision of high-quality care at the lowest possible prices. Antitrust enforcement policies are designed to promote competition, and thus to facilitate the provision of high quality care at the lowest possible prices, by making sure firms compete fairly. Government regulations that mandate the availability of information on provider quality (for example, at least seven states have passed "physician-profile laws" that require the release of physician-specific malpractice lawsuit payouts or hospital disciplinary actions)[30] or treatment efficacy are designed to promote competition by helping physicians and health consumers make better production (treatment and referral) and consumption decisions, respectively. Accordingly, enforcement of the antitrust laws and these other government interventions can be thought of as complementary.

Regulation and antitrust policy "often cohabit a market in which competition is partly possible and partly not."[31] Just as in other markets, unleashing market forces to allocate resources in health care markets is consistent with governments continuing to intervene in certain aspects of those markets.

## Why Is This Transformation Occurring Now?

The extraordinary transformation currently under way in the health care industry is the product of a confluence of at least two factors: private and public choices to rely more heavily on market forces, and recent technological innovations in the collection and dissemination of information about health care quality and treatment efficacy. These new information technologies have provided the opportunity for health care consumers to become better informed about quality and treatment efficacy. At the same time, these new technologies have increased health care firms' opportunities to compete on the basis of both price and quality.

## Choices to Rely More Heavily on Markets

Private and public choices to rely more heavily on market forces in health care markets are consistent with our increasing knowledge about the benefits of reducing the role of government as a regulator (or our better understanding of past failures of government regulation), and the benefits of allowing market forces to take the government's place. This view was summarized by the economist Thomas Rice as follows: "Since the Reagan administration in the 1980s there has been an increasing belief that markets are good and government involvement is not; in the health arena and more broadly, markets are viewed as 'efficient' and government 'inefficient.'"[32]

Consistent with this new thinking, the transformation in health care markets has been fueled by legislation to promote selective contracting and the growth of health maintenance organizations (HMOs). Selective contracting stimulates competition among those hospitals and physicians vying for inclusion in provider networks for insurance purposes. Examples of this sort of legislation include the Omnibus Budget Reconciliation Act of 1981, which allowed states to contract selectively with health care providers for care of the medically indigent. Likewise, in 1982 the California legislature enacted A.B. 3480 and overturned previous prohibitions on selective contracting with hospitals and physicians by insurers. The HMO Act of 1973 required employers with more than 25 employees to offer an HMO option to employees if there was a federally qualified HMO in the area.

The courts have also facilitated the health care transformation. For example, a 1963 court decision is credited with decreasing "the ability of organized medicine to hinder physician and hospital competition."[33] Prior to this court decision hospitals were required for accreditation to exclude from their medical staffs those physicians who were not members of local medical societies. The medical societies used this requirement to hinder competition by denying membership to physicians practicing with HMOs. The court decision decreased the power of local medical societies by eliminating this specific hospital accreditation requirement.

The transformation has also been fueled by more rigorous enforcement of the antitrust laws in health care markets. After decades of exemption, hospitals and physicians are now considered within the purview of the antitrust laws, and many of the guild practices of physicians have been interpreted as illegal collusion. Law professor Clark Havighurst stated that prior to the 1970s "both government and the private sector had largely acquiesced in the medical profession's view of itself as a self-regulating body and accepted the profession's hegemony over major portions of the health care system. Thus, nearly everyone discounted any substantial role for competition in the health care industry and tolerated some significant infringements on the operation of market forces."[34]

More specifically, prior to 1975 federal and state antitrust enforcement officials had largely ignored the health care industry.[35] In fact, as late as the mid-1970s, ethical standards of the American Medical Association (AMA) prohibited physicians from engaging in many competitive behaviors that are now considered commonplace. For example, the "AMA's ethical restrictions used to prohibit physicians from providing services to patients under a salaried contract with a 'lay' hospital or HMO, 'underbidding' for a contract or agreeing to accept compensation that was 'inadequate' compared to the 'usual' fees in the community, or entering into arrangements whereby patients were denied a 'reasonable' degree of choice among physicians."[36]

It was antitrust litigation that led to the abolition of these AMA ethical codes. "Antitrust has served as the nurse midwife to competition-based health care reform. Litigation has removed professional barriers to discounting, competitive contracting, and affiliation with HMOs; stopped dozens of private boycotts aimed at innovative financing plans; and discouraged provider collectives from engaging in collusive bidding."[37]

Specifically, two Supreme Court decisions in the 1970s, *Goldfarb v. Virginia State Bar* and *U.S. v. National Society of Professional Engineers*, made it very clear that the "learned professions" are not exempt from the antitrust laws. In *Goldfarb* the Court ruled that the "learned professions" are engaged in "trade or commerce." In the latter case "the Court rejected the claim that markets could not adequately provide for public health, welfare, and safety as 'nothing less than a frontal assault on the basic policy of the Sherman Act.'"[38] Then in *Arizona v. Maricopa County Medical Society*, the Supreme Court ruled in 1982 that the unique features of health care markets do not entitle physicians to unique antitrust rules. The Court held that neither "the fact that doctors rather than nonprofessionals" were involved nor the view that "the health care industry was . . . far removed from the competitive model" justified unique antitrust rules for physicians.[39]

However, support for allowing markets to allocate scarce health care resources is not unanimous, especially among physicians. For example, Michael DeBakey, a surgeon at the DeBakey Heart Center, wrote, "Today patients are called 'consumers,' physicians are 'providers,' and health care is a 'product'—all terms of commerce, not of a profession, and certainly not of a humanitarian profession. . . . Physicians do not provide inanimate commodities, as salespeople and service people do; they treat human beings. They deal with our most precious possession—our health and well-being—and to apply rules of commerce to such activities is unsound, indeed disastrous."[40]

## New Information Technologies

Markets tend to work best when market participants are well informed. Thus the extraordinary transformation currently under way in the health care industry has been facilitated by innovations in information technologies—high-speed computer systems, medical business decision software, clinical expert systems, and computerized medical records—that are rapidly being adopted by insurers, hospitals, and physician organizations.[41]

The development of standardized, computerized medical records has made the collection and analysis of clinical and administrative data feasible. This, in turn, is fueling the move to increased evidence-based practice of medicine.[42] The Institute of Medicine, managed care companies, physician organizations, and others are developing evidence-based clinical practice guidelines.[43] The hope is that practice guidelines will provide guidance to physicians and patients on what procedures are appropriate for patients with particular diagnoses, and thus reduce the likelihood that physicians will provide unnecessary services and increase the likelihood that they will provide necessary services.

These new information technologies are changing the ways physicians practice medicine. For physicians faced with decisions concerning the best treatment for their patients, technological innovations are reducing the costs of obtaining information on the appropriateness and efficacy of different health care treatments for patients with varying medical histories.

By making it possible to use objective data to evaluate a physician's performance relative to peers, new information technologies have also increased opportunities for quality improvement within health care firms. Michael Millenson, a health care journalist and consultant, stated: "Information age medicine remains on the doorstep of its greatest accomplishments. Still, what it has achieved so far represents nothing less than a paradigm shift. We have finally gone from a system that fiercely defended the idea that medical accountability must be defined by the opinions of doctors to a system that accepts the principle that doctors can be held accountable by outsiders using objective data."[44] Similarly, David Blumenthal, a physician and professor of medicine and health care policy, wrote that "the installation of computerized medical records and associated decision support systems creates the opportunity to monitor processes of care at a very detailed level and also to provide feedback for quality improvement in real time. Using process-related data from these systems, providers may be able to generate reasonably accurate statistics on the frequency with which individual physicians and groups follow accepted practice and achieve desired clinical end points in managing a range of diagnoses."[45]

Increasingly, health plans profile individual physicians' practices on the basis of how often they provide certain recommended treatments to patients. For example, with the stated goal of increasing quality of care, United HealthCare, a Minnesota-based health plan, distributes clinical profiles to all internists and cardiologists participating in its physician networks.[46] These profiles include data on each physician's provision of glycolated hemoglobin tests for diabetic patients, biennial mammograms for women 52 to 64 years of age, potassium level screenings for patients on diuretics, beta-blocker therapy for heart attack patients, and ACE inhibitor therapy for patients with congestive heart failure. Physicians can then compare their rates against those of their peers in the same specialty, health plan, and geographic region.

There is evidence that physicians are making changes in order to improve their performance on measured aspects of quality. For example, after health plans started monitoring and reporting the percentage of enrollees receiving beta-blocker treatment after a heart attack, the average rate increased to 80 percent in 1999 from 62 percent in 1996.[47] What is not known is whether these improvements have come at the expense of aspects of quality that are not measurable. Lawrence Casalino, a physician practicing in California, wrote, "Since most of what physicians do in caring for patients is not measured, rewarding a limited number of activities may lead to less effort—and lower quality—in areas of care that are equally or more important."[48]

There is also evidence of hospitals in combination with their physicians making changes to improve their performance on measured aspects of quality as a result of report cards. In Pennsylvania, where the Health Care Cost Containment Council issues reports on hospital-specific and physician-specific mortality rates for coronary artery bypass graft (CABG) surgery, not only have some hospitals dropped certain physician practices because the physicians' results were not up to snuff, but others have stopped providing the CABG surgery.[49] In California the publication of hospital-specific inpatient mortality rates for acute myocardial infarction (AMI) in 1996 led two hospitals to change the medical staff members assigned to treating AMI patients in the emergency room, and three other hospitals to evaluate their overall use and timeliness of thrombolytic therapy in the emergency room.[50] In Cleveland mortality rates for six medical diagnoses (pneumonia, stroke, heart attack, heart failure, gastrointestinal bleeding, and obstructive lung disease) decreased from 7.8 percent in 1991 to 5.4 percent in 1996 (the fourth year of publication for the hospital-specific report cards).[51] In the state of New York, where the Cardiac Surgery Reporting System publishes hospital-specific and surgeon-specific mortality rates for CABG surgery, there was a 41 percent reduction in risk-adjusted mortality rates[52] (the rate declined from 4.17 percent to 2.45 percent) among CABG surgery patients between the time the system was implemented in 1989 and 1992.[53]

Unfortunately, what is not known is whether these decreases in mortality rates are the result of physicians and hospitals improving their quality of care (and/or higher-quality physicians and hospitals gaining market share at the expense of their lower-quality competitors), or the result of physicians and hospitals "gaming the system"—seeking healthier patients with lower mortality risks and avoiding sicker patients with higher mortality risks. At least one paper examining the population of elderly heart attack patients (as opposed to just those patients receiving CABG surgeries) found evidence of this sort of gaming or selection of patients after the implementation of cardiac surgery report cards in New York and Pennsylvania.[54]

These innovations in information technologies have also led to the dissemination of hospital-specific quality information and health care treatment information to individuals over the Internet. Report cards on hospitals in the United States are readily available on the Internet.[55] Similarly, information on treatment effectiveness or the ability of alternative treatments to restore health is easy to find on the Internet.[56]

## Three Interrelated Changes Characterize This Transformation

### *The Growth of Managed Care*

Of individuals with employer-sponsored health insurance, 95 percent were covered by some form of managed care in 2002, relative to 92 percent in 2000 and only 73 percent in 1996.[57] Traditional health insurance plans do not restrict either the provider or the treatment choices of patients or physicians. In contrast, managed care plans influence health care delivery decisions through network development (exclusion of certain providers) and utilization and quality management (exclusion of certain treatments and requirements to provide others). Managed care involves methods of financing and delivering health care services that manage, or intervene in, patients' and physicians' choices of providers and treatments with the hope of reducing unnecessary utilization of services, decreasing health care costs, and increasing health care quality. The various forms of intervention include limiting the types and numbers of providers from whom treatment can be obtained, requiring advance approval of certain types of treatment, and reviewing treatments provided. The common feature of all managed care plans is that insurance coverage is provided for health care obtained from a predetermined group of hospitals and physicians, commonly referred to as the network, which is selected by the plan. Enrollees who receive treatment from providers outside the network must pay a higher share (sometimes all) of their treatment costs.

Managed care plans come in various shapes and sizes. Three of the most common types are HMOs, preferred provider organizations (PPOs), and point-of-service plans (POSs). Although these various types of plans have been thought of as distinct and mutually exclusive mechanisms for providing health care insurance, the differences among them are increasingly difficult to discern.[58]

PPOs appear to be the most popular type of managed care plan among persons with employer-sponsored health insurance. In 2002, approximately 52 percent of individuals with employer-sponsored health insurance were enrolled in PPOs, 26 percent in HMOs, and 18 percent in POS plans.[59] Government statistics suggest a similar picture. The Bureau of Labor Statistics' 1996 survey of small private firms (fewer than 100 employees) found 35 percent of employees enrolled in PPOs in 1996 (up from 13 percent in 1990) and 27 percent of employees enrolled in HMOs (up from 14 percent in 1990).[60] Likewise, the Bureau of Labor Statistics' 1997 survey of medium and large private firms (more than 100 employees) found 40 percent of employees enrolled in PPOs in 1997 (up from 16 percent in 1991) and 33 percent of employees enrolled in HMOs (up from 17 percent in 1991).[61]

The growth of managed care is also visible on the supply side. For example, 91 percent of physicians were in practices that had managed care contracts in 2001, compared with 88 percent in 1996 and 61 percent in 1990.[62]

Interestingly, managed care has grown at different rates across the country. A high percentage of people are enrolled in HMOs in some states, such as Massachusetts with 45 percent and California with 52 percent in 2001, while many fewer people are enrolled in HMOs in other states, such as Alaska with 0 percent and Wyoming with 2 percent in 2001.[63]

With the growth of managed care, health care providers are bearing more risk.[64] Health plans, employers, and physicians or hospitals (in the context of global capitation) can shift risk to provider organizations through various risk-shifting reimbursement mechanisms, including capitation, fee-for-service reimbursement with withholds, and a fixed percentage of premium reimbursement.[65] Under capitated payments the insurer reimburses the hospital or the physician organization a monthly payment for each of its enrollees, and this payment is independent of the quantity of medical services provided to those enrollees. If a patient requires hospitalization or if a patient requires no treatment, the hospital or the physician organization receives the same capitated payment. Just as health insurers accept the risk that the costs of their enrollees' medical care will exceed premium payments, under capitated reimbursement systems the provider organizations bear the risk that the costs of their patients' medical care will exceed their reimbursements from health plans and other payers.

In 2001 about 49 percent of physicians were in practices that accepted capitated contracts, and among those physicians accepting capitated contracts, approximately 30 percent of their practice revenue came from capitation.[66] In California many provider organizations, including physician organizations such as Brown and Toland Medical Group, and hospital-based systems, such as St. Joseph's Provider Network, have obtained limited Knox-Keene licenses that allow these provider organizations to accept globally capitated contracts from HMOs.[67] Under globally capitated contracts with HMOs the provider organization bears the risk for treatment costs associated with both physician and hospital services.[68] As another example of a private insurer shifting risk to its affiliated provider organizations, PacifiCare Health Systems (one of the largest firms in the Medicare-risk HMO business) capitates most providers. In 1998 over 70 percent of the medical groups providing services to enrollees in PacifiCare's Medicare HMOs were capitated.[69]

The extent to which provider organizations will bear insurance risk in the future is unknown. There is some evidence that health plans are losing interest in risk-contracting arrangements with hospitals and physician organizations.[70] Consistent with this is evidence that physician organizations are now moving away from capitation arrangements, particularly global capitation arrangements.[71]

Further, it is unclear exactly how much risk individual physicians, even those associated with the medical groups, independent practice associations (IPAs), and physician-hospital organizations (PHOs) that accept risk-shifting reimbursement payments from health plans or employers, are actually bearing. First, the impact of shifting risk to providers in large organizations is limited by the free rider problem. Individual physicians in large organizations face only a small consequence for their treatment decisions because all members of the organization share the risk. Second, there is evidence that some of the organizations accepting risk-shifting reimbursement payments pay their individual physicians on a fee-for-service basis. For example, in the Twin Cities area in Minnesota individual physicians may not be bearing significant risk because risk-sharing arrangements tend to be between health plans and umbrella organizations representing many small group practices, and these umbrella organizations tend to pay the small group practices on a fee-for-service basis.[72]

Third, those individual physicians who receive risk-shifting reimbursement payments may not be bearing significant risk because they purchase reinsurance or what is also called stop-loss protection. Reinsurance provides insurance protection against the partial or complete loss of money from high medical claims or claims in excess of specified dollar limits. Typically stop-loss insurance policies limit policyholders' risks for high medical claims beyond a certain dollar amount. Reinsurance can be bought by providers, employers, and insurance companies themselves.

It is also unclear how much risk individual hospitals are actually bearing for private-sector patients. In California it is rare for HMOs to capitate hospitals, and most medical groups pay hospitals on a per diem basis.[73]

Finally, it has been thought that health care providers contracting directly with employers, and thereby eliminating health plans as the "middlemen," bear significant risk. However, to the extent that these employers are self-insured, the providers involved in direct contracting may not be taking on additional risk.

The growth of managed care has been associated with vertical consolidation (mergers, acquisitions, joint ventures, exclusive dealing contracts, tying restrictions, and most-favored nation clauses) among hospitals and physicians. For example, between 1994 and 1998 hospitals in markets with high or growing managed care penetration were more likely to form PHOs with physicians than hospitals in markets with low managed care penetration.[74]

With the growth of managed care it was also expected that vertical consolidation among plans and providers would become commonplace.[75] Interestingly, this sort of vertical integration has not been widespread, and many of the mergers, acquisitions, joint ventures, and internal expansions that initially increased vertical integration between insurers and providers during the 1990s have unraveled. Between 1996 and 2000 the number of hospitals owning HMOs and PPOs decreased by 31 percent, from 2,741 to 1,898.[76] By 2000 17.7 percent or 870 of the 4,915 community hospitals owned HMOs, and 1,028 or 20.9 percent owned PPOs.[77]

Many provider-owned plans have been sold to major insurers.[78] For example, CareAmerica Health Plans, the largest provider-owned HMO (in terms of both revenue and enrollment) in *Modern Health-care*'s 1997 survey of provider-owned plans, was sold to Blue Shield of California in late 1997.[79] In 1997 two provider-sponsored HMOs in New Hampshire, Healthsource and Matthew Thorton Health Plan, were sold to national insurers, Cigna and Blue Cross and Blue Shield of New Hampshire, respectively.[80]

Likewise, many insurers are exiting the markets for physician and hospital services. The insurer Humana sold its hospitals in 1992 and then six years later sold 23 of its physician clinics.[81] Other insurers, such as FHP International, Foundation Health, Aetna US Healthcare, PacifiCare Health Systems, and Blue Cross/Blue Shield of Massachusetts, also sold their physician practices in the 1990s.[82]

At least two reasons have been given for these sales. First, provider-insurer integration (or joint venture) makes it difficult for those providers to compete for business from other insurers who view the vertically integrated providers as competitors in the insurance market. Second, providers and insurers have conflicting interests. For example, providers' interests may be best served by health plans with narrow provider networks (in order to direct more business to themselves), while insurers' interests may be best served by plans with broader networks (in order to increase marketability to consumers). In Humana's case it is argued that this insurer's demands for discounts from physicians alienated physicians, who responded by decreasing admissions to Humana's hospitals.[83]

## Horizontal Consolidation in Health Care Markets

Horizontal consolidation (mergers, acquisitions, and joint ventures among firms in the same product market, such as the market for health care financing, the market for hospital services, or the market for phy-

sician services) was a common phenomenon in the 1990s. Even allowing for the fact that available estimates of the numbers of health care
mergers/acquisitions include some double counting and some deals
that were announced but never consummated, the numbers of health
care mergers and acquisitions are quite large. It is estimated that there
were 623, 997, 1,183, and 1,131 health care mergers/acquisitions in the
United States in 1995, 1996, 1997, and 1998 respectively.[84]

### HOSPITAL SERVICES

Hospital closures, mergers, and downsizing have significantly altered
the supply of hospital services. Between 1994 and 1999 the number
of medical/surgical beds declined from 533,848 to 439,426, or by 18
percent; the number of intensive care beds declined from 72,229 to
70,215, or by almost 3 percent; and the number of hospital emergency
departments decreased from 4,547 to 4,177, or by 8 percent.[85] Data
compiled by *Modern Healthcare* suggest that approximately two-fifths
of hospitals in the United States were involved in mergers, acquisitions, joint ventures, lease agreements, or partnerships between 1994
and 1996, and another 14 percent were involved in these kinds of consolidation in 1998.[86] More recent data suggest that the trend toward
consolidation among hospitals is continuing, although at a much
slower pace.[87]

Membership in multihospital systems is especially widespread in cer-
tain geographic areas. For example, almost all hospitals located in San
Francisco became part of one of four not-for-profit hospital systems—
Kaiser Permanente, Sutter Health, Catholic Healthcare West, and
UCSF—by 1999.[88] In Cleveland two not-for-profit hospital systems,
Cleveland Clinic Health System and University Hospitals Health Sys-
tem, controlled 68 percent of the area's inpatient capacity by 2000.[89]

The largest hospital systems are often the result of mergers and acquisitions. For example, in 1997 Tenet Healthcare merged with OrNda
Health, creating the second largest hospital company in the country.
Tenet Healthcare operated 114 hospitals in 2002.[90] The largest hospital
system, HCA (previously called Columbia/HCA Healthcare), was
formed when Columbia Hospital Corporation merged with or acquired the hospitals of Hospital Corporation of America, Healthtrust,
Humana, Epic Healthcare Group, and many other smaller systems.[91]
HCA operated 181 hospitals in 2002.[92]

Similarly, during the 1990s there was major consolidation among Catholic hospitals. For example, Catholic Health East, based in Pennsylvania, was formed in 1997 by the merger of 17-hospital Eastern Mercy Health System in Pennsylvania, 6-hospital Franciscan Sisters of Allegany Health System in Florida, and 2-hospital Sisters of Providence Health System in Massachusetts.[93]

PHYSICIAN SERVICES

Markets for physician services are also undergoing tremendous horizontal restructuring. The emergence of new types of organizations in markets for physician services, such as IPAs, physician practice management companies (PPMs), and disease-specific management companies (DSM), is facilitating different degrees of consolidation among physicians. IPAs allow physicians to own and operate their separate practices, but to contract jointly with managed care plans. Rather than directly employing physicians, PPMs tend to buy physicians' practice assets, such as buildings and office equipment, and then to sign long-term (20 to 40 years) management contracts with the associated physicians. DSMs often contract with physicians on an exclusive basis. For example, US Oncology, Inc., the largest cancer-management company (and the result of a merger between two cancer-management companies, American Oncology Resources and Physician Reliance Network), has exclusive contracts with approximately 700 oncologists, radiation oncologists, and other cancer specialists, or more than 9 percent of the 7,500 cancer physicians in the country.[94]

The number of medical groups and the proportion of physicians practicing in those medical groups are increasing. Between 1984 and 1994 the number of medical groups and the percentage of physicians practicing in them increased from 28 percent in 15,485 groups to 32 percent in 19,478 groups.[95] By 1999, 62 percent of physicians in the United States practiced in groups.[96] While most medical groups are classified as small (between two and eight physicians), mergers and acquisitions between physician groups are fueling the growth of larger practices. In 1998 there were 631 publicly announced mergers and acquisitions of physician practices.[97] By 1999, approximately 23 percent of physicians in the United States practiced in medical groups with more than eight physicians.[98]

There has also been tremendous growth in IPAs. By 1996 there were approximately 4,000 IPAs in this country with an average of 300 physicians each, up from approximately 1,500 in 1990.[99] As with medical groups, mergers between IPAs are common. For example, Brown and Toland Medical Group, one of California's largest IPAs with approximately 2,000 affiliated physicians and contracts with 14 HMOs in 1998,[100] is the product of a 1992 merger between the two physician organizations associated with the two largest hospitals in the San Francisco area.[101]

Until the mad dash out of the physician-management business in the late 1990s, PPMs had been growing rapidly. Prior to 1998, it was estimated that approximately 42,000 physicians, or 8 percent of the physicians in the United States, were affiliated with PPMs.[102] Then in a single year (1998), Medpartner (the largest PPM) decided to sell its 238 physician clinics with more than 10,000 affiliated physicians and to focus instead on pharmaceutical services;[103] FPA Medical Management (the second largest PPM) filed for Chapter 11 bankruptcy protection; and PhyMatrix decided to divest parts of its physician practice management business and to focus instead on clinical research.[104] This trend has continued, with other PPMs (for example, ProMedCo Management Company of Fort Worth, Texas, and Response Oncology of Memphis, Tennessee, in 2001) filing for Chapter 11 bankruptcy protection.[105]

HEALTH CARE FINANCING

The trend is toward larger and larger managed care companies (MCCs). The largest health insurance company in the United States is Aetna—the result of Aetna's acquisition of U.S. Healthcare in 1996 and Prudential's health insurance division in 1999. Aetna provided health care benefits to approximately 18.3 million people in 2001.[106]

Other large managed care companies are also the product of mergers and acquisitions. In 1997 PacifiCare Health System acquired FHP International Corp. In 1998 the merger of two companies in the business of operating PPOs, utilization review, and case management, Beech Street and Capp Care, created the nation's largest PPO network.[107] Prior to the merger Beech Street operated in all 50 states and contracted with over 4,300 health care facilities and more than 320,000 provider locations.[108] Similarly, Capp Care operated in 43 states and contracted with over 4,700 health care facilities and more than 265,000 provider locations prior to the merger.[109] Consolidation among Blue

Cross and Blue Shield carriers has also resulted in fewer (43 in 2002, down from 114 carriers in 1980) but larger independent carriers.[110]

The flip side of this trend is that HMOs, POS plans, and PPOs increasingly are owned by or affiliated with national or regional companies. In 1997 regional and national managed care companies owned more than half of the existing HMOs and PPOs.[111]

Despite this trend toward horizontal consolidation, there are still at least eight large managed care companies operating in most large cities, and many cities have twice that number. For example, Chicago and San Diego had 18 and 16 MCCs in 1998, respectively. The exceptions are Buffalo and Norfolk/Virginia Beach/Newport News with six MCCs each, and Pittsburgh with only three MCCs in 1998.[112]

In a few geographic areas a small number of HMOs provide a large share of HMO services; however, these areas typically include multiple PPOs. For example, three HMOs—Blue Cross and Blue Shield of Massachusetts, Harvard Pilgrim Health Care, and Tufts Health Plan—have provided a large share of HMO services in the Boston area for years.[113] Likewise, three HMOs account for 80 percent of HMO services in the Minneapolis area, and six HMOs account for 75 percent of HMO services in southern California.[114]

## Quality Differentiation and Brand Names

The third change characterizing the transformation of the health care system is greater quality-based differentiation and competition. Increasingly health care providers and insurers are trying to differentiate themselves from their competitors on the basis of measurable aspects of quality and to compete for consumers on this basis. Variations in quality across providers and insurers have always existed in health care markets; what is new is the documentation of these differences in quality and the quality-based competition for consumers.

Insurers are starting to publish information on the relative performance of their affiliated physician organizations. For example, Health Net, a large insurer in California, began disseminating regional rankings of its more than 125 physician organizations in March 1998. Physician organizations are categorized as good, very good, or excellent based on the results of a 17-question satisfaction survey sent to enrollees. The 17 satisfaction parameters include thoroughness of the examination, skill/experience of the physician, outcome of care, access to care whenever needed, and access to specialty care.[115] In August 1998, PacifiCare Health Systems began publishing a "quality index" that ranks the relative performance of its largest medical groups in California. The medical groups in the top 10 percent, on the basis of 12 measures of clinical care and service (for example, cervical-cancer and mammography screening rates and enrollees' satisfaction with their primary care physicians), will have blue-ribbon icons next to their names in PacifiCare's directory of providers.[116]

In addition, insurers have started to try to improve the quality of care provided by their affiliated provider organizations. In 1998 United HealthCare, one of the largest managed care companies in the United States, began evaluating the drug prescribing and diagnostic testing practices of its physicians relative to accepted practice guidelines. Based on an initial sample of cardiologists and internists, United HealthCare plans to get its physicians to perform more tests and prescribe more drugs because the results suggest that many cardiologists do not prescribe widely recommended drugs, such as beta blockers for heart attack survivors and ACE inhibitors for chronic heart-failure patients, and many internists do not perform the glucose-monitoring tests necessary for diabetic patients.[117]

Insurers have also attempted to improve the quality of care provided by their affiliated provider organizations by linking provider compensation to various measures of quality. Providers, like everyone else, are influenced by self-interest, and thus, this linkage creates financial incentives for hospitals and physicians to provide higher-quality care. For example, Aetna US Healthcare started using payment incentives based on quality of care (and quantity of care, which has more to do with productivity) in its contracts with primary care physicians. Primary care physicians are capitated, and the capitation rate is adjusted on the basis of medical chart reviews, member transfer rates, practice growth rates, and number of scheduled office hours.[118] HealthPartners, an MCC in Minnesota, has an "Outcome Recognition Program" that awards bonuses of $2 million to provider groups and networks that meet certain health quality goals in the areas of patient satisfaction, pediatric immunization rates, and mammography screening rates.[119] Blue Cross and Blue Shield of New Hampshire has a "Quality Improvement Incentive Program" that reimburses primary care physician organizations more (a $20 bonus per member) if the organization scores in the top quartile on certain measures, such as breast cancer screening, cervical cancer screening, and childhood immunizations.[120]

More recently, six health insurers in California launched a "Pay for Performance" initiative where the insurers collect information on a common set of physician-specific quality measures, such as breast and cervical cancer screening rates, effective management of blood sugar levels for diabetics, and patient satisfaction, and then use financial incentives to reward physician organizations having the highest scores on these measures.[121]

Provider groups and networks have also begun to base compensation on quality. Results of a survey of IPAs in California suggest that approximately half of the 53 IPAs used financial incentives related to quality of care and patient satisfaction in 1996.[122] Southern California Permanente Medical Group awards bonuses ranging from $1,000 to $3,000 to physicians on the basis of physicians' scores on patient satisfaction and the Health Plan Employer Data and Information Set (HEDIS) standards in mammography, cervical exams, and childhood immunization rates.[123] Prairie Medical Group in Los Angeles puts up to one-quarter of physician compensation at risk for quality measures.[124] Paragon Health System, which operates three provider networks in the Cincinnati area, bases physician compensation in part on physicians' scores on patient satisfaction, compliance with pharmacy formularies, and HEDIS standards in mammography, cervical exams, and childhood immunization rates.[125]

Related to quality differentiation is the fact that some hospitals, physicians, and insurers are starting to develop and promote their own brand names. These brand names have the potential to convey information about the quality of hospitals or insurance plans to consumers, similar to the way the brand names McDonalds and Burger King convey information about the quality of hamburgers and french fries. Many Blue Cross/Blue Shield carriers use "Blues branding," such as renaming insurance products as BlueSelect or BlueCare.[126] At the national Blue Cross/Blue Shield Association in Chicago, there is a vice-president in charge of brand enhancement.[127] In 1996, prior to the discovery of its legal and management problems, Columbia/HCA renamed many of its hospitals to begin with the word "Columbia" and launched a $26 million campaign to promote the Columbia brand name.[128] At Memorial Health Services, a four-hospital system in southern California, actions are being taken to standardize care across the four hospitals (to ensure that patients are treated the same at each of the hospitals) and to develop and promote the brand name of MemorialCare.[129]

Quality-based competition in markets for health care financing, however, is limited by current trends in managed care contracting (specifically, the lack of selective contracting).[130] When managed care plans are associated with most physicians and hospitals, these plans are less able to differentiate themselves by offering insured access to particular physicians or hospitals that other plans do not offer.

There is evidence that managed care plans in many markets, including some areas with the highest penetration of managed care such as Boston and the Twin Cities, currently are contracting with most physicians.[131] Robert Berenson noted that "in many markets a busy primary care physician may have six to ten HMO contracts and an equal number of PPO network contracts. Specialist groups usually have many more, often twenty-five, sometimes fifty, and maybe even a hundred."[132]

Likewise, there is evidence that managed care plans in many markets are contracting with most hospitals. For example, in the New York City metropolitan statistical area (MSA) there are 71 hospitals, and the average number of hospital contracts per managed care product is 66.[133] In the Fort Lauderdale MSA there are 15 hospitals, and the average number of hospital contracts per managed care product is 13.[134]

Quality-based competition in markets for physician and hospital services is limited by the extent to which physicians and hospitals contract with multiple provider networks. A lack of selectivity on the part of provider networks translates into networks being associated with most physicians and hospitals, and thus networks that are less able to differentiate themselves by offering access to a subset of particular physicians or hospitals. There is evidence of physicians contracting with multiple provider networks in the Twin Cities and throughout California.[135]

## What's Next?

Today's health care markets tend to be characterized by fewer competitors. National and regional managed care companies are playing an increasingly important role in most local markets for health care financing; more and more physicians are members of groups or IPAs; greater numbers of hospitals are members of multihospital systems.

When otherwise competitive markets become more concentrated—fewer incumbent competitors with larger market shares—enforcement of the antitrust laws is often viewed as the best public policy. Does this view hold in health care markets? Does enforcement of the antitrust laws in health care markets make good public policy sense? To address these questions, the following chapter includes a discussion of the meaning of health care competition and the wisdom of using competition in health care markets to allocate our scarce health care resources.[136]

Markets for hospital, physician, and health care financing services are characterized by multiple imperfections and differences from standard markets, in large part deriving from the asymmetry of information between physicians and patients and the uncertainty inherent in the nature of medical care.[137] It is difficult for patients to determine how much and what kinds of medical services they need and to determine which hospitals and physicians offer the highest-quality services.

It has been argued that the special nature of medical care means that competitive markets for health care services cannot work well. In the following chapter I will examine the theoretical arguments against competitive health care markets and the empirical evidence on the question of how well health care markets actually work. The answer is not a simple one, as there are numerous empirical ambiguities.[138]

If the specific conditions of the health care industry prevent competitive health care markets from working well, then antitrust enforcement makes little sense. The enforcement of the antitrust laws in health care markets is good public policy only if antitrust enforcement has the potential to facilitate the realization of the benefits of competition in health care markets.[139] If, on the other hand, the specific conditions of the health care industry do not prevent competitive health care markets from working well in general, but health care markets are not working well (for example, prices are too high) because they are becoming too concentrated, then enforcement of the antitrust laws does make good public policy sense. In this case, enforcement of the antitrust laws has the potential to prevent the small number of physician organizations, hospitals, or insurers from exercising monopoly power.

# 2

# The Current Treatment:
# A Strong Dose of Competition

In health care as in no other area, there appears to be a recurring need to
return to first principles, and to talk about why competition
and antitrust enforcement make sense.

~ Robert Pitofsky, 1997[1]

I have no doubt that market forces can enable patients to obtain the highest
quality care at low prices, while encouraging providers to
be efficient and innovative.

~ David Dranove, 2000[2]

Simply stated, there is no inherent inconsistency between vigorous competition
and the delivery of high quality health care. Theory and practice confirm that
quite the opposite is true—when vigorous competition prevails, consumer
welfare is maximized in health care and elsewhere in the economy.

~ Timothy J. Muris, Chairman, Federal Trade Commission, 2002[3]

ANTITRUST POLICY IS premised on the judgment that competitive markets, relative to other methods of allocating scarce resources, do the best job and thus make consumers as well off as possible. Competition maximizes consumer welfare by providing sellers with incentives to produce the best mix of products and to sell those products at the lowest possible prices. This chapter addresses the issue of whether competition can provide these benefits in health care markets—that is, can competition in health care markets provide hospitals, physicians, and insurers with incentives to produce the best mix of health care products and to sell those products at the lowest prices? The answer to this question is crucial in determining whether it is good public policy to increase competition in health care markets.

## What Is Market Competition?

Market competition refers to the rivalry between sellers for consumers. Accordingly, the first step in understanding the competitive process is identifying who is doing the selling and who is making the consumption choices.

The growth of managed care has put managed care companies in the health care consumer driver's seat in the markets for hospital and physician services. Hospitals and physicians compete first for contracts with (or for inclusion in the networks of) MCCs, and second for individual patients. MCCs select which hospitals and physicians to contract with, and thus which hospitals and physicians will provide services to their enrollees. Under managed care it is the role of MCCs, rather than individual consumers, to search for and contract with the best buys in the markets for physician services and hospital services.[4] This makes hospitals and physicians the sellers, and managed care companies (on behalf of their enrollees) and then individual patients (often in consultation with their physicians) the ones making the consumption choices in markets for hospital and physician services.

In the market for health care financing, most people purchase their health insurance through their employers. Employers select which health insurance carriers to use (Blue Cross/Blue Shield, CIGNA, Kaiser Permanente, Aetna US Healthcare, and so on) and then which health plans of those carriers to offer their employees. Then in firms offering multiple plans, employees select one of the offered plans. Estimates suggest that in 1999, 55 percent of persons in large firms and 25 percent of those in small firms had the opportunity to choose between two or more health plans.[5] Thus, insurers compete to be included in employees' health benefits packages and then compete to be chosen by individual employees. Insurers are the sellers, while employers and employees are the consumers in the employment-based system of insurance.

Sellers (hospitals, physician organizations, and insurers) may compete for consumers by differentiating their products from their rivals' products, by developing new production and distribution techniques that decrease costs and thus prices, and by developing new and better products.

Market competition can also be thought of as a method for allocating society's scarce resources, such as land, labor, capital, and natural resources, among alternative uses. Relying on markets and market competition or the "invisible hand" to determine the prices of goods and services is one way to allocate society's resources, or more specifically, to answer the following questions:

1. Which goods and services should be produced? The concept of allocative efficiency deals with the economic reality that the production of unlimited quantities of all products is not possible. How much can be produced is limited by a finite supply of resources. The goal is to produce those goods and services that consumers value most highly. This goal, and thus allocative efficiency, is achieved when each good is produced up to the point where the value consumers place on the last unit produced is equal to the cost of producing that last unit.

2. How should those goods and services be produced? The concept of production efficiency deals with the fact that wasted resources are not available to produce goods and services that consumers value, and this makes consumers worse off. If resources are wasted in the production of hospital services, those wasted resources are not available to produce more hospital services or any other product. The goal is to maximize total output, or the quantity of all products produced. Production efficiency is achieved when each and every product is produced in the most cost-efficient manner.

When an industry is regulated, market forces and administrative processes codetermine these allocation decisions.

## The Potential Benefits of Market Competition

When markets are working well, the first benefit of market competition is that a society's scarce resources will be directed into the production of those goods and services that consumers value most highly. In an economy based on market competition (as opposed to a planned or a highly regulated economy) consumers' demands for different products indirectly determine which products and how much of each product are produced. Consumers effectively vote with their wallets and their feet, deciding which products to buy and from which sellers. As a result, market competition between sellers for consumers will naturally result in resources being directed into the production of those products that consumers value most highly.

The second and third potential benefits of market competition are that each and every product will be produced at its lowest possible average cost (so that no resources are wasted) and sold at its lowest possible price. Market competition provides sellers with incentives to minimize their costs of production and to keep their prices as low as possible. If sellers do not keep their costs or prices as low as possible, then consumers will purchase the product from rival sellers.

Taken together, this means that consumers will make their purchases from the sellers offering the most desirable products at the lowest quality-adjusted prices, and this provides the incentive for sellers to compete on the basis of both price and quality. Accordingly, when markets are working well, allocative and production efficiency are achieved and consumers are the winners: they are made as well off as possible. In health care markets, efficiency can be thought of as "providing the right care, at the right time, in the right place, with the right use of resources, to the right people."[6]

## When Does Market Competition Result in These Benefits?

Five conditions make the realization of these benefits from competition most likely—well-informed consumers, price-sensitive consumers,[7] well-informed sellers, easy market entry and exit, and last, but certainly not least, the condition that the market *not* be characterized by natural monopoly.[8] In other words, competition works best when (1) consumers know about or can learn about the prices and qualities of products offered by various sellers; (2) consumers have the incentive to search for the sellers offering the best deals; (3) sellers know about or can learn about their consumers; (4) sellers can enter profitable markets and exit unprofitable ones; and (5) the technology of production dictates that, relative to one large firm, two or more smaller firms can produce at the same cost or at lower cost.

Unfortunately, if one or more of these five conditions are not present in a market, then competition may not work well in that market. Imperfectly informed consumers, price-insensitive consumers, imperfectly informed sellers, entry barriers (any factor that prevents the entry of new competitors in markets where incumbent firms are earning excess profits), and natural monopoly conditions could each cause "market failure." If any one of these causes of market failure is present in the market, then competition may fail to produce the benefits described in the previous section.

Are the conditions necessary to realize the benefits of competition present in health care markets? Some researchers believe they are not, arguing that specific conditions of the health care industry, such as insured and thus less price-sensitive individual consumers, make competitive health care markets ineffective or undesirable. Specifically, this argument holds that insured, less price-sensitive health care consumers may not search (or may spend less time searching) for the physicians or hospitals offering the lowest prices, and this reduces health care providers' incentives to keep prices and production costs low.

It is true that individuals with health insurance are not particularly price-sensitive in regard to changes in the prices of hospital and physician services. Multiple empirical studies have demonstrated that insured consumers' use of health care services responds minimally to changes in the amount paid out-of-pocket. The Rand Health Insurance Experiment (HIE)[9] provides the best available estimates of the price sensitivity of health care consumers.[10] HIE estimates based on data from the 1970s and early 1980s suggest that if the price of outpatient care increased by 10 percent, the quantity of outpatient care demanded by consumers would decrease by approximately 1 to 3 percent. Likewise, if the price of inpatient care increased by 10 percent, the quantity of inpatient care demanded by consumers would decrease by approximately 1 to 2 percent.[11]

With the growth of managed care, however, there is less need for individuals to be price-sensitive because MCCs are taking on this role in markets for hospital and physician services. Compared with insured individuals, MCCs are thought to be more price-sensitive because MCCs pay the full contracted prices of the hospital and physician services that their enrollees consume.[12] Accordingly, through the selective contracting process MCCs can stimulate price competition among physicians or hospitals and thus greatly increase the odds that competitive health care markets will provide physicians and hospitals with incentives to offer medical care at the lowest possible prices. There is empirical evidence that allowing MCCs to contract selectively with the physicians and hospitals offering the best deals stimulates price competition: three studies of hospital markets in California suggest that the nature of competition in markets for hospital services underwent a structural change as a result of legislation allowing MCCs to contract selectively with health care providers.[13] These studies confirm that putting MCCs in the health care consumer driver's seat stimulated price competition among hospitals.

At least five additional arguments are heard against competitive health care markets; they involve the issues of moral hazard, supplier-induced demand, the medical arms race, quality deterioration, and adverse selection. With the exception of the adverse selection argument, however, the thesis of this chapter is that the changes associated with the health care transformation are making markets for physician and hospital services more like "standard" markets, and thus the realization of the benefits of competition in markets for physician and hospital services more likely.

## Potential Problems of Competitive Health Care Markets

### Moral Hazard

The special nature of health care, in particular consumers' uncertainty concerning the occurrence of disease and injuries, leads consumers to purchase insurance. The first argument against competitive health care markets is that competitive markets, in combination with insured consumers, result in too many of society's scarce resources going into the production and consumption of health care goods and services.[14] Insurance reduces the out-of-pocket prices paid by insured consumers (below the costs of producing the health care goods and services),[15] and as a result, insured health care consumers purchase too many physician and hospital services from society's perspective. That is, insured consumers purchase too many medical services in the sense that they purchase physician visits, hospital days, diagnostic tests, and so on for which the additional benefits derived from their consumption are less than the additional costs of their production. This is called the moral hazard problem of health insurance.[16]

## Supplier-Induced Demand

The potential for moral hazard in health care markets may be exacerbated by consumers' lack of information concerning which and how much medical services to consume. Rather than trying to make consumption choices on their own, imperfectly informed consumers often rely on the advice of sellers (usually physicians) to determine which medical services or treatments and how much of each medical service or treatment to consume. Patients seek information about what is causing their illnesses and symptoms (diagnostic information), and given their diagnoses, they seek information about the effectiveness of various treatments to restore their health (treatment information).

Physicians' crucial role as providers of diagnostic and treatment information creates the opportunity for physicians to induce demand for their services or the opportunity to provide extra and less necessary physician services. Moreover, when the additional fee received for providing an additional physician service is greater than the extra cost of providing that service, the fee-for-service system of physician reimbursement creates the financial incentive for physicians to induce demand for their services.

Accordingly, the second argument against competitive health care markets is that competitive markets, in combination with poorly informed consumers and the fee-for-service reimbursement system, result in too many of society's scarce resources going into the production and consumption of medical services. There is general agreement among health economists and practicing physicians that physicians have the ability to influence their patients' utilization of health care services.[17]

IMPACT OF MORAL HAZARD AND SUPPLIER-INDUCED
DEMAND

There is plenty of empirical evidence suggesting that moral hazard and supplier-induced demand have resulted in the overconsumption of medical services by insured consumers.[18] Studies published in the 1980s found that up to one-third of medical tests and procedures performed were inappropriate or their benefits to consumers were less than their risks. More specifically, approximately 14 percent of coronary bypass surgeries, 17 percent of coronary angiograms, 20 percent of pacemaker insertions, 32 percent of carotid artery surgeries, and 17 percent of upper G.I. endoscopies were judged inappropriate.[19] In another study, retrospective reviews of the charts of adults discharged from a large teaching hospital in 1991 revealed that 28 percent of standard laboratory tests (for example, arterial blood gases, routine cultures, and dioxin levels) were repeated earlier than the recommended test-specific intervals and thus were redundant.[20] Other empirical studies suggest that too many cardiac catheterizations, in the sense that the marginal catheterization has little benefit for the patient, are still performed.[21]

## CONSTRAINTS ON MORAL HAZARD AND SUPPLIER-INDUCED DEMAND

As just discussed, moral hazard and supplier-induced demand are associated with fee-for-service reimbursement of providers and patients' lack of diagnostic and treatment information. Therefore, better informed patients and other forms of provider reimbursement may be effective weapons against moral hazard and supplier-induced demand.

In theory, provider risk bearing can change the financial incentives facing health care providers, and thus the behavior of health care providers. The shifting of insurance risk from insurers to physicians can provide physicians with incentives to recommend only those medical services for which the additional benefits to the consumer are greater than or equal to the additional costs of providing the service. Unfortunately, there is very little empirical evidence on the relationship between provider risk bearing and provider behavior. One study suggests that risk bearing by physician groups, measured as the physician groups' share of patients from HMOs, increases the probability that physician groups will use clinical algorithms specifying which tests are necessary or appropriate for particular medical problems.[22]

While patients will continue to depend on their physicians for diagnostic information, new scientific evidence regarding the effectiveness of various medical treatments and new sources of this treatment information are reducing the asymmetry of information between physicians and patients. It is becoming more and more common for patients to go online and find treatment information for their specific diagnoses. These Web sites are operated by universities, government agencies, and others.[23]

These new sources of treatment information also facilitate physicians' and third-parties' oversight and management of physician practices (or micromanagement of physician decisions). Aided by this tremendous increase in the availability of scientific evidence regarding the effectiveness of various medical treatments, managed care companies and physician organizations have instituted numerous methods for increasing the odds that the care provided is necessary and appropriate. These controls include, for example, utilization review,[24] preadmission certification,[25] standardized disease management protocols (for early diagnosis and coordinated treatment of chronic conditions, such as asthma, diabetes, congestive heart failure, and cancer), clinical practice guidelines, physician profiling,[26] and case management. A 1994 survey of managed care plans in 20 states found that 74 percent of plans use physician profiling and 63 percent use practice guidelines.[27] Using data on 94 physician groups and IPAs in California that accepted capitation from HMOs in 1993, another study found that all the groups and IPAs had adopted utilization management methods, such as gatekeeping (100 percent), preauthorization for certain tests or referrals (100 percent), retrospective profiling of individual physician's utilization patterns (79 percent), and guidelines (70 percent).[28]

There is anecdotal evidence that suggests adoption of clinical practice guidelines and disease management protocols has been associated with lower health care utilization and costs.[29] Humana's national program of disease management for persons with congestive heart failure reduced inpatient costs by 61 percent and the number of inpatient days by 58 percent.[30] At the University of Pennsylvania Health System in Philadelphia, the use of disease management protocols reduced the average length of stay for renal transplants from 14.8 days to 8.7 days.[31] At the Phoebe Putney Memorial Hospital in Albany, Georgia, 16 clinical protocols were introduced to standardize the care of patients in the intensive care unit. After the introduction of these protocols, median hospital length of stay for patients with acute respiratory failure requiring mechanical ventilation fell to 10 days from 11 days, median ICU length of stay for acute respiratory failure requiring mechanical ventilation fell to 5 days from 7.5 days, and median time on the ventilator fell to 3 days from 5.5 days.[32]

## The Medical Arms Race

Since physicians often have a great deal of influence over consumers' hospital choices, hospitals may compete indirectly for patients by offering physicians the latest technologies and services that complement physicians' work effort. It has been argued that this competition for physicians (which is quite different from price competition for consumers), in combination with insured and less price-sensitive patients, has led to excessive duplication of services and medical technologies in markets with more hospitals. This potential market failure has been labeled the "medical arms race" in the market for hospital services, and it constitutes the third argument against increasing competition in health care markets.

MAGNITUDE

The question of the magnitude of the medical arms race is difficult to address empirically because it requires determination of, first, the optimal level of service and technology availability, and second, the difference between this optimal level and the actual level of service and technology availability. What is labeled excessive duplication of hospital services by one observer may be viewed as excellent access to hospital services by another.

In theory, the optimal level of service/technology availability depends on the consumer benefits derived from increases in service/technology availability and the costs of providing that higher level of availability. Service/technology availability should be increased until the extra benefit to consumers of raising availability is equal to the extra costs of providing that increased availability. As one can imagine, in practice the optimal level of service/technology availability is extremely difficult to quantify and measure.

Empirical research based on data from earlier periods (the 1970s and 1980s) suggests that markets for hospital services with more competitors were characterized by greater availability of specialized hospital services.[33] These empirical findings of a direct relationship between competition and service/technology availability have been interpreted as evidence of the medical arms race; however, since we do not know the optimal level of service/technology availability, it is unclear whether this greater availability of specialized hospital services is bad or good for consumers. The best balance between greater access, on the one hand, and higher hospital costs and prices, on the other, has not been established. We do not know whether markets with more hospitals provided too much or too little service/technology availability relative to this unknown optimum. It is possible that these increases in the availability of specialized hospital services associated with more hospital-competitors make consumers better off, not worse off.

### CONSTRAINTS ON THE MEDICAL ARMS RACE

Stimulating price competition among hospitals may be the best method to protect against hospitals providing excessively high levels of services or technologies. Consider the case where more service- or technology-intense medical care is more expensive to provide, and when hospitals increase service- or technology-intensity, they also have to raise their prices to break even. Only when health care consumers (in particular, the MCCs making network decisions) value the increase in service- or technology-intensive care more than they mind the higher price, will the strategy of providing higher service- or technology-intense medical services at higher prices increase the hospital's profits. Under price competition the level of market investment in these sorts of non-price attributes is likely to reflect the preferences of consumers, at least consumer preferences as aggregated by employers or MCCs.[34] Price competition may be the best protection against the medical arms race.

On the other hand, if MCCs select hospitals to include in their networks on the basis of price and the availability of services and technologies, hospitals may adopt new technologies that are unprofitable in and of themselves in order to get contracts with MCCs.

With respect to the empirical evidence on the relationship between managed care and the availability of hospital services and technologies, the results are mixed. There is some evidence that managed care is decreasing service/technology availability, and some evidence that managed care has had little impact on such availability. In support of the hypothesis that managed care decreases hospitals' incentives to compete by offering greater service/technology availability, one study found that markets with higher HMO market shares were characterized by fewer mammography facilities per 100,000 population.[35] Likewise, another study found that increases in HMO market share were associated with (1) slower diffusion of MRI equipment into hospitals between 1983 and 1993, and (2) slower growth of MRIs per capita operated in and outside of hospitals between 1993 and 1995.[36]

The results of another study, however, using an index of technology availability in hospitals between 1983 and 1993, suggest there is no relationship between HMO market share and the within-markets dispersion of technology availability.[37] In other words, this study did not find significant differences in the availability of technologies across hospitals in markets with high and low HMO market shares. This result, however, must be qualified because there are limits to what can be learned from aggregate measures of technology availability, as opposed to measures of the availability of one or a few related technologies. The impact of managed care on technology adoption by hospitals is likely to vary by technology. Technologies with the potential to lower hospital costs may be adopted more readily in areas of high managed care penetration, whereas technologies that increase hospital costs might diffuse less rapidly.

## Quality Deterioration

The fourth argument against competitive health care markets is that health care plans and providers practicing in increasingly price-competitive markets may compete by simultaneously lowering price and quality of care. This creates a problem when consumers are not able to differentiate between the plans, physicians, or hospitals offering high quality and those offering low quality. Economic theory suggests that in this case health care firms may sell low-quality services at high-quality prices,[38] and as price competition among health care firms increases (relative to quality competition), health care firms will select suboptimal levels of quality.[39] Even though consumers value higher-quality products, competitive markets may underprovide higher-quality products in this case.[40]

This is an especially difficult argument to address because health care quality is a multidimensional construct that is extremely difficult to define and measure.[41] There is general agreement, however, that quality deficiencies can be classified into at least two types: underuse and misuse of medical services. (Overuse can also be considered a quality deficiency.)[42] Misuse occurs when the right service is provided badly and an avoidable complication reduces the patient's benefit from the service. Underuse or "stinting" occurs when too few services are provided or health care providers fail to provide a service for which the additional benefits to a patient are greater than the additional costs of providing the service.

Increasing competition in health care markets may involve a trade-off between these two types of quality deficiencies. Increasing competition may lead to more underuse, but less misuse of medical services. Prior to the growth of managed care, most physicians worked in relatively isolated environments with few opportunities to monitor and correct the misuses of medical services. The empirical evidence reviewed in the next section suggests that misuse of health care services has been a significant problem. Consolidation among physicians, increasing competition among providers and among health plans, and advances in information technology, however, may increase health care quality by decreasing the misuse of health care services. This possibility is discussed in the following sections.

MAGNITUDE OF THE QUALITY PROBLEM

Quality problems have existed in health care markets characterized both by intense competition and by lackadaisical competition.[43] Independent of the level of market competition, empirical studies have documented serious quality deficiencies, measured as both misuse of services (medical errors) and underuse of services, in the health care system in the United States.[44] According to an Institute of Medicine report, medical errors during hospitalization are responsible for between 44,000 and 98,000 deaths in the United States each year.[45]

The jury is still out on the underprovision of health care services because we are just starting to develop methods to measure the extent of stinting. Unfortunately, the available news is not good. Studies suggest that underprovision of medical care services may be a significant problem in our health care system. For example, a 1988 study by the U.S. General Accounting Office found evidence that many cancer patients are receiving too few services. The study concluded, "20 percent of those with Hodgkin's disease, 25 percent of those with one type of lung cancer, 60 percent of those with rectum cancer, 94 percent of colon cancer patients did not receive what [the National Cancer Institute] considers state-of-the-art treatment."[46] A 1993 study of elderly heart attack patients in four states documented underprovision of treatment relative to the voluntary guidelines issued by the American Heart Association and the American College of Cardiology.[47] One-fifth of heart attack patients who needed thrombolytic clot busters did not receive them. A four-year study of Medicare recipients in New Jersey documented underprovision of beta-blocker drugs.[48] Only one-fifth of eligible, hospitalized patients received the drugs, and those who did not receive the drugs had a 43 percent greater chance of dying.

We do not know whether stinting increases or decreases with the competitiveness of markets. Only one study directly examines the relationship between price competition and quality in the market for hospital services. Using data on hospitalized heart-attack patients before and after the dissolution of the hospital rate-setting program in New Jersey, this study found that elimination of the hospital rate-setting program and the associated increase in price competition among hospitals was associated with lower hospital quality, measured as lower utilization of inpatient cardiac procedures (cardiac catheterization) and higher inpatient mortality rates.[49] This finding on the impact of deregulation, however, may not apply to hospitals that have not been recently subject to rate regulation and instead are located in markets transitioning from some price competition to more intense price competition. It is also unclear whether the lower use of inpatient cardiac procedures associated with deregulation made consumers better or worse off; it is possible that unnecessary inpatient cardiac procedures were performed under the rate-setting program. The relationship between price regulation and quality is discussed further in Chapter 3.

Studies examining the relationship between managed care and quality have not found evidence of greater stinting under managed care. For example, a study using national data from 1996 and 1997 did not find evidence of reduced use of hospital days, surgeries, or emergency room visits among enrollees in HMOs as compared with persons with other types of insurance.[50] In fact, enrollees in HMOs made more visits to physician and nonphysician practitioners and were more likely to obtain flu shots and (for women over 40) mammograms than persons with other types of insurance.[51]

Theory suggests that provider reimbursement method influences the extent of stinting. Reimbursing providers on a prospective basis (for example, Medicare's system which pays hospitals on the basis of patients' Diagnosis Related Group or HMOs' systems which pay hospitals on the basis of a fixed per diem payment) may result in hospitals and physicians providing too few services to high-cost patients as well as the "dumping" of high-cost patients.[52]

On a more positive note, partial capitation, rather than full capitation, can eliminate plans' and providers' incentives to stint[53] (and to cream-skim low-risk individuals, as discussed later in this chapter). Under partial capitation, health care firms are paid partly on the basis of risk-adjusted capitation payments and partly on the basis of the actual services delivered. Partial capitation reduces plans' and providers' incentives to stint (and cream-skim) by reducing the financial losses on high-risk, high-cost individuals. Further, in California there is evidence that many capitated physician organizations have quality assurance programs to monitor underuse of preventive services.[54]

CONSTRAINTS ON DECLINING HEALTH CARE QUALITY

The newest and possibly most effective constraint is the increasing capability of consumers to learn about plan- and provider-specific quality, and thus their increasing abilities to punish those plans, hospitals, and physicians providing too little quality and to reward those plans, hospitals, and physicians providing the best care. Economic theory suggests that when consumers are informed and thus can make their consumption choices based on seller-specific quality, sellers will provide high-quality products.[55] Sellers will have the incentive to compete for consumers on the basis of both price and nonprice variables, such as quality. When consumers are capable of determining which sellers offer higher-quality products and which ones offer lower-quality products, sellers offering higher quality will be able to charge higher prices.[56]

Consumers have always been able to ask their friends, relatives, co-workers, physicians, and others for recommendations concerning which health plans, physicians, and hospitals provide high-quality care. In this way consumers have been able to learn about plans' and providers' reputations based on the quality of care provided in the past. In addition to reputations, consumers have been able to use other quality indicators, such as brand name, teaching status,[57] or medical school affiliation, to learn about quality.[58]

Advances in information technology and research methods[59] have made reliable and precise measurement of plan- and provider-specific quality more feasible. As discussed in Chapter 1, the development of high-speed computer systems and standardized, computerized medical records has made the collection and analysis of clinical and administrative data feasible. This, in turn, has made measurement and comparison of quality within and across insurance plans, hospitals, and physician organizations feasible.

PLAN-LEVEL INFORMATION

The most prominent example of a health-plan-specific report card is the Quality Compass, based on enrollee satisfaction surveys and performance data from the Health Plan Employer Data and Information Set (HEDIS). The Quality Compass, directed by the National Committee on Quality Assurance (NCQA), is a collaborative effort between public and private buyers and the managed care industry. The performance data in HEDIS includes measures of the effectiveness of care (for instance, the proportion of adult women receiving Pap smears and the proportion of children who are up to date on their immunizations), the availability and accessibility of health care providers, use of services, and health plan stability (disenrollment rates and physician turnover rates).[60]

State governments have been quite active on the report card front as well. In 1997 both Maryland and New Jersey released their first report cards on commercial HMOs.[61] The California Public Employees Retirement System (CalPERS), which provides health insurance for over a million California public employees, retirees, and their dependents, began issuing plan-level report cards in 1995. CalPERS participates in the California Cooperative Healthcare Reporting Initiative (CCHRI), an organization that collects, analyzes, and reports data on health plan performance. Twenty-two health plans (representing 95 percent of commercially enrolled HMO members in California) provide data, including HEDIS indicators, to CCHRI.[62] Similarly, starting in 1998 the Texas Health Care Information Council has issued reports on whether local HMOs' performances are higher, lower, or equal to state averages on rates of childhood immunizations, breast and cervical cancer screening, chlamydia screening, cholesterol management after acute cardiovascular events, comprehensive diabetic care, prenatal care, and other measures of service delivery.[63]

There are also examples of plan-level report cards developed by private employers and purchasing groups.[64]

PROVIDER-LEVEL INFORMATION

Provider-specific information is collected and disseminated by state government agencies, employer groups, and health plans; it is published in report cards and is increasingly available on the Internet.[65] Examples of state government agencies active in this area include the California Office of Statewide Health Planning and Development, which publishes reports comparing hospitals on the basis of risk-adjusted mortality rates of heart attack patients.[66] Similarly, the New York State Department of Health began publishing a report on hospital-specific coronary artery bypass graft (CABG) surgery outcomes in 1990 and surgeon-specific CABG surgery outcomes in 1991. The New York reports contain information on the number of cases, the number of deaths, observed mortality rates, expected mortality rates, and risk-adjusted mortality rates.[67]

Examples of employer groups active in this area include the Pacific Business Group on Health, a group of 33 employers which publishes a study of patient satisfaction with medical groups and physician networks in California and the Pacific Northwest.[68] This report ranks groups and networks on patient satisfaction, ease of getting referrals, and their records of keeping blood pressure and cholesterol under control and counseling patients on preventive care. Likewise, in Cleveland, Ohio, a report on local hospitals' relative performance on such measures as adjusted in-hospital mortality rates, patient satisfaction, costs, cesarean-section rates, and length of stay was published on the front page of the *Plain Dealer* (Cleveland's local newspaper) for many years. Hospitals were rated as better than expected, as expected, or worse than expected in surgery, general medicine, intensive care, and obstetrics and gynecology.[69] Unfortunately, this program was terminated in 1999 after the Cleveland Clinic, one of the largest hospitals in the area, decided to stop supplying the program with quality data.[70] More recently, the Leapfrog Group, a group of Fortune 500 companies and other large purchasers of medical care, began publishing information on hospitals' relative performance in three areas deemed to reduce medical errors—whether hospitals computerize physicians' orders, staff their intensive care units with physicians who are intensive care specialists, and have extensive experience providing particular medical procedures, such as coronary-artery bypass surgeries.[71]

In addition to the provider-specific information disseminated by state agencies and employer groups, health plans are publishing information on the relative performance of their affiliated physician organizations. Examples of this were presented in Chapter 1, along with health plans' experiments with the use of financial rewards based on the relative performance of physician organizations.

Physician organizations also use physician-specific information to encourage physicians to provide higher-quality care. Data from a nationally representative sample of physician organizations in 2001 suggest that physician organizations pay individual physicians based, at least in part, on the individual physician's measures of patient satisfaction (24 percent) and specific measures of quality, such as rates of preventive care services for their patients (17 percent).[72]

## IS PLAN- AND PROVIDER-SPECIFIC INFORMATION WORTH READING?

David Eddy, a mathematician and physician, wrote that available measures of quality can be "blunt, expensive, incomplete, and distorting. And unless great care is taken, they can easily be inaccurate and misleading."[73]

At least in theory, risk-adjusted quality measures can reveal differences in quality of care across providers, since all hospitals and physician organizations face similar constraints with respect to the availability of effective medical treatments. Risk-adjustment is necessary because patients' health outcomes are a function of multiple factors, including some which are under providers' control (the quality of care provided) and some which are not (random chance and patients' risk factors, such as age or severity of illness). Recent studies support the validity of risk-adjusted mortality rates as a measure of hospital performance. The California Office of Statewide Health Planning and Development, for example, found that patients in hospitals with low heart attack mortality rates were more likely to receive high-quality care, measured as good treatment for heart attacks—the receipt of aspirin therapy within six hours, heparin, revascularization, coronary angiography, and pulmonary artery catheterization.[74]

Our current ability to risk-adjust, however, is quite limited. As a result, even risk-adjusted mortality rates may not be valid measures of providers' actual performance with respect to quality. One study found that the use of different risk-adjustment methods resulted in dramatically different rankings of hospitals and concluded that the current methods used to produce comparisons of risk-adjusted mortality rates across hospitals are inadequate to isolate quality differences.[75] In other words, currently available risk-adjusted mortality rates may not be able to distinguish accurately between hospitals providing high-quality and those providing poor-quality care.

Specific criticisms of plan-level report cards include the view that the reported measures of quality are invalid because they are self-reported by the plans[76] or subjective. Inclusion of subjective information, such as patient satisfaction data, will create problems if the subjective measures of quality are unrelated to other measures of quality. If, for example, health outcomes and patient satisfaction are not related, then health care consumers cannot be confident that health plans (or providers) with the highest patient satisfaction ratings are actually the highest-quality plans (or providers).

The evidence suggests at best a weak relationship between patient satisfaction and clinical measures of quality, as illustrated by a report by the NCQA based on the 1999 HEDIS. Specifically, 63 percent of individuals in health plans that scored in the top 25 percent on the HEDIS measures gave their plans high marks on patient satisfaction, while 55 percent of individuals in health plans that scored in the bottom 75 percent on the HEDIS measures gave their plans high marks on patient satisfaction.[77] Consistent with this, there is other evidence that patient satisfaction and clinical measures of quality are not highly correlated.[78]

## WILL HEALTH CARE CONSUMERS USE THE AVAILABLE INFORMATION?

It is really too early to answer this question, as few individual health care consumers even have access to plan- or provider-specific information on quality. The results of a 1997 survey of over 1,500 private and public employers with 200 or more employees suggest that just 1 percent provided HEDIS data to assist their employees in choosing among health plans.[79] A more recent survey of Fortune 500 companies found that although 93 percent of those companies collected quality information on health carriers and 83 percent used this information on quality in the selection of health carriers for their employees, only 35 percent of those companies disseminated these quality data to their employees in 1999.[80]

However, based on the experiences of some of the pioneers in this area, such as the federal government, General Motors, and the Buyers' Health Care Action Group in Minnesota (a coalition of 26 large employers who contract directly with provider care systems), it appears that individuals, if given the opportunity, will use the available price and quality information to select their health plans and providers.[81] Starting in 1996 General Motors began distributing report cards[82] indicating health plan performance in many areas including NCQA accreditation, access to care (appointment waiting time and access to mental health services), patient satisfaction with an HMO's physicians and overall care, and performance in caring for patients with chronic illnesses.[83] In addition, General Motors began separating HMOs into categories based on costs and quality, and setting employees' premium contributions according to HMOs in the best category, the benchmark HMOs. Thus, in 1998 a family in a benchmark HMO paid a premium of $19/month, while a family in a poor-performing HMO paid $175/month.[84]

General Motors' information and benchmarking program resulted in a large migration of enrollees to the highest-rated HMOs. Between 1996 and 1998 enrollment in the benchmark HMOs grew by 30 percent, while fair-performing plans lost 23 percent of their GM enrollees and poor-performing plans lost 82 percent of their GM enrollees.[85]

It is no surprise that individuals switched from the higher-priced and lower-quality plans to the lower-priced and higher-quality plans. Yet it is unclear whether they made the switch to avoid the relatively high out-of-pocket prices or to avoid the relatively lower-quality plans. One study addressed this issue, or more specifically examined the impact of the report card information on plan enrollment in 1996 and 1997 while controlling for out-of-pocket price differences across plans, and found that the quality ratings do matter: specifically, that employees tended to avoid plans with many below-average ratings relative to plans with average ratings. However, employees were not attracted to plans with many superior ratings.[86]

Consistent with the General Motors case, preliminary evidence from the Buyers' Health Care Action Group suggests that when employees receive comparative information on member satisfaction with provider care systems and when they pay higher premiums for higher-cost provider care systems, employees vote with their feet. Among the medium-cost provider systems, the one with the highest member satisfaction rating in 1997 had the largest gain in market share in 1998.[87]

One study did find that at one Fortune 100 company, provision of comparative health plan information for the first time had little impact on employees' health plan choices.[88] This result, however, should be interpreted with caution because individuals may decline to use comparative plan (or provider) information when it is first introduced for reasons that can be expected to disappear with time and experience, such as lack of understanding of the quality measures[89] and the often correct belief that the newly developed measures are not very helpful.[90] With time and experience quality measures will become more accurate and reliable, and thus more helpful.

### OTHER CONSTRAINTS ON QUALITY DETERIORATION

The other mechanisms in health care markets that protect consumers against quality deficiencies, such as medical errors and systematic underprovision of care, include the selective contracting process; the American Medical Society's *Code of Medical Ethics*;[91] licensure as a condition of practice; peer review; accreditation or certification of hospitals, physicians, and managed care organizations; and the medical malpractice laws.

MCCs (possibly the best informed shoppers) can use the selective contracting process to exclude those hospitals or physician organizations providing lower-quality care. For example, Anthem recently created coronary-care networks in Ohio, Kentucky, and Indiana that exclude hospitals that fail to meet benchmarks for keeping death and complication rates low in cardiac surgery and angioplasty.[92] However, this sort of quality-based contracting by MCCs may not be happening consistently across states. A study of patients in New York State between 1993 and 1996 suggests that patients with managed care insurance were less likely to undergo CABG surgery at lower-mortality hospitals compared with patients with fee-for-service insurance.[93]

If one looks at HMOs in particular, there is again variation across states in quality-based contracting. The evidence from California suggests that HMOs are shopping for high-quality providers on behalf of their enrollees, while the evidence from Florida suggests otherwise. A survey of four HMOs in California found that the HMOs used measures of quality, in addition to geographic location and price, to identify potential tertiary care hospitals for contracting purposes.[94] The surveyed HMOs used a combination of methods to assess quality of care, including outcomes data, hospital reputation, and the development of quality assurance programs by hospitals. In addition, the results of two other studies suggest that HMOs in California are using quality measures to selectively contract with higher-quality hospitals. The first of these found that HMO patients who underwent CABG surgery in California in 1991 were more likely to receive care at hospitals with lower than expected CABG mortality (higher measured quality) than insured non-HMO patients.[95] Similarly, the second study found that HMO patients who underwent CABG surgery in California in 1994 were more likely to obtain their surgeries in hospitals with lower death rates for that surgery than insured non-HMO patients.[96] However, in contrast to these results for California, the second study found that HMO and non-HMO patients in Florida were similarly distributed across hospitals with high and low death rates for CABG surgery.

The AMA's *Code of Medical Ethics* covers many subjects, including the patient-physician relationship and professional responsibilities. Some view these ethical guidelines as attempts to use moral suasion to persuade physicians to adopt the role of agent for patients—to provide the care that patients would choose if they had the same information as the physician.[97] The AMA and state medical societies enforce the AMA's ethical guidelines, but unfortunately studies of their effect on physicians' practices do not exist.[98] Interestingly, the current *Code* also encourages competition: "Competition between and among physicians and other health care practitioners on the basis of competitive factors such as quality of services, skill, experience, miscellaneous conveniences offered to patients, credit terms, fees charged, etc., is not only ethical but is encouraged."[99]

Hospitals are required to obtain a state license to operate and are required to undergo review by Peer Review Organizations. In addition, most hospitals voluntarily seek accreditation by the JCAHO. To be accredited, hospitals must comply with JCAHO standards for patient safety and quality of care. The ability of the JCAHO to detect substandard patterns of care, however, has been recently questioned.[100]

State regulation of insurers ensures the financial solvency of insurance companies and mandates the coverage of certain insurance benefits. Further, health plans can voluntarily seek accreditation from the NCQA and the JCAHO. By early 1997 approximately 50 percent of licensed HMOs had been reviewed for accreditation by the NCQA.[101] The NCQA sends a survey team to review how a health plan manages its delivery system and its administrative services. As of 1997 only about 40 percent of health plans reviewed by NCQA had received full three-year accreditation. Of the remaining plans, 37 percent received a one-year accreditation, 11 percent received "provisional" accreditation, and 11 percent were denied accreditation.[102] However, a 1997 survey of large employers found that only 35 percent of these firms were familiar with NCQA's accreditation system, and even fewer firms (9 percent) required NCQA accreditation for health plan selection.[103]

Physicians are required to obtain a license to practice medicine. While licensure cannot distinguish high-quality from low-quality physicians, it can be thought of as a means to create a floor on quality of care. State medical boards ensure that all licensed physicians have adequate education and can revoke, suspend, or restrict physicians' licenses for misconduct and negligence. In 1997 state medical boards revoked the licenses of 1,639 physicians for various reasons, including substandard care, unprofessional conduct, substance abuse, and negligence.[104] The NCQA also has a physician organization certification program that certifies that a medical office is in compliance with specific standards.

The medical malpractice laws may also create incentives for physicians and, in a few states, health plans[105] to provide higher-quality care. Tort law holds physicians liable for conduct that falls below a certain standard of care. Under most circumstances this standard is defined by reference to the usual and customary practice among medical providers in the same specialty and in similar circumstances.

However, it is believed that the deterrence benefits of the malpractice system or the extent to which this system and its threat of liability makes physicians more careful are quite small. The malpractice system's lack of effectiveness at promoting quality may be due to the discrepancy between deserving plaintiffs and judicial outcomes and the inability of malpractice insurers to experience rate liability policies.[106] There is some evidence, however, that the malpractice system induces physicians to spend more time per patient visit and induces older physicians and generalists to see fewer high-risk cases.[107]

Some believe that medical malpractice laws that would give health plans responsibility for medical malpractice would result in higher-quality care. According to William Sage, a physician and law professor, "The most important benefit of enterprise liability is that it could act as a potent counterweight to incentives to underserve captive populations of patients enrolled in managed care. . . . If health plans are held liable for patient injury, they might contract with providers and evaluate practice patterns based on quality instead of engaging in economic credentialing. At the same time, physicians—relieved of many concerns over individual liability—might participate more readily in cooperative decision making and might be less resistant to clinical practice guidelines and other efforts by health plans to induce cost-effective practice on a system-wide basis."[108]

## Selection in Markets for Insurance

The fifth argument against increasing competition in health care markets is the potential for either adverse or favorable selection in health insurance markets. In the extreme, adverse selection can lead to the disappearance of competitive markets for the most generous types of insurance.[109] In less extreme cases, adverse selection can lead to some individuals buying too little insurance (relative to the amount of insurance that would have been purchased in the absence of adverse selection).

Adverse selection is the result of poorly informed sellers of health insurance and better informed buyers. When sellers of health care insurance cannot determine the health status or risk type of individuals (or when the transaction costs of doing so are extremely high), both high-risk individuals (for example, those with chronic diseases such as heart disease, multiple sclerosis, or depression) and low-risk individuals are charged the same premiums. Individuals, on the other hand, have information about their own health and risk status (for instance, history of heart disease, cancer, or other health problems). Only those individuals who think the insurance is a good deal because the benefits of being insured are greater than the premium payments (most likely higher-risk individuals) will purchase the insurance. Accordingly, the pooling of high-risk and low-risk individuals in the same insurance plan is less likely to occur.

Consider the case where all individuals pay $200/month for a less generous health plan that does *not* contract with the hospitals and physicians best known for treating chronic conditions, and $500/month for a more generous plan that contracts with these particular providers. Facing these insurance premiums, some lower-risk individuals will underinsure (purchase the $200/month health plan despite their preferences for more generous insurance coverage) or will not purchase any insurance at all. The premium for the more generous plan is especially high because of this tendency and the tendency of individuals who are less healthy, and thus more expensive to insure, to purchase the more generous health plan.

This is the market failure of adverse selection. In a competitive market with consumer choice of health plan, those plans associated with provider networks with the best reputations for treating chronic conditions or plans offering the most generous benefits will suffer from adverse selection.

In addition to the potential market failure of adverse selection by individuals, there is the potential for "cream skimming," "cherry picking," or favorable selection by insurers—that is, insurers' attempts to attract good risks and discourage bad ones. If the premiums that insurers are paid do not fully reflect the risks of insuring their enrollees, then insurers have incentives to attract healthy, low-risk individuals and to "weed out" the sickest, highest-risk individuals. Insurers may be able to design their plans to make them more attractive to low-risk individuals and less attractive to high-risk individuals. For example, health plans with high deductibles may be more attractive to healthier, low-risk individuals and less attractive to high-risk individuals. Health plans with gatekeeper physicians may be less attractive to high-risk individuals who wish to see many specialist physicians. In order to attract good risks, health plans may include memberships in health clubs or subsidized items such as bicycle helmets. In addition, health plans may use marketing techniques or screening devices to encourage enrollment of healthier individuals and discourage enrollment of less healthy individuals.

The inefficiency associated with risk selection by individuals and insurers is that high-risk and low-risk individuals may not end up with their desired level of health insurance. Even though individuals might be willing to pay higher premiums for insured access to the best cancer care, it is possible that no health plan will provide it because offering this sort of insured access to outstanding oncology programs might attract the worst risks. Likewise, even though some individuals do not value highly insured access to the local hospital with the best obstetric program, and thus would prefer lower premiums and a more limited network of hospitals, it is possible that no health plan will provide this option because offering such a plan might attract an older and thus higher-risk population.

The implications of adverse selection by individuals and favorable risk selection by insurers for increasing competition in the market for health care financing appear to be profound. One implication is that increasing competition by increasing consumers' choices among competing health plans or increasing consumers' incentives to search for the "best-buy" in health plans will increase risk segregation and the probability that the most generous insurance plans will cease to be sold in competitive markets. Further, because one health plan's lower cost and premium may be the result of its less generous benefit package, its more efficient operation, or its ability to attract lower-risk enrollees,[110] increasing consumer choice among health plans will not necessarily increase efficiency. Holding benefits constant, if differences in premiums across health plans reflect differences in the risk characteristics of enrollees (rather than differences in plan efficiency), then encouraging choice among health plans will not necessarily result in the more efficient plans gaining market share at the expense of the less efficient ones.

There is yet another problem with competitive markets for health care financing. Even if insurers could determine the expected future health care spending of individuals or groups (thus potentially eliminating the problem of adverse selection),[111] competitive health insurance markets may still not work well. If insurers set premiums based on the expected future spending of an insured group (known as experience rating), then the sickest, highest-risk groups will face the highest premiums. Those born less fortunate may be charged higher insurance premiums throughout their lives. This leads to a market failure over time because people will be unable to insure against future health risks.[112]

How serious are the problems of adverse and favorable selection in real world markets? The majority of the empirical evidence suggests that adverse selection by individuals and favorable selection by insurers is a significant problem.

Risk segregation, such as higher-risk, less healthy individuals (individuals with poorer health status and large previous health expenditures) enrolled in the more generous health plans, supports the hypothesis of adverse selection by individuals. Empirical studies provide evidence of risk segregation in markets for health insurance. A review of the literature on risk selection in HMOs and PPOs concluded that among the elderly and the nonelderly populations, healthier individuals are more likely to enroll in health plans that restrict enrollees' choices of health care providers.[113] Consistent with this, a more recent study found that, compared with the elderly in traditional fee-for-service Medicare plans, elderly enrollees in Medicare HMOs had better functional status, fared better in activity limitations, and were less likely to report their health status as fair or poor in 1994.[114]

Similarly, recent case studies of two groups of employees (the Group Insurance Commission of Massachusetts, which serves state and local employees and Harvard University) provide evidence of adverse selection: the healthiest, lowest-risk employees moved out of the most generous plans as the cost of the less generous plans decreased. Using data on people insured through the Group Insurance Commission of Massachusetts, one study estimated that people leaving the most generous indemnity plan for the HMO in 1994 and 1995 spent 30 to 36 percent less than people who stayed in the more generous indemnity plan.[115] Another study showed that after Harvard University's switch to a system of paying a fixed contribution independent of health plan choice (increasing consumers' incentives to search for the most efficient health plans), adverse selection became a significant problem (individuals leaving the most generous plan were healthier than those who stayed in that plan), and this adverse selection eliminated the market for the most generous insurance plan.[116]

Recent evidence suggests that cream skimming by insurers also may be a serious problem. An unreleased federal report found that 18 percent of Medicare beneficiaries in HMOs were illegally pre-screened.[117] A recent General Accounting Office report found that some insurers told insurance agents that they would cut or eliminate commissions to agents who sold policies to high-risk individuals eligible for insurance under the Health Insurance Portability and Accountability Act.[118] Additional evidence of favorable selection is provided by the finding that those Medicaid enrollees in New York City who learned about their managed care plans from plan representatives were more likely to report excellent or very good health than those who learned about plans in other ways, such as from staff at city income support centers.[119]

CONSTRAINTS ON SELECTION

Health plans enroll both high-risk and low-risk individuals. We observe this risk pooling for multiple reasons. First, our employment-based system of insurance encourages risk pooling. Moreover, there are factors that limit adverse and favorable selection in real world markets for health insurance. For example, if insurers must incur large costs to write insurance contracts that disproportionately attract low-risk individuals, then such contracts might not be offered and risk pooling will occur.[120]

## Conclusion

Competitive markets for hospital and physician services are working reasonably well, despite the special nature of medical care and the potential problems of moral hazard, supplier-induced demand, the medical arms race, and quality deterioration.

Managed care companies are playing the critically important role of price-sensitive consumers in markets for hospital and physician services. Competition among hospitals or physicians for inclusion in MCCs' provider networks is providing hospitals and physician organizations with incentives to keep their costs and prices low, and, it is hoped, to provide appropriate care and limit their participation in medical arms races.

New sources of information on medical effectiveness and provider-specific quality are providing the means to limit the potential problem of quality deterioration in markets for hospital and physician services.

Information on the effectiveness of various medical treatments facilitates physicians' abilities to provide (and possibly patients' abilities to check that their physicians are providing) the best possible treatments for specific diseases. At the same time, new information on provider-specific quality facilitates both MCCs' and enrollees' selections of high-quality providers, and this provides the incentive for hospitals and physicians to provide desired levels of quality.

Since competitive markets for physician and hospital services are working reasonably well, it is reasonable to conclude that the antitrust laws written a century ago for application to "smokestack industries" can and should be applied to these health care markets. In the following chapter I provide an introduction to U.S. antitrust laws and a discussion of their enforcement in health care markets.

3

# Antitrust Policy in
# Health Care Markets

*Antitrust laws . . . are the Magna Carta of free enterprise. They are as important to the preservation of economic freedom and our free enterprise system as the Bill of Rights is to the protection of our fundamental personal freedoms.*
— U.S. Supreme Court, 1972[1]

THE THREE MAIN pieces of federal antitrust legislation are the Sherman Act of 1890 (of particular importance are Sections 1 and 2), the Clayton Act of 1914 (particularly Sections 3 and 7), and the Federal Trade Commission Act of 1914 (particularly Section 5).[2] These antitrust laws were enacted to protect and promote both market competition (as the means to achieve an efficient allocation of our scarce resources) and consumer welfare.[3] The hope is that by protecting and promoting competition, the antitrust laws will protect consumers from private firms with the ability to exercise monopoly or market power (the power to increase price above competitive levels). When properly enforced, the antitrust laws can protect competition and consumers by prohibiting anticompetitive business conduct (conduct that has a negative impact on consumers) as well as anticompetitive consolidation (consolidation that has a negative impact on consumers).

There are four potential actors who can initiate enforcement of the federal antitrust laws: the Antitrust Division of the United States Department of Justice (DOJ), the Federal Trade Commission (FTC),[4] states' attorneys general,[5] and private plaintiffs (including consumers) who have suffered from anticompetitive practices. Interestingly, most actions brought under the federal antitrust laws are brought by private parties rather than by the FTC or DOJ. Of the 539 published judicial opinions concerning health care antitrust disputes between 1985 and 1999, the vast majority (95 percent) were brought by private parties.[6]

The DOJ tends to bring criminal prosecutions and civil actions for injunctive relief in the federal courts, while the FTC tends to conduct its own administrative hearings and adjudications, which the parties can later appeal to the federal courts.[7] The FTC has sole responsibility for enforcing the Federal Trade Commission Act. The DOJ prosecutes violations of the Sherman Act, and both the DOJ and the FTC prosecute violations of the Clayton Act.

The outcomes of antitrust cases vary, although the most common outcome is settlement to avoid costly trials with uncertain outcomes. Settlements in private antitrust cases most frequently take the form of agreements by the defendant to pay damages to the plaintiff, but these damages are usually less than those claimed by the plaintiff. Settlements in government antitrust cases most often take the form of consent decrees or orders outlining the specific actions the defendant will or will not take in the future. Settlements in merger cases often take the form of agreements by the merging parties to "spin off" particular products, divisions, or firms and agreements by the government not to prosecute the case further.

### Anticompetitive Business Conduct

Anticompetitive conduct harms consumers by facilitating firms' abilities to exercise market power. Anticompetitive business conduct includes some (but not all) attempts to monopolize a market, some (but not all) tying requirements and exclusive dealing arrangements, and all written and verbal agreements among competitors to restrict output, fix prices, or divide markets. Tying requirements are requirements that the purchaser of one product (the tying product) purchase a second, tied product from the same seller. Under exclusive dealing contracts, at least one of the parties in the exchange agrees to trade only with the other. The antitrust laws deal separately with each of these types of potentially anticompetitive behaviors.

Monopolization, tying restrictions, and exclusive dealing agreements are considered under rule of reason analysis. Under this type of analysis, the court generally follows a two-step process: first, the court determines the extent to which the challenged conduct decreases competition; second, if competition has been lessened, then the court attempts to weigh the procompetitive and anticompetitive impacts of the challenged conduct to determine if, on balance, the challenged conduct violates the antitrust laws.

Accordingly, monopolization can be illegal under certain conditions and legal under others. Under Section 2 of the Sherman Act and rule of reason analysis, illegal monopolization requires proof of three factors: substantial market power,[8] injury to competition, and intent to monopolize through predatory or unreasonable exclusionary conduct. The net effect of monopolization on consumers is assumed to be negative only when the monopoly position is obtained through unreasonable exclusionary conduct. What this means is that obtaining a monopoly position or exercising monopoly power is not unlawful if the monopoly position or power was obtained through competition on the merits or by being the best competitor—using the most efficient production, distribution, and marketing methods.

Exclusive dealing agreements are not uncommon in health care markets. These sorts of contracts exist between insurers and hospitals, insurers and physician organizations, and hospitals and physician organizations. For example, an exclusive dealing contract between $HMO_x$ and hospital$_x$ may stipulate that the insurer will provide its enrollees with insured access to hospital services only at hospital$_x$ and thus rival hospitals will be prevented from entering into contracts with $HMO_x$. Or an exclusive dealing contract between $HMO_y$ and physician organization$_y$ may stipulate that physician organization$_y$ will treat only patients insured by $HMO_y$ and thus rival insurers will be prevented from entering into contracts with physician organization$_y$. Under certain conditions these sorts of exclusive dealing contracts can lessen competition in markets for hospital services and health care financing services, respectively, and thus can harm consumers of hospital services and health care financing services. The conditions under which this can happen are analyzed in Chapter 7.

The Clayton Act, Section 3, prohibits tying requirements and exclusive dealing arrangements when the effect of these contracts may be to lessen competition substantially or to tend to create a monopoly. Exclusive dealing agreements can also be challenged under Section 1 of the Sherman Act (Section 1 prohibits "every contract, combination, . . . and conspiracy in restraint of trade or commerce") and Section 5 of the Federal Trade Commission Act.

There has been extensive antitrust litigation involving exclusive dealing arrangements that inhibit other physicians' access to a vertically consolidated hospital. However, challenges to these sorts of exclusive contracts on antitrust grounds are rarely successful.[9] For example, in *Jefferson Parish Hospital District No. 2 v. Hyde*,[10] one anesthesiologist who was denied admission to the hospital staff challenged the hospital's exclusive contract with a group of anesthesiologists. The Supreme Court ruled that the challenged exclusive contract did not violate the Sherman Act because there was no evidence that competition was restrained. Evidence was presented showing that 70 percent of patients residing in the parish went to hospitals other than Jefferson Parish Hospital, and thus Jefferson Parish Hospital lacked market power and local residents could obtain their anesthesiologist of choice by going to other local hospitals.

One successful challenge occurred in *Oltz v. St. Peter's Community Hospital*.[11] In this case a nurse anesthetist challenged an exclusive contract between anesthesiologists and the hospital. Evidence was presented showing that (1) the nurse anesthetist lost privileges after the anesthesiologists threatened to leave the hospital if the nurse anesthetist was not terminated; (2) the hospital provided 84 percent of the general surgical services in the town, and patients could not go elsewhere for alternative sources of anesthesia services; and (3) after the termination of the nurse anesthetist, each of the anesthesiologists' annual earnings increased by 40 to 50 percent. The court determined that this exclusive contract was harmful to competition and thus found the anesthesiologists and the hospital guilty of an illegal conspiracy under Section 1 of the Sherman Act.

There has been little antitrust litigation involving exclusive dealing arrangements that inhibit other hospitals' access to vertically consolidated physicians, and even less involving tying requirements. In 1999, however, the 225-bed St. Luke's Hospital in San Francisco filed an antitrust lawsuit charging the 613-bed California Pacific Medical Center (CPMC) with entering into illegal tying and exclusive dealing contracts with Brown & Tolland (B&T), the largest IPA in San Francisco. The complaint alleged that contracts between CPMC and B&T effectively tied the hospital services provided by CPMC to the physician services provided by B&T and thereby eliminated other hospitals' abilities to compete for risk contracts with B&T. This case was settled out of court.

Written and verbal agreements among "competitors" to restrict output, fix prices, or divide markets (assign each competitor certain buyers, geographic markets, or products) are *per se* illegal (presumed illegal without elaborate inquiry into the precise harm caused or the business excuse for their use). These agreements among "competitors" to act jointly (as if they were a monopolist) are believed to cause the same harm to competition and consumers as an illegal monopoly. Therefore, the courts presume that these sorts of horizontal agreements harm consumers in all circumstances, and thus that they are anticompetitive and unlawful in all circumstances. Accordingly, unlike Sherman Act, Section 2 cases, some Section 1 cases are judged under the more stringent *per se* rule.[12]

Another potential *per se* violation is the group boycott (an agreement among competitors not to deal with another competitor or to preclude that competitor from a competitive advantage). The courts have analyzed the exclusion of certain providers by a provider-controlled health plan as a group boycott.[13] Similarly, the courts have examined health plans' refusals to allow certain providers to become participating providers as group boycotts.[14]

Until recently there were only a few cases involving allegations of price fixing among hospitals.[15] In 2000 two hospitals in Poughkeepsie, New York, were found guilty of jointly fixing prices. The hospitals' use of a common and exclusive agent to negotiate the terms and rates that they charged third-party payers was found to be a *per se* violation of the Sherman Act.[16] Similarly, the DOJ in *U.S. v. Classic Care Network, Inc. et al.*[17] charged Classic Care Network, a corporation established by eight member hospitals, and those eight hospitals with conspiring to coordinate contracting with HMOs to avoid discounting their rates for services. The DOJ alleged that the hospitals agreed to refrain from accepting any discount off inpatient rates and to accept no more than 10 percent off outpatient rates. In 1995 the parties signed a settlement agreement enjoining the hospitals from engaging in any collective activities to set fees.

On the other hand, there have been multiple cases of price fixing among physicians and other health care professionals. In 1982 the Supreme Court ruled that the maximum schedule of fees agreed upon by the physicians of two medical foundations constituted illegal price fixing by those physicians.[18] This case has been referred to as the "alpha and omega" of antitrust enforcement in the market for physician services. These physicians had agreed by majority vote to accept fee schedules drafted by the Medical Society as the maximum prices they would charge to subscribers of certain health plans: "The rank-and-file vote of the Medical Society members accounting for 70 percent of the physicians in the geographic market left little doubt that (1) there was 'an agreement among hundreds of competing doctors concerning price at which each will offer his own services to a substantial number of competitors,' and (2) the members of the Medical Society could collectively exercise market power."[19]

In *U.S. v. Lake Country Optometric Society*[20] the DOJ charged a Texas trade association of optometrists with participating in a conspiracy to fix prices for eye examinations between November 1992 and February 1994. The optometrists were charged with meeting to discuss prices for eye examinations, agreeing to raise the prices charged, raising prices, and monitoring and enforcing compliance with the price agreement. In 1995 the optometrists pled guilty.

The issue of price fixing has also arisen in connection with medical associations' creation of relative value scales, indices that assign weights to various medical services to determine the relative fees assigned to those services. However, in the only case in which the FTC's challenge to a relative value scale was fully litigated, the court found that the relative value scale did not facilitate price fixing and thus did not violate the Sherman Act.[21]

Recently the courts confronted the issue of illegal market allocations among physicians. In *Blue Cross & Blue Shield of Wisconsin v. Marshfield Clinic*, the Marshfield Clinic and its associated health plan were accused of agreeing with some of its competitors to divide markets (two plans agreed not to open offices in each other's territories). On appeal, Richard Posner, Chief Judge of the U.S. Court of Appeals for the Seventh Circuit, wrote: "The charge of a division of markets in this case is backed by some pretty strong documents. . . . We think the evidence of a division of markets, though a little scanty, was sufficient to sustain the jury's verdict on this."[22]

Likewise, in a recent case *(State of New York v. St. Francis Hospital et al.)* the defendant hospitals were found guilty of eliminating competition by allocating markets. The hospitals' agreement to (1) designate one of the hospitals as the site for cardiology, obstetric, gynecology, cancer, and medical pediatric services and the other hospital as the site for orthopedics/neurology, ambulatory surgery, plastic surgery, and emergency and trauma services and (2) not to compete for consumers of these services was found to be a *per se* violation of the Sherman Act.

Even in the absence of written or verbal horizontal agreements between competitors, it may still be possible for competitors to coordinate their behavior and jointly increase their prices. Coordination involves competitors' adoption, with or without communication with rivals, of business strategies that recognize their historical and future interdependence. In a market that is conducive to coordination, an agreement is unnecessary for coordination between firms and harm to competition and consumers to occur.[23] However, interfirm coordination or the exercise of market power by a group of competitors without proof of a written or verbal agreement is not necessarily illegal under Section 1 of the Sherman Act.

Are markets for health insurance, physician services, and hospital services conducive to this sort of tacit coordination? Although increasing concentration (the degree to which the market is dominated by a small number of large firms) in health care markets certainly increases the likelihood that health care firms will recognize their mutual interdependence and thus coordinate their behaviors, there is not a clear-cut answer to the question of tacit coordination. Certain characteristics of health care markets may make coordination difficult.

Tacit coordination is neither easy nor costless. Firms must devise ways to signal to each other (without a written or verbal agreement) the need to change prices or outputs. Further, the firms involved in the coordination must be able to detect and prevent "cheating" among themselves. "Cheating" occurs when a firm(s) undermines the coordinated interaction by lowering its price or increasing its output. Firms often have the incentive to cheat because cheating will increase that firm's profit, assuming the other firms do not cheat. Detection of cheating is easier when (1) there are few firms and many buyers in the market, (2) firms have information about one another, such as the information collected and disseminated by trade associations, (3) prices are public knowledge, (4) products are homogeneous, and (5) sales are frequent.[24]

Interfirm coordination in health care may be especially difficult and costly for a few reasons. First, coordination is more difficult when there are differences between firms in terms of their products or their costs.

For example, when firms produce multiple and differentiated products (as insurers, hospitals, and physicians do), successful coordination may involve coordinating a whole schedule of prices, rather than coordination of a single price. Coordinated interaction is also made more difficult in industries characterized by rapid technological change, as is the health care industry. Technological innovations, such as new products or new lower-cost methods of production, make it particularly difficult to coordinate because each innovation alters the prices or outputs that maximize firms' joint profits. Finally, coordination is more difficult when firms compete on multiple dimensions, such as competition based on price, quality, customer services, advertising, and other nonprice variables. As Richard Posner observed, "If other forms of competition—inventory, product quality, service, or whatever—are very important, the only effect of eliminating price competition may be to channel competitive energies into other, and costly, forms of competition. Indeed, . . . firms may increase their expenditures on the other forms of competition until they have competed away all of the higher profit that they hoped to obtain by increasing prices above the competitive level."[25]

## Anticompetitive Consolidation

The antitrust laws also provide the basis for enforcers and the courts to interdict changes in market structure (the number and size distribution of firms). In theory this will decrease the likelihood of interfirm coordination or tacit collusion among competitors. Specifically, the Clayton Act, Section 7,[26] prohibits mergers or acquisitions when the likely effect of the consolidation is "substantially to lessen competition, or tend to create a monopoly." Successful challenges maintain the number of independent competitors in markets that are susceptible to interfirm coordination and the exercise of market power. In health care markets, these sorts of antitrust cases usually have involved challenges to consolidations among hospitals.

Anticompetitive consolidation harms consumers by facilitating firms' abilities to exercise market power. A significant body of research has established a clear relationship between market concentration and market power.[27] The economist Timothy Bresnahan reviewed the empirical literature based on data from multiple industries and concluded:

"There is a great deal of market power, in the sense of price-cost margins, in some concentrated industries."[28] Consistent with this, one study found that 42 percent of the DOJ's price-fixing cases between January 1963 and December 1972 involved markets with four firm concentration ratios (the sum of the market shares of the four largest firms) that were over 75 percent, and another 34 percent of the cases involved markets with four firm concentration ratios between 51 and 75 percent.[29]

One would also expect to find a link between more concentrated markets and higher prices in health care. In geographic areas characterized by one or only a few hospitals or physician organizations, MCCs and employers (in the case of employers contracting directly with providers) have less bargaining power—less ability to divert enrollees to other hospitals or physician organizations. In markets characterized by many hospitals or physician organizations, on the other hand, MCCs and employers can bargain for lower reimbursements to providers by threatening to: (1) drop the more expensive provider from their networks; (2) keep the more expensive hospital in their networks, but give physicians financial incentives to admit patients at cheaper hospitals (for example, global capitation contracts whereby physicians are responsible for hospitalization expenses) or give individual patients financial incentives to use cheaper hospitals; or (3) keep the more expensive provider in their networks, but carve out certain services, such as cardiac services, and separately contract for those services with other providers. Under carve-out contracts separate, specialized organizations provide health care services for particular conditions/diseases (heart disease, cancer, diabetes, asthma) or procedures/treatments (cardiovascular treatments).[30]

A growing number of studies establish a direct relationship between market concentration and higher health care prices, providing justification and ammunition for antitrust enforcement in these markets. The most relevant research on concentration, market power, and output levels in health care markets is reviewed in Chapters 6 and 7.

As with monopolization and exclusive dealing agreements, however, not all mergers and joint ventures are anticompetitive. In fact, the vast majority of mergers, acquisitions, and joint ventures will have neutral or positive net impacts on competition. Moreover, there may be efficiency justifications for not only allowing, but also desiring larger competitors. For example, larger insurers or health care providers may be able to produce at lower costs. Efficiency gains resulting from consolidation may lead to lower prices, increased output, and additional increases in competition in the market(s) in which the associated firm(s) operates.[31]

The most controversial cases include those where the merger, acquisition, or joint venture will likely increase both economic efficiency and the potential for firms to exercise market power. In these cases the net effect on market price may be either positive or negative because lower costs may induce health care firms to expand output, which will reduce the market price, while increased concentration may induce collusion, which will increase the market price. Allowing the consolidation may result in both lower long-run costs of production and higher prices to consumers.

Ideally, one would want antitrust enforcers to challenge and the courts to disallow only those mergers, acquisitions, and joint ventures in which the efficiency gains from the consolidation are less than the losses due to increased market power. However, antitrust enforcers and the courts face the perplexing problem of having to decide whether to challenge or to allow a merger, acquisition, or joint venture at a time when the alleged anticompetitive effects and the alleged efficiencies of the proposed consolidation are highly uncertain. Prior to the consolidation, economists and others can make reasonably well-informed predictions about the likely effects of particular mergers, acquisitions, and joint ventures. It is impossible to know with certainty, however, the exact effects on prices, outputs, and efficiencies, especially in markets that are changing very rapidly. The best that can be expected in antitrust cases where consolidation will simultaneously create market power and promote efficiencies is a judgment about predominant effects based on informed economic intuition and the best available estimates. The weight and significance given to different types of efficiencies in antitrust cases should depend on the magnitude and probability of the efficiencies, and the degree to which the efficiencies will enhance competition in the relevant market.[32]

## The Harm to Consumers

Both anticompetitive business conduct and consolidation increase the ability of firms to exercise market power, which in turn decreases the welfare of consumers in at least two ways: by reducing the availability of products and by raising their prices. Relative to competitive firms, firms with the willingness and ability to exercise market power produce too little output from consumers' perspectives. When the firm(s) with market power reduces output below the competitive level, some consumers are denied the opportunity to consume this product. These consumers would have chosen to consume this product if the firm(s) had not used its market power to decrease the product's availability in the market. The decrease in production thus decreases the welfare of those consumers who would have consumed the product under competitive market conditions, but are denied access to the product as a result of the exercise of market power. There is agreement among economists that this loss in consumer welfare (often called the deadweight loss) is a cost of market power.[33]

The second source of harm is that, relative to competitive firms, firms with the willingness and ability to exercise market power set prices too high from the perspective of consumers. When a firm with market power raises its price above the competitive level, consumers pay higher prices and the firm with the market power earns higher profits. The consumers are worse off, but the owners of the firm (or whoever earns the extra profit from the exercise of market power) are better off.

Whether this transfer from consumers to producers (sometimes called the monopoly profit) should be considered a cost of market power is an issue of debate among economists. Many economists argue that the monopoly profit is merely a transfer from consumers to producers, and thus should not be considered a cost (to society) of market power. According to this view, this transfer represents redistribution from consumers to producers, and therefore society as a whole is no better or worse off. However, proponents of the "pure consumer welfare standard" argue that this transfer from consumers to producers represents a real harm to consumers and thus should be considered a cost of market power. Richard Posner makes an additional argument for this latter view, contending that this monopoly profit is a cost of market power because firms will expend society's scarce resources (for example, resources used to lobby politicians) in attempts to gain market power and thus the opportunity to obtain this extra profit.[34] The costs of resources used to gain market power are costs to society as a whole because these resources are not available to produce other goods and services that consumers value. In 1997, for example, the American Medical Association spent $17 million on lobbying, the Blue Cross and Blue Shield Association spent $8.8 million, and the American Hospital Association spent $7.9 million.[35]

Further, proponents of active antitrust enforcement in health care markets often argue that allowing health care firms to operate in less competitive or more concentrated markets will make consumers worse off in at least three additional ways: by lowering health care quality, decreasing product differentiation (fewer choices or varieties of products), and reducing rates of innovation.[36] This may or may not be the case; neither theoretical nor empirical research has established a clear relationship between market concentration and quality, between market concentration and product differentiation, or between market concentration and technological innovation.

The effect of increased market concentration on product quality is theoretically indeterminable. Depending on firms' cost structures and the elasticity of demand, the level of quality produced under monopoly conditions may be lower or higher than the level of quality produced in competitive markets.[37] This unsettled issue has huge implications in the markets for hospital and physician services, where in some cases, small changes in quality can mean the difference between life and death.

The quality issue in health care antitrust analysis is further complicated by the fact that in industries characterized by price regulation (like the health care industry, with its regulated prices under Medicare), it may be socially optimal for firms with market power to lower quality.[38] Firms subject to minimum price regulation cannot compete by lowering their prices and thus may compete more vigorously on the basis of quality. This may lead to excessively high quality, in the sense that the benefits of the increases in quality are less than the costs of producing those increases. In the airline industry prior to deregulation, for example, price regulation induced airlines to compete on the basis of service quality, and this led to socially excessive flight frequency (frequent but rather empty flights).[39]

The effect of market concentration on product differentiation or variety is also theoretically indeterminable.[40] A monopolist may or may not provide less product differentiation (or less product variety) relative to the optimal level and relative to the level provided by firms in markets characterized by more competitors.[41] Additional unknowns further complicate the variety issue in health care antitrust analysis. Specifically, recent empirical evidence on product differentiation, measured as hospital service and technology availability, is mixed.[42] It is unclear whether managed care and competition are decreasing or increasing service and technology availability. On a more superficial level, product differentiation has increased. For example, many hospitals have been "revamping" their food service, with some hospitals offering hotel-style room service, others hiring gourmet chefs, and still others offering "visiting chef" series.

Consumers clearly have different preferences for medical care. Some women prefer to have physicians deliver their babies in hospitals with neonatal intensive care units, while others prefer to have nurse-midwives deliver their babies in outpatient facilities or in their homes. Some patients choose to obtain inpatient care in large teaching hospitals or Catholic or Jewish hospitals, while others prefer to receive their care in smaller community hospitals. Despite these variations in consumers' preferences, it is unclear whether increases in product variety make consumers better or worse off. With greater product variety, individual consumers will be better able to find and purchase the medical services that match their individual tastes and thus yield the most satisfaction. However, if the technology of producing and marketing medical services is such that there are variety-specific economies of scale (increases in production of one variety are associated with decreases in the average costs of producing and marketing that variety of the product), then increases in the number of different varieties produced will be associated with higher average costs. Economies of scale mean that, on a second level, health care consumers will be worse off if markets produce a large variety of health care products because average costs and possibly prices will be higher.

Another issue concerning quality and product differentiation is that the economic models which are the basis of antitrust enforcement analyses focus on price competition. Thus the traditional approach to antitrust may have inherent difficulties in evaluating markets, such as health care markets, where there is substantial product differentiation and issues of quality are especially important.[43] It has been argued, however, that in the absence of generally applicable models of nonprice competition, antitrust enforcement best protects quality competition by protecting price competition.[44]

Finally, neither theoretical nor empirical research has established a clear relationship between market concentration and innovation (rate of technological progress). Health care innovation includes both the development of new products, such as drugs, devices, and clinical procedures, and the development of new, lower-cost methods of financing and delivering health care services. On the one hand, market concentration may be inimical to innovation because a monopolist without rivals has less incentive to invest in research and development.[45] On the other hand, it has also been argued that a monopolist has a greater ability to innovate. Specifically, a monopolist may have (1) better access to low-cost internal sources of funding for research and development projects, (2) greater potential to innovate at lower average costs if there are scale economies in research and development, and (3) greater potential to appropriate the full value of its innovations.[46]

Empirical evidence suggests that in some industries large firms are the most innovative, while in other industries it is the small firms that are most innovative.[47] For example, Kodak introduced amateur photography products in the 1970s, while Royal Crown, not Coke or Pepsi, introduced diet cola, caffeine-free soft drinks, and soft drinks in cans.[48] Other evidence indicates that the impact of firm size and market concentration on innovation may be small or nonexistent. In an extensive review of the empirical literature on the effects of firm size and market concentration on the rate of innovation, the economists Wesley Cohen and Richard Levin concluded that (1) the results are "inconclusive" and "fragile," in large part because of methodological difficulties and data problems, and (2) "the effects of firm size and concentration on innovation, if they exist at all, do not appear to be important."[49]

New medical technologies are produced by physicians and other medical researchers associated with academic health centers, pharmaceutical companies, medical device companies, and the biotechnology industry. As a result of recent mergers and acquisitions, the pharmaceutical industry is now characterized by large multinational firms such as Novartis, GlaxoSmithKline, Pfizer-Warner-Lambert, SmithKline Beecham, and Bristol-Meyers Squibb. The medical device industry, on the other hand, consists of many small firms. This industry includes approximately 16,000 firms, and the vast majority (80 percent) employ fewer than 50 persons.[50] Similarly, the biotechnology industry is characterized by numerous firms (over 2,000), many of which are investor-funded research ventures.[51]

The recent trend toward large pharmaceutical companies partnering with smaller biotechnology firms highlights the advantages of both small and large firms in the research and development process. To share development risks, many large firms are outsourcing some of their research and development to smaller, newer start-ups that concentrate their research and development on specific molecules, proteins, diseases, or drug-delivery systems. The advantages to the small biotechnology firm with these sorts of partnerships are access to the resources of the larger partner (often in exchange for selling or licensing promising technologies to the larger partner) and less "need to invest in marketing or distribution areas that require a large amount of money and expertise."[52]

In the health care industry there is extremely high public and private commitment to research and development. National spending on health-related research and development was $35.8 billion in fiscal year 1995.[53] The National Institutes of Health has the largest basic research budget of all the federal agencies.[54] Likewise, both the U.S. pharmaceutical and medical device industries spend a larger percentage of their sales revenues on research and development (18 and 12 percent, respectively)[55] than the aircraft, electronics, and chemical industries. Not surprisingly, the rate of technological innovation in the health care industry, measured as the number of new drugs and medical devices introduced, is very high. For example, in 1990 approximately 5,000 new medical devices were introduced in the United States.[56] The pace of development is also very high for new pharmaceutical products. In 1997, 316 new medications were in development for the treatment of cancer, 124 new medications and vaccines were in development for the treatment of AIDS, and 96 new medications were in development for the treatment of heart diseases.[57]

Perhaps because it would be very difficult to sort out the impact of firm size on innovativeness in health care, there has been no empirical investigation on this topic. However, in the market for insurance it has been small third-party administrators (firms specializing in claims processing) and consulting firms, rather than the large insurers, that have been the innovators of products such as the PPO.[58] It is also interesting to note that many medical devices (lasers, ultrasound, magnetic resonance spectroscopy) are not the result of medical research, but rather the result of adapting technologies developed for other uses. Likewise, the CT scanner was invented by an engineer who "was not involved with anything having to do with medicine or diagnostics," while working at a research firm "having nothing to do at that point with medical technologies."[59] Accordingly, concentration in health care markets may have little impact on the rate of innovation, at least in medical devices.

In summary, if insurers, physicians, or hospitals were to obtain market power, it is unclear what sort of impact this would have on health care quality, on the variety of health care services available to consumers, or on the rate of technological innovation in health care markets. The literature shows with certainty, however, that if insurers, physicians, or hospitals were to obtain market power, these parties would raise their prices. As the discussion in the next section indicates, this is true for both for-profit and nonprofit health care firms.

## Special Considerations in Health Care Markets

### The McCarran-Ferguson Act

The McCarran-Ferguson Act limits enforcement of the federal antitrust laws in markets for health care financing. Specifically, the Act exempts certain insurance-related conduct, in particular "the business of insurance" or activities that involve spreading or transferring risk or that implicate relationships between policyholders and insurers, from the federal antitrust laws. Insurers' relationships and transactions with health care providers, however, are not necessarily "the business of insurance" and thus probably do not qualify for McCarran-Ferguson protection.[60] There are no similar exemptions in markets for hospital and physician services.

### Efficiency versus Equity

Hospitals and physicians often provide care to patients despite those patients' inability to pay (they are both poor and uninsured or underinsured). In fact many public policies, such as those that determine incorporation as a charitable organization, those that determine nonprofit organizations' exemptions from payment of taxes, and those dealing with accreditation, licensing, and malpractice liability standards, require hospitals and physicians to provide charity care.[61] It is estimated that physicians provided $11 billion worth of uncompensated care in 1994, and that 77 percent of the physicians practicing in the United States in 1996 and 1997 provided some charity care.[62] More recent estimates suggest that 71.5 percent of physicians provided charity care in 2001, and among those providing charity care 70.2 percent spent less than 5 percent of their practice time on this care.[63] American Hospital Association estimates suggest that hospitals provided $21.6 billion worth of uncompensated care (charity care plus bad debt) in 2000.[64] Further, uncompensated care provided by hospitals as a percentage of total hospital expenses remained relatively constant at 6 percent between 1990 and 2000.[65] Charity care is care given without the expectation of payment, while bad debt is care for which payment is expected but not received.

Traditionally, hospitals and physicians have used the profits earned by treating patients with private insurance to finance charity care. Hospitals and physicians have cross-subsidized across patients or have engaged in price discrimination—charging higher prices to certain groups of consumers, such as individuals with private insurance, and lower prices (free care or care at subsidized prices) to other groups of consumers.

Some people question the wisdom of enforcing the antitrust laws in health care markets because increasing competition may affect the ability of hospitals and physicians to cross-subsidize and thus to provide charity care to the medically indigent. Increasing price competition may reduce hospitals' and physicians' abilities to earn the revenues necessary to cross-subsidize. On the other hand, increasing competition may increase hospitals' and physicians' incentive to achieve greater efficiency and lower their costs. The net effect on hospitals' abilities to cross-subsidize depends on the relative changes in revenues and costs.

Empirical studies provide modest support for an inverse relationship between price competition and charity care. The first study, using data on hospitals after the passage of legislation in California that allowed selective contracting (1984–1988), found that hospitals in more competitive markets lowered their compensated care charges relative to hospitals in less competitive markets.[66] However, "the relative fall in financial measures of uncompensated care may not be directly interpretable as a reduction in the level of care delivered to the uninsured, for two reasons. First, changes in uncompensated care will reflect both changes in the level of care to the uninsured and changes in hospital pricing policy. . . . Second, hospitals may have responded to competitive pressure by collecting more of their unpaid debts. This would yield reduced dollars of uncompensated care with no reduced units of care to the uninsured."[67]

The second study, while confirming the association between increased price competition and decreased compensated care charges, suggests that hospitals continue to provide higher levels of charity care in more competitive markets, compared with less competitive markets.[68] Specifically, this study found that prior to legislation allowing selective contracting in California (1980 to 1982), compensated care charges at private, general acute care hospitals in highly competitive markets in California were about 21 percent higher than at hospitals in the least competitive markets in California. By 1989 (after approximately six years of selective contracting) compensated care charges at private, general acute care hospitals in highly competitive markets were about 13 percent higher than at hospitals in the least competitive markets.

The third study, using data from 1996 and 1997, found that in areas with higher managed care penetration (including HMOs, PPOs, and POS plans), physicians provided about 25 percent fewer hours of charity care compared with physicians practicing in areas with lower managed care penetration.[69]

Even if increasing price competition among hospitals and physicians is associated with decreases in the quantity of charity care provided by hospitals and physicians, this is not a valid argument against antitrust enforcement in health care markets. We have to ask a second question: Is it good public policy to finance charity care by charging prices above costs to individuals who are well-insured? Current methods of financing charity care effectively "tax" the well-insured to pay for the care of persons who are uninsured or underinsured.

While many view access to medical services as a fundamental right or at least as something a civilized society provides to its members, there is no consensus on how to finance those services. There are two basic choices—fund health care services for the medically indigent through cross-subsidies (from the well-insured) or through direct subsidies (paid for by government taxation). Economic theory demonstrates that it is not good public policy to fund care for the medically indigent through cross-subsidies. "Taxing" well-insured persons to subsidize others' consumption of hospital and physician services generates multiple inefficiencies.[70] Accordingly, society's desire to provide medical care to all of its members does not conflict with using antitrust policy to facilitate competitive health care markets.

## Nonprofit Institutions

Some people argue that health care antitrust enforcement is complicated by the prevalence of nonprofit institutions. In two recent hospital merger cases, the notion that nonprofit hospitals (compared to for-profit hospitals) might be less likely to exercise monopoly power influenced the courts' decisions. In one court's decision to allow the merger of the two largest hospitals in Grand Rapids, Michigan, it was argued that nonprofit hospitals would not exercise monopoly power, even given the opportunity to do so.[71] The court argued that nonprofit hospitals act in the best interests of the community, or at least are constrained by boards of trustees composed of members of the local community.

Similarly, the district court in *FTC v. Freeman Hospital* stated: "Arguably, a private nonprofit hospital that is sponsored and directed by the local community is similar to a consumer cooperative. It is highly unlikely that a cooperative will arbitrarily raise prices merely to earn higher profits because the owners of such an organization are also its consumers. . . . Similarly, if a nonprofit organization is controlled by the very people who depend on it for service, there is no rational economic incentive for such an organization to raise its prices to the monopoly level even if it has the power to do so."[72]

It is possible that nonprofit institutions behave differently from for-profit institutions; however, the majority of the evidence (three out of four studies) suggests that nonprofit hospitals, just like their for-profit counterparts, are willing and able to exercise monopoly power in more concentrated markets.[73] Using data on California hospitals in 1986, 1989, 1992, and 1994, one study found that nonprofit hospital mergers resulted in higher prices in every year except 1986, and further, that the price-increasing impact of nonprofit hospital mergers is getting larger over time.[74] The price effects of nonprofit hospital mergers went from nil in 1986 to 2.8, 3.9, and 7.3 percent higher in 1989, 1992, and 1994, respectively. Similarly, two other studies found a positive relationship between market concentration and the prices charged by nonprofit hospitals.[75]

In addition to the argument that nonprofit hospitals are less likely to exercise monopoly power in concentrated markets, it has been suggested that compared with for-profit hospitals, nonprofit hospitals provide higher-quality services, devote more resources to research and education, and supply more charity care to the poor and needy. While it is true that nonprofit hospitals as a class devote more of their resources to research and education,[76] there is little support for the other two claims. The evidence on quality differentials between nonprofit and for-profit hospitals is clear-cut: there do not appear to be measurable differences in quality.[77]

Studies have found that many factors, including nonprofit versus for-profit, urban versus rural, and teaching versus nonteaching, influence hospitals' provision of charity care. Recent data suggest that private nonprofit and for-profit hospitals spend similar percentages of their revenues on uncompensated care. Specifically, private nonprofits spent 4.5 percent of revenue on uncompensated care in 1994, compared with 4.0 percent by for-profit hospitals.[78]

After reviewing the empirical literature on the effects of hospital ownership on hospital performance, measured as costs, pricing patterns, uncompensated care, technology diffusion, quality of care, and capital funds and investment, the economist Frank Sloan wrote under the heading "Bottom line": "Overall, one is struck by the similarity between private not-for-profit and for-profit performance, except in the areas, such as capital structure, where there must be differences for institutional reasons."[79]

Interestingly, despite the growth of national, for-profit hospital systems, the proportion of hospitals that are for-profit, as opposed to nonprofit or public, has remained relatively stable. Between 1985 and 2001 the proportion of for-profit community hospitals increased only slightly, from 14.0 percent to 15.4 percent.[80]

## Current Antitrust Policies of the DOJ and FTC

The FTC and DOJ have provided hospitals, physicians, and insurers with guidelines regarding their enforcement policies in health care markets. Specifically, the publication *Statements of Antitrust Enforcement Policy in Health Care* (August 1996) includes guidelines of enforcement policy in the following areas: (1) mergers between hospitals, (2) hospital joint ventures involving health care equipment, (3) hospital joint ventures involving specialized clinic services, (4) providers' joint provision of nonprice information to purchasers of health care services, (5) providers' joint provision of price information to purchasers of health services, (6) provider participation in exchanges of price and cost information, (7) joint purchasing arrangements among providers, (8) physician networks, and (9) multiprovider networks.[81]

The guidelines include "antitrust safety zones" or descriptions of the circumstances under which the agencies will not challenge mergers, acquisitions, joint ventures, and other transactions under the antitrust laws. For example, the agencies will not challenge non-exclusive physician networks comprising 30 percent or less of the physicians in each physician specialty who practice in the relevant geographic market and share substantial financial risk (capitation, withholds, percentage of premiums/revenues, or all-inclusive case rates) or engage in significant clinical integration (programs to monitor, evaluate, and change the clinical practices of the network's physicians). In addition, the guidelines describe the ways in which the agencies will analyze mergers, acquisitions, and joint ventures that fall outside the antitrust safety zones. Conduct falling outside the safety zones may or may not be challenged. The agencies also respond to health care firms' requests for staff advisory opinions and business review letters in 90 to 120 days after receipt of the information considered necessary to evaluate the request.

The *Horizontal Merger Guidelines* (April 2, 1992) articulate the FTC/DOJ's analytical framework for determining whether a merger "is likely to create or enhance market power or facilitate its exercise." Consolidation-associated changes in firms' abilities to exercise market power are typically assessed indirectly by looking at pre- and post-consolidation market shares, concentration levels, and entry conditions. The FTC and DOJ calculate pre-merger and post-merger market concentration using the Herfindhal-Hirschman Index (HHI). The HHI is the sum of the squared market shares of all firms currently operating in the relevant market. It is considered to be the best measure of market concentration for at least two reasons: the HHI reflects the distribution of firm sizes across all firms in the market, and it gives the greatest weight to the largest firms in the market. In addition, the agencies assess whether entry will be likely, timely, and sufficient to inhibit the ability of the incumbent firm(s) to exercise market power.

## *Alternative Methods to Assess Market Power*

In actual antitrust cases, estimates of a firm's own demand elasticity have been the most important source of evidence on the firm's ability to exercise market power.[82] The firm's own elasticity of demand measures the sensitivity of customers to the firm's own price increases. When consumers are more sensitive and responsive to price increases (that is, many consumers purchase less and possibly none of the firm's product in response to the price increase), demand tends to be elastic. When demand is elastic and the firm increases its price by 5 percent, the firm will lose more than 5 percent of its sales.[83] Accordingly, the firm's revenue from sales (but not necessarily its profit) will fall. Profit does not necessarily fall as the firm increases price because in addition to selling less, the firm produces less, so that both its costs and revenues fall. Therefore, the more elastic a firm's demand curve is, the less able the firm is to exercise market power.

In addition, critical sales loss calculations have been used as evidence of a firm's ability to raise its prices and thus have played a prominent role in recent hospital merger cases. In the event that the merged hospital increases its price, the break-even critical sales loss measures the percentage of customers that would have to use a different hospital to make the merged hospital's price increase unprofitable. The break-even critical sales loss decreases with increases in the hospital's price-cost margin [(price − cost)/price] and increases with increases in the merged hospital's price increase [(future price − current price)/current price]. If the merged hospital increases its price by 10 percent rather than 5 percent, a larger percentage of customers would have to start using alternative hospitals to make the 10 percent price increase unprofitable. The more the merged hospital marks its prices above its costs, the smaller the percentage of customers that would have to start using alternative hospitals to make a price increase unprofitable.

In *U.S. v. Mercy Health Services* the defendants used an estimate of the break-even critical sales loss to convince the judge that even a 5 percent price increase would be unprofitable for the merged hospital. The defendants' economic expert calculated an 8 percent break-even critical sales loss for a 5 percent price increase, and the judge concluded that "the total of those likely to switch in the event of a 5% price rise is higher than the 8% necessary to make the price rise unprofitable."[84]

## Federal Challenges to Anticompetitive Consolidations

In the area of health care consolidations the federal antitrust agencies have been most active in markets for hospital services (as compared to markets for physician services and health care financing), yet they have challenged very few hospital mergers. Of the 956 required initial filings of notice of proposed general acute care hospital mergers received by the FTC and DOJ (pursuant to the Hart-Scott-Rodino Act) between 1981 and 1997, only about 2 percent were challenged.[85]

In June of 1999 for the first time one of the federal agencies challenged a merger/acquisition between MCCs;[86] specifically, the DOJ challenged the acquisition of Prudential by Aetna US Healthcare. This matter was settled by a consent order specifying that Aetna US Healthcare would sell certain health plans in Dallas and Houston.

The federal agencies have also been quite lenient regarding the formation of health care provider networks. Between 1991 and 1996 the FTC and DOJ approved the formation and activities of almost every health care provider network (31 out of 34) reviewed in the FTC's process of writing staff advisory opinions and the DOJ's Business Review Procedure.[87] Moreover, the agencies rarely recommend challenges to conduct falling outside the safety zones. For example, in 1998 the FTC decided not to recommend a challenge to the formation of a physician network in Erie, Pennsylvania, despite the evidence suggesting that the proposed nonexclusive network would include far more than 30 percent of the physicians in many specialties.[88] Specifically, the proposed network included 100 percent of the specialists in colon and rectal surgery, 66 percent of the specialists in cardiovascular disease, 69 percent of the specialists in cardiovascular/thoracic surgery, and 67 percent of the specialists in infectious diseases in a 10-county area.[89] Likewise, in 1997 the DOJ decided not to challenge the proposed operation of a physician organization in Rutland, Vermont, that included 100 percent of the general surgeons, 100 percent of the gastroenterologists, and 63 percent of the ophthalmologists practicing in the Rutland area.[90]

The federal agencies have also been quite lenient toward vertical consolidation. For example, in 1998 the DOJ decided not to challenge the formation of a joint venture between the largest gatekeeper-type HMO in northeastern Pennsylvania and a limited partnership of 166 physicians, despite the evidence suggesting that First Priority Health System (FPHS), the proposed, jointly owned "service delivery organization" to provide and manage medical services to the HMO's enrollees, would include exclusive contracts with about 31 percent of the primary care physicians (GPs, FPs, and internists) in one county and that FPHS would be the exclusive provider of medical services to the HMO.[91]

Despite this leniency, some have criticized the federal agencies for their use of regulatory techniques in health care markets. Thomas Kauper, a law professor at the University of Michigan, argues that the FTC and DOJ increasingly use negotiated consent decrees, other settlements of actual and threatened litigations, policy statements, and advisory opinions/review letters to regulate the allowable conduct of health care firms.[92] One response to this criticism is that the agencies' policy statements, staff advisory opinions, and business review letters are only "helpful guideposts."[93] They do not carry the force of judicial decisions. Health care firms have the option of taking their cases to court, and it is the courts that ultimately decide the legality of mergers, acquisitions, joint ventures, and other transactions between health care firms.

Interestingly, this is also an issue for antitrust enforcement at the state level. There are numerous examples of state attorneys general negotiating hospital merger agreements in which the merging hospitals agree to state-level oversight of future price increases or blueprints for future negotiations between health plans and the merged hospitals. For example, in Pennsylvania the state attorney general allowed the merger of Children's Hospital of Pittsburgh and the UPMC Health System with the following conditions: UPMC will go to binding arbitration if negotiations with health plans fail; UPMC will not limit access to Children's Hospital to health plans that contract with the other UPMC hospitals; and UPMC will not offer lower rates to its own UPMC Health Plan.[94]

## Conclusion

While it is clear that consolidation among health care firms can lead to higher prices, the impact of consolidation (and thus of antitrust enforcement policies) on health care costs, health care quality, the variety of available health care services and technologies, and rates of technological innovation is ambiguous. The ambiguities with respect to the impact of consolidation on costs, quality, product differentiation, and technological innovation, however, are not unique to health care markets, and thus they do *not* justify a revision of basic antitrust enforcement principles for health care markets. The same principles that guide antitrust enforcement in other markets should guide enforcement in health care markets as well.

The next chapter includes a discussion of the issues involved in defining health care markets in antitrust cases. Market definition is one of the most important components of antitrust analyses because it often determines whether a merger, acquisition, or other conduct will be found illegal under the antitrust laws. It entails finding answers to multiple questions, including how far health care consumers will travel to obtain care, and thus which health care providers or insurers will be able to constrain the consolidated health care firm's attempts to raise prices or lower quality of care in the future.

Market definition has become more challenging and controversial as a result of the changes occurring in health care markets. Traditional methods of market definition in health care antitrust cases, such as defining the product market as a cluster of services in hospital cases (for example, acute care inpatient hospital services) or defining the geographic market on the basis of historical patient flows, are called into question when those markets are characterized by managed care and selective contracting. Some argue that the use of these traditional methods in health care markets characterized by managed care and selective contracting results in market definitions that are too broad, and thus in court decisions based on underestimates of the antitrust risks associated with consolidation of health care firms.[95] Others argue just the opposite—that the use of these traditional methods results in market definitions that are too narrow, and thus in court decisions based on overestimates of the potential for anticompetitive effects.[96] These issues will be explored in the following chapter.

# 4

# Market Definition in Health Care Antitrust Cases Involving Consolidation

There is no subject in antitrust law more confusing than market definition.
~ First Circuit Court of Appeals, 1993[1]

IF THERE WERE A crystal ball capable of revealing the future (post-consolidation) ability and willingness of firms to exercise monopoly power, then the highly controversial and cumbersome process of defining the relevant product and geographic markets in these antitrust cases could be discarded. If we could somehow observe a consolidated firm's future choices, for example its costs, qualities, and prices in the future, we could discard all the steps involved in estimating consolidated firms' potential to exercise monopoly power in the future.

Unfortunately we lack this sort of crystal ball, and therefore correctly defining the market in which the consolidated firm will compete is the essential first step in the process of estimating the likelihood of future anticompetitive behavior. The court's answer to the question of whether the defendant currently possesses monopoly power or will possess monopoly power after the consolidation (and thus the court's decision to allow or stop the consolidation) often depends on how the market is defined. If the market is defined too broadly (by including firms that are not true competitors of the consolidating firms), then the court may err in the direction of allowing a merger, acquisition, or joint venture that will have anticompetitive effects. If the market is defined too narrowly (by excluding firms that are true competitors of the consolidating firms), then the court may err in the direction of not allowing a merger, acquisition, or joint venture that would have had procompetitive effects.

## Why Is Market Definition So Controversial?

Market definition is not an exact science. Consolidating firms tend to argue for relatively broad market definitions, including many competitors, while plaintiffs tend to argue for more narrow definitions. This was the case in four of the last five federal challenges to hospital mergers. These federal challenges are summarized in Table 1.

In 1995 the FTC lost its challenge to the proposed merger of two of the three acute care hospitals in Joplin, Missouri. Although the parties agreed upon the product market definition of acute care inpatient hospital services, they disagreed about the relevant geographic market. Specifically, the hospitals argued that the geographic market extended up to 54 miles from Joplin, while the FTC argued that it extended only 27 miles from Joplin. The district court agreed with the hospitals,[2] and on appeal, the court of appeals affirmed and wrote that the government provided only a static analysis of the geographic market and did not address the crucial question of where patients could go for hospital services in the event of a post-merger price increase.[3]

In 1995 the DOJ sought to block the merger of the only two general acute care hospitals in Dubuque, Iowa. The parties agreed on the relevant product market of acute care inpatient services, but as in the case of Joplin, they disagreed over the relevant geographic market. Specifically, the hospitals argued that the geographic market extended 70 to 100 miles from Dubuque, while the DOJ argued that it extended only 15 miles from Dubuque. The hospitals presented evidence suggesting that many hospital patients do not have established relationships with physicians, and thus loyalty to a particular physician would not prevent patients from using more distant hospitals, particularly if encouraged by the financial incentives of managed care organizations.

**Table 1** Most recent federal challenges to hospital mergers

| Case | Agency | Year | Reason for court's rejection |
|------|--------|------|------------------------------|
| Joplin, Missouri | FTC | 1995 | Geographic market definition |
| Dubuque, Iowa | DOJ | 1995 | Geographic market definition |
| Grand Rapids, Michigan | FTC | 1996 | Not-for-profit hospitals |
| Long Island, New York | DOJ | 1997 | Product market definition |
| Poplar Bluff, Missouri | FTC | 1999 | Geographic market definition |

Again the district court agreed with the hospitals, stating that "the government's case rests too heavily on past health care conditions, . . . makes invalid assumptions as to the reactions of third-party payers and patients to price changes," and "fails to undergo a dynamic approach to antitrust analysis, choosing instead to look at the situation as it currently exists within a competitive market."[4] The DOJ appealed the ruling to the Eighth Circuit Court of Appeals; but since the hospitals abandoned the proposed merger while the case was on appeal, the court deemed the case moot.[5]

Similarly, in a 1999 decision concerning the proposed merger of the only two acute care hospitals in Poplar Bluff, Missouri, the Eighth Circuit Court of Appeals rejected the government's more narrow geographic market definition (a 50-mile radius around Poplar Bluff, as opposed to the defendants' wider definition of a 65-mile radius, which can be up to 95 driving miles) and accordingly, allowed the merger to proceed. "The proximity of many patients to hospitals in other towns, coupled with the compelling and essentially unrefuted evidence that the switch to another provider by a small percentage of patients would constrain a price increase, shows the FTC's proposed market is too narrow."[6]

Again in this case the FTC and the hospitals agreed on the product market definition (general acute care inpatient hospital services, including primary and secondary services, but not tertiary or quaternary care hospital services) but disagreed on the geographic market definition. The hospitals provided evidence that, even at current prices, many commercially insured patients were seeking care at hospitals outside the 50-mile radius. Further, the hospitals' analysis suggested that if the merged hospital attempted to exercise its monopoly power by raising prices in the future, enough patients would seek care at alternative hospitals to render this price increase unprofitable.

Product market definition was quite controversial in the DOJ's challenge to the merger of two teaching hospitals in Long Island, New York. The government contended that the relevant product market should be defined as the cluster of services of "anchor hospitals" or the bundle of acute inpatient services provided by a subset of hospitals with prestigious reputations for offering an extensive range of high-quality services to managed care plans.[7] The DOJ argued that any managed care plan would have to include one or the other of the two merging hospitals to "anchor" its provider network in order to attract consumers. Other local hospitals that provide similar services but have less prestigious reputations, the DOJ argued, are not substitutes for anchor hospitals in the formation of provider networks for managed care plans.

The court rejected the DOJ's proposed product market definition of anchor hospitals on the basis that it was "unnecessarily restrictive," arguing that the services provided at so-called anchor hospitals are not unique and are not a separate product market. Approximately 85 percent of the services provided by the merging hospitals, the court noted, are offered by numerous other hospitals in the defendants' counties.

As these examples illustrate, defining the relevant market has been a very controversial part of recent health care antitrust analyses. There has been a great deal of disagreement about the best methods to define market boundaries with limited data and in markets characterized by managed care. Further, quality differentials between hospitals played a small role in the geographic market analyses in the Joplin, Dubuque, and Poplar Bluff cases, although the Appeals Court in the Poplar Bluff case noted that more distant and expensive hospitals could be practical alternatives to the merged hospital when the former hospitals are perceived to provide higher-quality care than the merged hospital. In the future, as more and more information on hospital-specific quality of care becomes available, physicians' and patients' perceptions of quality differentials across hospitals will most likely have a larger influence on hospital choices and thus will play an increasingly important role in product and geographic market definition.

A correctly defined market is essential to ensure that the antitrust enforcement process protects and promotes consumer welfare. Accordingly, in this chapter I discuss some of these controversies and review the issues that are integral to defining health care markets. Since geographic market analysis is heavily dependent on the product market definition, I will begin by addressing product markets in health care.

## The Product Market in Health Care Antitrust Cases

Consumers play a very important role in limiting the boundaries of product markets for antitrust analyses. The product market consists of all the goods and services that *consumers* consider to be reasonably interchangeable with the goods and services of the consolidating firms.

This general definition of a product market is easier to state than to apply. Actually specifying the product market is a complex task that involves analyzing current consumer and seller behavior and estimating future consumer and seller behavior. More specifically, defining the product market requires determining (1) who are the consumers, (2) which firms currently supply the same product(s) as the consolidating firms, (3) which firms currently supply products that consumers consider to be close substitutes to the product(s) of the consolidating firms, (4) which incumbent firms could increase supply of the product(s) or a close substitute if the consolidated firm attempted to exercise market power, and (5) which new firms could begin to supply with relative ease the product(s) or a close substitute if the consolidated firm attempted to exercise market power (that is, which firms are potential entrants).

## *Identifying the Consumers of Hospital and Physician Services*

Prior to managed care, when individuals required medical treatment, they would choose (often in conjunction with their physicians) which specialists or hospitals to use from the set of all available physicians and hospitals. MCCs or employers did not limit individuals' choices among physicians or hospitals, and thus individual patients together with their physicians made the choices concerning which hospital or which physician to receive treatment from.

Under managed care, the answer to the question—who are the consumers of hospital and physician services—is more complicated. In this situation both individuals in conjunction with their physicians, and MCCs or employers (involved in direct contracting with hospitals and physicians), can be thought of as the consumers of hospital and physician services.

Under managed care MCCs (or employers involved in direct contracting with providers) often impose restrictions, of varying degrees, on enrollees (or employees) with respect to which hospitals and physician organizations are covered by their health insurance plans. Accordingly, the decision to consume hospital or physician services under managed care can be thought of as a two-stage process.[8] It is the MCC (on behalf of its enrollees) or the employer (on behalf of its employees) that initially chooses which hospitals, physician organizations, and combinations of the two to include in its provider network. Thus, in the first stage MCCs are consumers of hospital and physician services in the sense that these organizations shop for and negotiate reimbursement rates with local hospitals and physician organizations. It is the MCC that decides which hospitals and physician organizations to contract with, and thus which hospitals and physician organizations its enrollees will have insured access to.

The second stage, after MCCs and employers have made their consumption selections (created their networks), involves enrollees or employees (in consultation with their physicians) making their consumption decisions among those hospitals or physicians in the network.

The implication of this two-stage consumption process under managed care is that a consolidated hospital or physician organization may compete with a different set of hospitals or physician organizations at the first stage than it does at the second stage. In other words, under managed care the relevant product and geographic markets for antitrust analyses involving consolidation among hospitals or physician organizations may differ between the first and second stages of the consumption process.

According to Gregory Vistnes, an economist, "Distinguishing between these different stages of competition and their different consumers helps resolve several controversies between the Agencies and hospitals in recent mergers. In effect, the Agencies have focused largely on first-stage competition, while the merging hospitals often emphasize evidence more relevant to second-stage competition. This can lead each side to different conclusions about market definition and competitive effects. Moreover, *both* sides may be correct: a hospital merger could reduce first-stage competition without significantly reducing second-stage competition. Nevertheless, even if a merger has little effect on second-stage competition, a reduction in first-stage competition is sufficient to conclude a hospital merger is anticompetitive."[9]

## *Identifying the Consumers of Health Care Financing*

Most privately insured individuals purchase health insurance through their employers. Thus, health plan choice for most privately insured consumers is determined, in part, by employers' decisions concerning which health insurance carriers and then which health plans of those carriers to offer their employees.

Accordingly, the decision to consume health insurance can be thought of as a two-step process involving at least two different consumers. First, employers decide which health insurance carriers and plans to offer their employees, and second, employees choose a health plan from the limited set of plans offered by their employers.

The implication of this two-stage consumption process in our employment-based health insurance system is that a consolidated insurance carrier competes with a different set of insurance carriers at the first stage than at the second stage. In other words, the relevant product and geographic markets for antitrust analyses involving consolidation among sellers of health care financing may differ between the first and second stages of the consumption process.

### Determining Close Substitutes for the Product of the Consolidating Firms

Determining substitutes entails an assessment of demand substitutability—a measure of the extent to which consumers would substitute some other product for (or forgo consumption of) the product of the consolidated health care firm, if the consolidated firm raised its price or lowered its quality.

When there is adequate data, one can assess demand substitutability with estimates of the cross-price elasticity of demand,[10] as established in *Brown Shoe Co. v. United States.*[11] The cross-price elasticity of demand is a gauge of the extent to which consumers consider two goods (or services) to be substitutes for each other (or how close a substitute consumers consider one good to be for another). It actually measures the responsiveness of consumers' demand for one good to changes in the price of the other good. If an increase in the price of one good (for example, butter) is associated with an increase in demand for the other good (in this example, margarine), then the cross-price elasticity will be positive and one can conclude that (1) at least some consumers consider the two goods to be substitutes for each other, and (2) for antitrust purposes the two goods belong in the same product market. The larger the positive estimate, the better or closer the substitutes are considered to be by consumers.

Unfortunately, economists' abilities to estimate cross-price elasticities of demand between various health care services (or own price elasticities of demand) have been severely hampered by data limitations. Estimates of cross-price elasticities between various physician services, various hospital services, or various types of health plans often do not exist, and if they do exist they are often based on out-of-date data.

Evaluating the potential for substitution in antitrust cases involving hospitals and physicians as plaintiffs is further complicated by the fact that under managed care, consumption of hospital and physician services is a two-stage process and involves multiple parties. For example, if two hospitals merge and raise prices, the extent of demand substitutability at the first stage will depend on the extent to which MCCs are able to exclude the merged hospital from their provider networks and still have a commercially viable plan, and at the second stage (assuming the merged hospital is included in MCCs' networks) on the extent to which MCCs are able to use financial incentives to discourage patients and physicians from using this merged and higher-priced hospital.

For MCCs to be able to exclude the merged hospital from their provider networks, first, there have to be alternative hospitals in the local market, and second, physicians have to be able to treat patients at these alternative hospitals. Factors specific to the local market could inhibit physicians' abilities to treat patients at alternative hospitals and thus inhibit MCCs' abilities to exclude certain hospitals from their networks. For example, an exclusive dealing arrangement requiring physicians to admit their patients to a particular local hospital could inhibit MCCs' abilities to exclude that hospital from their networks.

Moreover, for the managed care plan to be commercially viable without the merged hospital, patients and physicians have to be willing to use the alternative hospitals. If the alternative hospitals are more specialized (offer treatments for fewer types of diseases), physicians may be less willing to use them, especially when they are uncertain about patients' precise needs and it is costly to transfer patients between hospitals.[12] If the alternative hospitals are perceived as lower-quality providers relative to the merged hospital, patients and physicians may be less willing to use these hospitals, and thus managed care plans excluding the merged hospital may not be commercially viable. Finally, if the alternative hospitals are located further from patients relative to the merged hospital, patients and physicians may be less willing to use these more distant hospitals, and again managed care plans excluding the merged hospital may not be commercially viable.

This is particularly relevant under payer-driven competition,[13] where individuals effectively select their health care providers before knowing their health care needs. In this situation individuals select their providers (at least the ones to which they have insured access) at the time they select their health plan. Under these circumstances, individuals will value highly health plans that offer insured access to a broad range of providers and also insured access to certain providers (possible tertiary care providers or teaching hospitals if individuals associate teaching hospitals with high-quality care). Accordingly, MCCs may not be able to market health plans that do not include a tertiary care hospital or a teaching hospital.[14]

In general, increasing quality differentiation in health care markets will affect the extent of demand substitutability among hospitals or physician organizations. As the availability of provider-specific information on quality increases, payers' selective contracting decisions and patients' and physicians' choices of hospitals or specialists within the network will be based increasingly on perceived quality differentials. More and more, payers,' physicians,' and patients' responsiveness to quality differentials will define health care market boundaries. Therefore, to correctly define health care markets for antitrust purposes, it is essential that the market definition methods incorporate quality differentials as well as price differentials.

As in the case of hospital and physician services, evaluating the potential for substitution in antitrust cases involving health care insurers as plaintiffs is complicated by the fact that consumption of health care financing is often a two-stage process that involves multiple parties. For example, if two MCCs merge and raise prices, the extent of demand substitutability at the first stage will depend on the extent to which employers are willing and able to exclude the health plans offered by the merged MCC from the menu of plans offered to employees, and at the second stage on the extent to which employers continue to offer the health plans of the merged MCC, but are able to use financial incentives to discourage employees from choosing the higher-priced plans.

## Determining Excess Capacity and Potential Entrants

Determining excess capacity and potential entrants entails an assessment of supply substitutability—a measure of the extent to which current competitors would increase production of the consolidated firm's product(s) and the extent to which potential entrants would begin to produce the consolidated firm's product(s), if the consolidating health care firm raised its price or lowered its quality.

Estimates of the elasticity of supply, when they are available, can be used to gauge the ability and willingness of current and potential sellers of the product to increase supply in the event that the consolidating firm attempts to raise its price. Unfortunately, like estimates of cross-price elasticity of demand, estimates of supply elasticities for hospital, physician, and health care financing services are rarely available.

The impact of managed care on supply substitutability has received little attention. If managed care plans, possibly in the interest of reducing transaction costs, contract with hospitals offering a wide range of services and technologies, then the growth of managed care may have little impact on supply substitutability. If, on the other hand, MCCs increasingly contract with "centers of excellence" (hospitals with higher volumes and greater experience in providing particular services),[15] as recently recommended by the Leapfrog Group, then the growth of managed care may reduce supply substitutability, especially for high-tech services. The Leapfrog Group is encouraging "evidence-based hospital referrals" or referrals to hospitals with a minimum level of experience in treating certain medical conditions (for example, hospitals providing 500 or more coronary artery bypass surgeries per year).

The direct effect of evidence-based hospital referrals is likely to be an increase in quality. An indirect effect may be less supply substitutability: evidence-based hospital referrals may reduce the extent to which entrants can begin to supply new hospital services in response to rivals' price increases. It will only be profitable for entrants to begin to supply new hospital services if consumers are willing to purchase those services from the new entrant. If individuals (in conjunction with their physicians) believe that higher-quality hospital services are provided at incumbent hospitals with more experience in providing those specific services, then hospitals just starting to offer these services will be at a competitive disadvantage, reducing the extent of supply substitutability.

## Current Practices

How are product markets actually defined in health care antitrust cases? The Supreme Court in *Brown Shoe* did not establish which method(s) should be used to define product markets when estimates of cross-price elasticities are unavailable. However, the Court suggested that within broad product markets, well-defined submarkets may exist, and the boundaries of those submarkets can be determined by a smorgasbord of tests or "examining such practical indicia as industry or public recognition of the submarket as a separate economic entity, the product's peculiar characteristics and uses, unique production facilities, distinct customers, distinct prices, sensitivity to price changes, and specialized vendors."[16]

The federal enforcement agencies have also suggested tests to determine the interchangeability of products, and thus the boundaries of product markets. The agencies stated in their 1992 *Horizontal Merger Guidelines* that they will consider at least three factors in order to predict consumers' responses to price increases by the consolidating firms: (1) evidence that consumers have shifted purchases between the products in response to relative price changes in the past, (2) evidence that sellers have based their pricing or other business decisions on the notion that consumers consider the products to be substitutes, and (3) evidence on the timing and costs of switching between products.

In the following subsections, current practices and thinking about product market definition in health care cases are reviewed.

### MARKETS FOR HOSPITAL SERVICES

In hospital merger cases there is a precedent for defining hospitals' product markets as very broad clusters of services, despite the fact that demand substitutability between many hospital services is generally quite limited (for example, a patient in need of an appendectomy would most likely not consider treatment for pneumonia to be a good substitute for the appendectomy). In relatively recent merger cases, hospital product markets have been defined as either one cluster of services—acute care inpatient hospital services;[17] two clusters of services—general acute and primary care inpatient hospital services;[18] or three clusters of services—primary, secondary, and tertiary care inpatient hospital services.[19] Interestingly, in nonmerger hospital cases (tying, monopolization, refusal to deal, and exclusive dealing claims) product markets have been defined more narrowly—for example, the market for anesthesiology services,[20] the market for invasive cardiology services, and the market for adult open heart surgery.

Primary inpatient hospital services include less complex services, such as general surgeries (for example, appendectomies), general medicine (for example, care of a patient with pneumonia), and other basic hospital services (for example, obstetrics). General acute care hospitals offer primary inpatient services. Secondary inpatient hospital services include services requiring more sophisticated equipment or personnel, such as intensive care services. Some nonhospital facilities, such as surgi-centers, offer some primary and secondary inpatient services. Tertiary care inpatient hospital services, such as coronary artery bypass surgery, neonatal intensive care, oncology and radiation oncology care, neurosurgery, solid organ and bone marrow transplants, pediatric cardiology and surgery, acquired immunodeficiency syndrome care, spinal surgery, chronic dialysis, burn care, and inpatient psychiatry,[21] require especially sophisticated technology and professional expertise.[22] Most tertiary services are provided by a small subset of hospitals, such as teaching hospitals in large urban areas.

There are at least two potential justifications for this precedent of defining hospitals' product markets as broad clusters of services, although recent developments in health care markets may be weakening both justifications. The first justification is that many MCCs, while not the ultimate consumers of hospital services, often contract for hospital services on an all-or-nothing basis. With all-or-nothing contracting, the hospital is either included or not included in the HMO/PPO's provider network. So in effect MCCs are not contracting for individual hospital services; rather, they are contracting to provide their enrollees access to the full range of services at each hospital in the network.

Consistent with this, some methods of hospital reimbursement, such as global capitation and per diem, involve one payment for all hospital services, rather than separate payments for individual services. Under a global capitation contract the hospital is reimbursed on a per-member per-month basis, regardless of actual hospital services used. Under a per diem reimbursement system the hospital is reimbursed on a per-day basis, regardless of actual hospital services used—for example, $1500 per day. Per diem reimbursement is the most common type of reimbursement arrangement between HMOs and hospitals.[23] As of July 1998, approximately 33 percent of HMOs used capitated contracts for some portion of their payments to hospitals; 72 percent of HMOs used fee-for-service payments for some portion of their payments to hospitals; 86 percent used per diem rates; and 50 percent used DRG-based payments or rates based on patients' diagnoses.[24]

In markets with three or more hospitals, however, there is some evidence that MCCs are starting to contract for specific hospital services.[25] For example, Anthem Blue Cross and Blue Shield of Ohio has a statewide program that identifies high-quality hospitals, based on clinical standards for the treatment of coronary diseases, and then reimburses these hospitals for each coronary artery bypass surgery, angioplasty, or other major cardiovascular procedure performed, based on global rates per discharge.[26]

In addition, consistent with the recommendations of the Leapfrog Group, there is some evidence that coalitions of employers contracting directly with hospitals are starting to contract for specific hospital services, rather than on an all-or-nothing basis. For example, the Health Action Council of Northeast Ohio, an alliance of 140 of Cleveland's largest employers, began to contract with 5 of the 30 local hospitals as preferred providers for 22 specific conditions in 1997. On the basis of data from the Cleveland Health Quality Choice project and hospital-provided data on hospital-specific outcomes for specific procedures, the Council selected MetroHealth Medical Center as its only designated hospital for burns; the Cleveland Clinic, University Hospitals, and PHS-Mt. Sinai Medical Center for treatment of pulmonary disease; the Cleveland Clinic as the only designated hospital for heart transplants; and University Hospitals as the only designated hospital for treatment of cystic fibrosis. Cleveland Clinic and University Hospitals were selected for most of the 22 procedures, while PHS-Mt. Sinai was selected for 10 procedures, and Columbia/St. Vincent Charity Hospital was selected for 5 procedures.[27] However, this program did not "fly" for long—for example, the Cleveland Clinic withdrew as of December 1998.[28]

The second justification for the precedent of defining hospital product markets based on broad clusters of services is the belief that supply substitutability between primary and secondary hospital services is quite high—that is, hospitals can introduce new primary and secondary services with relative ease, when rival hospitals raise their prices or lower their quality for those particular services. Most hospitals have in common the base of technologies or capabilities that are necessary to meet the surgical, medical, and other needs of inpatients, such as operating rooms, anesthesia, intensive care capabilities, 24-hour nursing care, and pharmaceuticals. With high supply substitutability between hospital services, it makes sense to include multiple services in the same product market because each hospital is capable of producing the full range of hospital services. However, because tertiary services require especially sophisticated technologies, facilities, and professional expertise, the supply substitutabilities for tertiary services are greatly reduced.

The broad cluster approach to market definition in hospital merger cases is not always in the public interest. Defining hospital product markets based on broad clusters of services can lead to overestimation of the competitive harm of hospital consolidation (and thus to enforcers stopping hospital consolidations that are in the public interest) in certain situations and to underestimation of the competitive harm of hospital consolidations (and thus to enforcers allowing hospital consolidations that are not in the public interest) in other situations.[29]

The broad cluster approach may underestimate the competitive harm of consolidation or mask the consolidated hospital's potential to exercise market power (in the form of higher prices for specific treatments under treatment-based reimbursement, or higher prices for the entire package of hospital services under capitation or per diem reimbursement) when the hospitals proposing consolidation are the main or only providers of certain hospital services in the local market and when supply substitutability between hospital services is limited. Under the broad cluster approach the consolidated hospital's ability to exercise market power is masked by the presence of local rivals offering relatively similar clusters of services; however, the consolidated hospital is not prevented from exercising market power because there are no rivals offering or able to start offering those particular services with relative ease. In this case the courts may err on the side of allowing hospital consolidation when, in fact, the consolidation is not in the public interest.

On the other hand, the broad cluster approach may overestimate the competitive harm of consolidation or mask the abilities of rival hospitals to constrain the exercise of market power by the consolidating hospitals when the consolidating hospitals' rivals are specialized. As the extent of specialization increases, hospitals look less and less alike and, at the extreme, specialization could result in each hospital being the sole provider of certain services. Already there are hospitals that specialize in cancer treatment (Memorial Sloan-Kettering in New York), while others specialize in the treatment of children (Children's Hospital of Philadelphia). Exclusion of these more specialized rivals, who in combination may offer the full range of acute care hospital services, from the product market definition may result in the courts not allowing hospital mergers that are, in fact, in the public interest.

There is some anecdotal evidence of increasing specialization in hospital markets. For example, there are increasing numbers of health care firms specializing in one or a few services, such as Salick Health Care with its cancer centers that treat only cancer patients, and "cataract factories" that offer only cataract removal operations.[30] Other examples include MedCath, a firm based in Charlotte, North Carolina, that builds and manages specialty heart hospitals, and MediSphere Health Partners, a firm based in Nashville, Tennessee, that specializes in developing centers of excellence for women's health care.[31]

There is also evidence, however, of decreasing specialization in hospital markets. Examining data from 321 Metropolitan Statistical Areas (MSAs), researchers found that the proportion of hospitals in each MSA offering 13 out of 17 specialized services (including open heart surgery, angioplasty, MRI, and women's health centers) actually increased between 1990 and 1994.[32] Only the proportion of hospitals offering diagnostic radioisotope services, alcohol units, emergency departments, and transplants declined between 1990 and 1994.[33]

In terms of empirical analysis, the results are mixed.[34] In general, increasing hospital specialization is limited by at least three factors. First, specialized hospitals have less potential to realize economies of scope or the lower costs associated with producing multiple products using shared inputs. The treatment of multiple diseases at a general hospital may result in lower costs through the realization of scope economies associated with shared inputs, such as diagnostic facilities and surgical suites. Second, many patients do not want to travel far from their homes and their regular physicians, and thus only the biggest cities may be large enough to support specialized hospitals. Third, many diseases are associated with other kinds of health problems (for example, diabetes often leads to eye, nerve, kidney, and heart problems), and thus it may make sense to treat patients with these diseases in general hospitals.

As stated earlier, a correctly defined product market is essential to ensure that antitrust enforcement protects and promotes the welfare of consumers. Accordingly, whether it makes good public policy sense to continue to use broad clusters of services to define hospital product markets in future merger cases depends on whether hospitals in the future can introduce new services with relative ease when rival hospitals raise their prices for those services, and whether managed care plans and other buyers of hospital services continue to contract and pay for hospital services on an all-or-nothing basis. If these factors change, then using the broad cluster approach to hospital product market definition may not result in correctly defined markets, and thus may hinder antitrust enforcers' abilities to protect and promote welfare.

## MARKETS FOR PHYSICIAN SERVICES

At present there is little precedent for defining physicians' product markets as broad clusters of services. This, however, may have more to do with the absence of antitrust cases involving multispecialty physician organizations in mature managed care markets than with the lack of justifications. If managed care organizations' tendency toward "all or nothing contracting" with hospitals justifies the use of broad clusters of hospital services for hospital product market definition, then evidence of this sort of contracting with multispecialty physician organizations may also justify defining the product markets for physician services as clusters of services. In some markets MCCs contract with (and reimburse using global capitation) physician organizations to provide their enrollees access to the full range of services at each physician organization in the network.

Likewise, if high supply substitutability between hospital services justifies the use of broad clusters of hospital services for hospital product market definition, then evidence of this sort of supply substitutability for physician services may justify defining markets for physician services as clusters of services. Supply substitutability between various physician services appears to be quite high—that is, multispecialty physician organizations appear able to introduce new services with relative ease by hiring additional physicians, when rival physician organizations raise their prices or lower their quality for those services.

Accordingly, in markets characterized by multispecialty physician organizations and global capitation reimbursement, these justifications suggest a broad cluster approach to market definition in antitrust cases involving physician organization consolidation.

Despite the potential justifications for using a broad cluster approach in certain markets for physician services, the FTC and DOJ typically start with the assumption that each physician specialty or type of physician service offered is a separate product market. In a business review letter (September 15, 1998) the DOJ stated: "The Department has found that in general all services provided by each physician specialty can be considered to be a separate relevant product (service) market." Taking this a step further, in its letter of March 8, 1996, regarding a proposed joint venture of anesthesiologists in California, the DOJ defined the product market as a subset of all anesthesiologists. Specifically, the product market was defined as "managed anesthesia services provided by adequately sized, financially integrated anesthesia medical groups that have a reputation and range of experience comparable to the existing Groups and are known and acceptable to the surgeons at the Affected Hospitals."

Similarly, in numerous advisory opinions the FTC has calculated the inclusiveness of proposed provider organizations based on the assumption that each physician specialty constitutes a separate product market. This includes hematologists/oncologists (September 21, 1995), otolaryngologists (August 15, 1995), general surgeons (May 14, 1997), obstetricians/gynecologists (May 14, 1997), urologists (January 23, 1996), and neurologists (August 13, 1998).

The agencies also consider, however, whether there are other services or specialties that are sufficiently close substitutes to justify including these other services or specialties in the product market.[35] For example, the agencies have found family practitioners (FPs), general practitioners (GPs), and internists to be good substitutes for one another, and thus the agencies have viewed these three types of physicians to be participants in a single product market.[36]

More generally, to define product markets for physician services one would like estimates of demand substitutability (for example, estimates of consumers' abilities and willingness to substitute the services of GPs or FPs for the services of gynecologists or pediatricians, if incumbent gynecologists or pediatricians increased their prices or lowered their quality of care) and supply substitutability (for example, estimates of general and family practitioners' willingness and ability to provide primary care services to women, infants, and children themselves or their willingness and ability to recruit additional gynecologists or pediatricians, if incumbent gynecologists or pediatricians increased their prices or lowered their quality of care). However, these sorts of estimates are rarely available.

Thus the question becomes: what do current patterns of service offerings tell us about the boundaries of product markets for physician services? Unfortunately, current patterns of service offerings by different specialists do not tell the complete story about demand and supply substitutability. The observation that gynecologists, GPs, and FPs are all currently providing primary care services to women may suggest that demand and supply substitutability are sufficiently high to include the three in one product market. However, merely observing that GPs and FPs do not currently provide primary care services to infants and children is not sufficient to determine that there is a separate product market for the services of pediatricians. To make this determination, one would need to know whether GPs and FPs would be willing to start to provide primary care services to infants and children, if the prices of those services increased.

The Court of Appeals in the Marshfield Clinic case[37] emphasized the importance of supply substitutability between various physician services in the definition of product markets for physician services and emphasized the problem of using current patterns of service offerings as an estimate of supply substitutability. At the District Court level, the plaintiff's expert had argued that specific procedures, called Diagnostic Related Groups (DRGs), such as circumcision of a male under 17 years, circumcision of a male 17 years or older, hysterectomy, and reconstructive surgery for the uterine system, define separate product markets for physician services. However, the Court of Appeals ruled that DRGs do not represent separate product markets because of supply substitutability: "Classification in a DRG is unrelated to the conditions of supply. Many, no doubt most, physicians perform or are capable of performing more than one procedure, and are therefore part of the market even if at present not active in it. If the Clinic overprices a particular procedure, other physicians capable of performing that procedure will have an added incentive to do so, knocking down the excessive price."[38]

A second pertinent question is what the opinions of buyers of physician services, such as health plan officials and employers, tell us about demand substitutability, and thus about the boundaries of product markets for physician services. In the absence of estimates of cross-price elasticities, the FTC and DOJ have been relying heavily on these sorts of opinions. For example, in its business review letter of March 1, 1996, the DOJ concluded, in part on the basis of interviews with local officials of health plans, that there is a separate product market for the services of pediatricians. Apparently, these officials did not view GPs and FPs as substitutes for pediatricians in the formation of local managed care physician networks: "Our investigation, including interviews with the medical directors and provider contracting officials of health benefits plans, leads us to the conclusion that it is impossible successfully to market a health plan that requires (or provides incentives to) its enrollees to use doctors other than pediatricians to care for their children, especially in the more affluent and populous areas of southern New Jersey."

Likewise, in its business review letter of July 7, 1997, the DOJ concluded, in part on the basis of the views of local buyers of physician services, that there is a separate product market for the services of board-certified gastroenterologists: "Particularly in this area of Pennsylvania (which we are told has a particularly large Medicare population that frequently requires the attention of gastroenterologists), the presence of a variety of gastroenterologists is a critical selling point. Payers stated that they could not market a product in the Lehigh Valley area that excluded gastroenterologists but included other types of doctors who also performed some of the procedures gastroenterologists perform." Accordingly, the relevant product market was defined as the services of board-certified gastroenterologists, and the DOJ concluded that the proposed merger of 12 of the 14 gastroenterologists in Allentown/Bethlehem, Pennsylvania, was likely to have anticompetitive effects.

Similarly, in its business review letter of July 1, 1996, the DOJ concluded, partly on the basis of interviews with buyers of physician services, that there is not a separate product market for the services of surgeons specializing in rectal and colon surgery. Apparently, those interviewed believed that, in the formation of managed care physician networks, general surgeons were close substitutes for surgeons specializing in rectal and colon surgery. "Based on [agency interviews with buyers] it is evident that managed care plans . . . do not consider it necessary to include dedicated colon and rectal specialists among their providers."

The courts appear to be approaching definition of product markets for physician services in a manner that is relatively similar to the approach of the FTC and DOJ. The courts have considered product market definition in markets for physician services in at least three recent private antitrust cases—one in Vicksburg, Mississippi, one in Lincoln, Nebraska, and one in Marshfield, Wisconsin.

In the Vicksburg case, the plaintiff sought to define four relevant product markets for physician services: primary care (including the services of GPs, FPs, and internists); general surgery; urology; and otolaryngology (ear, nose, and throat) services.[39] Further, the plaintiff argued that there were two relevant submarkets—the submarket of pediatric services and the submarket of multispecialty clinic services purchased by MCCs. While the defendant recognized the market for primary care as a relevant product market, there was disagreement over whether pediatricians and obstetricians/gynecologists should be included in the market for primary care services.[40]

To settle this issue, the court in the Vicksburg case relied on both current patterns of service offerings and the opinions of officials at managed care plans. The court noted that obstetricians/gynecologists do not provide primary care services to the population as a whole, and women do not use obstetricians/gynecologists for primary care purposes. Further, the court wrote that pediatricians "cannot substitute for internists or general practitioners in the formation of a managed care panel." This last argument is remarkably similar to the government's argument in its business review letter of March 1, 1996. Accordingly, the court agreed with the plaintiff and ruled that the market for primary care services includes the services of GPs, FPs, and internists, and excludes the services of pediatricians and obstetricians/gynecologists.[41]

Interestingly, neither the court in the Vicksburg case nor the court in a recent Long Island hospital merger case allowed the definition of separate product markets based entirely on the purchasing needs of managed care plans. In both cases the plaintiffs argued that managed care plans must purchase services from certain providers (specifically, physician services from multispecialty clinics and hospital services from anchor hospitals, respectively) to have a marketable provider network. The court in the Vicksburg case did not accept the plaintiff's submarket for multispecialty clinic services purchased by managed care plans. Likewise, the court in the Long Island case did not accept a separate product market for anchor hospital services purchased by managed care plans.

A major difference between the two cases is that in the Vicksburg case the court acknowledged that in communities with developed managed care markets, managed care plans may prefer to contract with multispecialty clinics, rather than with independent physicians and physicians associated with smaller clinics. However, the court found that managed care in Mississippi is in its infancy, and managed care plans are contracting with independent physicians and physicians associated with clinics of all sizes. Accordingly, the court concluded that the services offered by independent physicians and physicians associated with smaller clinics are substitutes for the services of the physicians associated with the two merging multispecialty clinics, and thus there is not a separate product market for the physician services bought by managed care plans.

MARKETS FOR HEALTH CARE FINANCING

It should come as no surprise that the boundaries of product markets for health care financing are also quite controversial. The controversy focuses on two issues: whether managed care health insurance constitutes a separate product market from traditional health insurance and, if so, whether HMOs constitute a separate product market from other forms of managed care health insurance, such as PPOs and POS plans.

Before getting into the issue of demand and supply substitutability for health care financing, we need to ask what the product is. Health care financing can consist of multiple components, including risk bearing, claims processing, utilization management, quality assurance, and insured access to the specific health care providers in the associated provider network. Each component can be purchased separately, or all can be purchased from one seller. Some sellers offer all the components, while some firms offer only some of these components. HMOs tend to offer all of the components. PPOs are increasingly likely to include utilization management and quality assurance.

As was true for hospital and physician services, the key issues in defining product markets for health insurance are demand substitutability (the extent to which consumers of insurance would substitute various types of health plans—HMOs, PPOs, POS, and conventional insurance—if the price of one type of plan increased or the quality of one type of plan deteriorated) and supply substitutability (the extent to which current and potential competitors would provide the various types of plans if the price of one type of plan increased or the quality of one type of plan decreased). If consumers of insurance are willing and able to switch between the various types of health plans, then demand substitutability is high and the various types of health plans should be included in the same product market for antitrust analyses. If sellers of insurance are willing and able to supply each of the various types of health plans, then supply substitutability is high and the various types of health plans should be included in the same product market for antitrust analyses.

There has been more empirical analysis of demand substitutability in markets for health care financing than in those for hospital and physician services. At least three recent studies suggest that price does matter—privately insured consumers switch plans in response to increases in their insurance premiums. Nonetheless, assessment of demand substitutability between various types of health plans is complicated by at least two factors. First, most privately insured individuals purchase health insurance through their employers, and thus health plan choice for these individuals is determined, in part, by employers' decisions concerning which health plans to offer their employees. Insured employees do not choose their health plans from the full set of plans offered in the market.

Second, choice of health plan is affected by adverse selection, or the propensity of the least healthy, highest-risk individuals to choose the most generous plans. The premiums of the most generous plans will be higher because of the higher costs of offering more generous benefits and the higher costs of insuring a less healthy group of enrollees. This increase in premiums due to adverse selection inefficiently induces some enrollees to leave the most generous plans because they are subsidizing the costs of insurance for the least healthy individuals. There-fore, cross-price elasticities between HMOs, PPOs, POS plans, and conventional plans may be measuring both the closeness of substitutes and the extent of adverse selection.

Empirical analysis of demand substitutability has been further ham-pered by lack of data. To correctly estimate cross-elasticities between HMOs, PPOs, POS plans, and conventional insurance plans, one would need representative data that include information on all avail-able health plans in the market, including differences in quality and the premiums paid by employers and their employees. Unfortunately, these data are not available. The best available estimates are based on employees' choice of health plans offered by a single employer;[42] how-ever, as just discussed, this is only part of the story. These studies do not directly answer the question of how consumers regard HMOs, PPOs, POS plans, and conventional insurance plans in terms of substitutabil-ity because employees are not choosing among all health plans in the market, and, as a result of employer subsidies, the relative prices of health plans available to employees may be quite different from the rel-ative market prices.

One study examined employees' choice of health plan within the University of California system in 1994, the year the university changed from paying the full premium for most plans to paying a fixed amount set equal to the lowest-priced health plan. Employees had a choice of at least two HMOs, a PPO, and an indemnity plan. Of the employees switching from "pay HMOs" (HMOs that required an em-ployee premium contribution), 94 percent switched to "free HMOs" (HMOs that did not require an employee contribution).[43] Moreover, of the employees switching from indemnity plans that became consider-ably more expensive, 50 percent switched to a PPO that did not require an employee contribution and 46 percent switched to "free HMOs." The generalizability of these results, however, is questionable because the University of California system may be different from most others; specifically, benefits in the University of California system are stan-dardized across plans, and many plans are characterized by overlapping provider networks (the exception is the Kaiser HMO with its closed panel).

Another study examined employees' choice of health plan at Har-vard University in 1995, the year Harvard changed its system from one of subsidizing more expensive insurance plans to a system of contributing an equal dollar amount to each plan.[44] This change increased the annual price of the PPO, the most generous plan, by $597 for an individual and $960 for a family. Although the researchers did not estimate cross-price elasticities between the PPO and HMO plans, their results suggest that demand for the PPO is quite sensitive to price. More specifically, they found that each 10 percent increase in the price of the PPO results in a 20 percent decrease in enrollment in the PPO.

Yet another study examined employees' choice of health plan at Stanford University in 1994 and 1995.[45] Employees were offered the choice of four major health plans (one POS plan, one group practice HMO, and two network model HMOs), with standardized benefits[46] and the university contributing a percentage of the cost of the lowest-cost plan. Between 1994 and 1995 the premiums for each of the plans decreased, although the size of the decrease varied across plans. The authors of the study did not estimate cross-price elasticities between the POS plan and the network and group HMOs, but their results suggest that employee demand for each of the four plans is price-sensitive. For example, they estimated that a 1 percent increase in premiums for the POS or group practice HMO plans would result in a 0.2 to 1 percent decrease in enrollment in those plans, and a 1 percent increase in premiums for the network model HMOs would result in a 0.3 to 1.5 percent decrease in enrollment in those HMOs.

In the absence of current estimates of cross-elasticities of demand between various types of health plans, there are at least two readily observable factors that can help in the assessment of the extent of demand substitutability. Both of these factors suggest a high degree of demand substitutability, and thus a broad definition of the product market including all types of health plans.

First, observations of businesses offering their employees choices among different types of health plans, such as HMOs, PPOs, and POS plans (more likely for large employers), and observations of businesses switching their offerings between different types of health plans provide some evidence that at least the health benefits managers and employees at these businesses view different types of plans as substitutes. It is estimated that 50 to 70 percent of employers offer their employees the health plans of only one insurance carrier, but most insurance carriers offer multiple types of health plans, including HMO, PPO, and POS plans.[47]

In the small-employer market (defined as firms with 50 or fewer em-

ployees) the vast majority of businesses (94 percent) offering health insurance in 1995 offered only one plan; however, between 1993 and
1995 there was a dramatic increase in the percentage of small businesses offering a managed care plan, rather than a traditional plan, as
their only choice for employees (from 19 to 61 percent).[48] Moreover,
price was the major factor in small businesses' decisions to switch. A 10
percent decrease in prices of managed care plans, relative to traditional
insurance plans, increased the probability that small businesses offered
a managed care plan by 2.4 percent in 1995. A more recent survey also
suggests that small businesses offering health insurance are very likely
to offer only one plan option and quite price-sensitive. More specifically, the Kaiser Family Foundation's survey of small businesses (defined as 3 to 24 employees) found that among small businesses offering
health insurance in 2001, 71 percent offered only one plan option and
28 percent switched health plans in the previous two years, with price
being the most important reason cited for the switch.[49]

Second, in the assessment of demand substitutability one can observe the extent of product differentiation between the various types of
health plans (the similarities and differences across plans' provider networks and other characteristics, such as benefit designs). The greater
the similarities and the smaller the differences between types of plans,
the more likely consumers are to view them as substitutes. For example, if the provider networks of HMOs and PPOs overlap to a large extent, then consumers will be more likely to view the HMOs and PPOs
as substitutes. Further, when plans have overlapping provider networks, consumers' costs of switching health plans are reduced. Accordingly, the extent of overlap between plans' provider networks is a very
important determinant of consumers' willingness to switch health
plans, and thus of the relevant product market.

Typically, traditional plans include insured access to all providers
(the associated provider network is unlimited), while in theory HMOs
and PPOs include insured access to a more limited network of providers. POS plans represent a hybrid of these other types of insurance in
the sense that the product includes insured access to all providers, but
the extent of coverage for particular providers varies based on the POS
plans' associated provider network.

Recent evidence, however, suggests HMOs and PPOs are offering
broad, overlapping networks that include almost all the providers in

each local market.[50] Consistent with this, the results of a 1995 national survey show that about half of all physicians had contracts with 5 or more separate health plans, and about one-quarter had contracts with 10 or more health plans.[51] Likewise, there is evidence that managed care plans in many markets are contracting with most hospitals. For example, in the New York City metropolitan statistical area (MSA) there are 71 hospitals, and the average number of hospital contracts per managed care product is 66.[52] In the Fort Lauderdale MSA there are 15 hospitals, and the average number of hospital contracts per managed care product is 13.[53]

There is also evidence indicating that the extent of supply substitutability between various types of health insurance plans is quite high. Most insurance carriers offer multiple types of insurance plans. For example, Aetna U.S. Healthcare, PacifiCare Health System, and United HealthCare Corp. all offer HMOs, PPOs, POS plans, and indemnity products.[54] The American Association of Health Plans estimated that 75 percent of the insurance carriers offering an HMO plan also offered a POS plan or other open-access plan (plan that allows members to use out-of-network providers without referral, but at added expense), 59 percent also offered a PPO product, and 59 percent also offered an indemnity product in 1996.[55]

All these factors suggest a single product market for health care financing; however, the role played by indemnity plans is shrinking, while the role played by managed care plans is growing. Some have argued that indemnity plans, being the most generous type of health insurance, are in an adverse selection death spiral and may cease to exist.[56] If indemnity plans continue to lose market share, then a new and more narrow definition of the product market may be required.

The current precedent for defining product markets in health care financing cases is consistent with this evidence on the extent of demand and supply substitutability between various types of insurance plans. Specifically, the courts have defined the relevant product market to be quite broad. In *Blue Cross and Blue Shield of Wisconsin v. Marshfield Clinic*[57] the Appeals Court reversed the district court's decision upholding a jury verdict based on a separate market for HMOs on the grounds that HMOs compete with other types of health plans. In *Ball Memorial Hospital et al. v. Mutual Hospital Insurance*[58] the court defined the product as health care financing: "The Blues, other insurance companies, hospitals offering PPOs, HMOs, and self-insuring employers all offer methods of financing health care. Employers and individual prospective patients easily may switch from one financing package to another; nothing binds an employer or patient to one plan."[59]

The DOJ, however, defined the product market more narrowly in its recent challenge to Aetna's purchase of Prudential.[60] More specifically, the DOJ defined a separate market for HMO and HMO/POS products that did not include PPO or indemnity plans. The government's argument was based primarily on benefit design differences, such as the tendency of HMOs to offer better preventive care benefits and greater limits on treatment options and referrals to specialists, relative to PPOs, as well as pricing differentials. Since the case was settled by consent order, it is still uncertain whether a court would accept this narrower product market definition.

## The Geographic Market in Health Care Antitrust Cases

The goal of geographic market definition is to specify the boundaries of the geographic area in which competition occurs. A correctly defined geographic market includes every location in which there is a seller capable of constraining the pricing and quality-setting behavior of the consolidated firm. In other words, a correctly defined geographic market includes those locations in which there are sellers to which enough consumers would be willing to go to obtain the product, if the consolidated firm raised its price or lowered its quality.

As this suggests, consumers play a very important role in limiting the size of geographic markets. For many health care services, the size of geographic markets is limited both by the willingness and ability of MCCs to include more distant sellers, rather than more local sellers, in their provider networks and by the willingness and ability of individuals (and their physicians) to travel to obtain (provide) health care services. The willingness and ability of individuals (and their physicians) to travel is, in turn, a function of multiple factors, including where local physicians have hospital admitting privileges, local physicians' referral patterns, real and perceived quality differences between closer and more distant providers, and the financial incentives embedded in managed care plans.

## Current Practices in Geographic Market Definition

The federal enforcement agencies in the 1992 *Horizontal Merger Guidelines* defined the relevant geographic market as the smallest geographic area in which a monopolist or group of sellers, if combined into a cartel, could profitably exercise market power. More specifically, the *Guidelines* define the geographic market as a region such that a hypothetical monopolist could "profitably impose at least a 'small but significant and nontransitory' increase in price, holding constant the terms of sale for all products produced elsewhere." As enumerated in the *Guidelines*, the DOJ and FTC will look at the following factors in attempting to predict whether a price increase will be profitable or the likely reaction of consumers to price increases: (1) evidence that consumers have shifted purchases between sellers in different geographic regions in response to relative price changes or changes in quality; (2) evidence that sellers base their business decisions on predictions concerning consumers' choices among sellers in different geographic regions; and (3) the timing and costs of switching between sellers in different geographic regions.

In the following subsections current practices and thinking about geographic market definition in health care cases are reviewed. Geographic markets for the services of certain physician specialists, such as cardiologists, or for tertiary care hospital services, such as open heart surgeries or kidney transplants, may be quite large, while geographic markets for the services of pediatricians or hospital-based emergency services may be quite small.

### MARKETS FOR HOSPITAL SERVICES

Until the mid-1990s, the precedent had been to rely, almost exclusively, on the Elzinga-Hogarty (E-H) test[61] to define geographic markets for hospital services. This test is based on analysis of readily available and historical "patient flow" data that describe where patients have traveled to obtain hospital services. According to the E-H test, a hospital's geographic market has been correctly defined if (1) the hospital(s) in that geographic area has treated most of the patients living in that area (that is, few local residents have traveled outside the geographic area to obtain the hospital service) and (2) most of the hospital's patients resided in that geographic area (few persons living outside the geographic area have traveled into the geographic area to obtain the hospital service).

The problems associated with this static (one point in time) and historical analysis are now widely recognized.[62] Exclusive use of the E-H test implies a decision to ignore factors that provide information on why consumers travel to more distant hospitals and where consumers could go for hospital services in the event that the consolidated hospital attempts to exercise monopoly power in the future.

When there are distant hospitals that consumers have not chosen under pre-consolidation prices, but that consumers might choose under higher post-consolidation prices, the E-H test may underestimate the geographic market for hospital services. Likewise, there are at least two reasons to believe that the E-H test can lead to overestimates of geographic markets for hospital services. First, when there are significant differences in consumers' perceptions of hospital-specific quality of care, then the E-H test may overestimate the geographic market for those hospitals perceived to be of higher quality. For example, if an urban hospital(s) is larger, more sophisticated, and provides a wider range of services and a higher perceived quality of care than the hospitals in the surrounding towns, then one-way migration from the surrounding towns to the more urban hospital will be observed. On the evidence of this one-way migration, the E-H test will define the geographic market for the urban hospital to include the hospitals in the surrounding towns. However, since no or few urban patients are willing to travel to the surrounding towns for hospital care, the urban hospital can exercise market power in a smaller geographic market (excluding the hospitals in the surrounding towns).

Use of the E-H test in combination with cluster-of-service methodology to define the product market can also lead to overestimates of the relevant market. If the product market is defined as acute care inpatient hospital services, then the patient flow statistics will include tertiary care patients who are most likely willing to travel longer distances than primary or secondary care patients. Empirical evidence suggests that travel distances are (1) lowest for services sought on an urgent basis, such as heart failure and shock, and routine, elective services, such as hernia repair and appendectomy; (2) higher for more complex procedures, such as back, joint, and vascular surgery; and (3) highest for the most complex procedures, such as open heart surgery and kidney transplants.[63] Therefore, use of the E-H test may lead to a geographic market definition that includes the more distant tertiary care providers when, in fact, the local hospital(s) are able to exercise market power in primary and secondary care services in a smaller geographic area.

More recently, economists have used critical loss analysis to delineate hospitals' geographic markets.[64] As discussed in the previous chapter, critical loss analysis is based on the idea that if the merged hospital increases its price, it will lose some of its patients to competitors. If, as the result of a small price increase, the hospital's loss of patients to competitors outside its currently defined geographic market is more than a certain amount, this suggests that the geographic market has been defined too narrowly. This method has its own problems and critics.[65]

The courts' decisions in the Joplin, Dubuque, and Poplar Bluff hospital merger cases (discussed earlier in this chapter) suggest a relatively large geographic market for hospital services. These decisions are based, in part, on controversial assumptions: first, that in response to hospitals' price increases, employers and MCCs are willing and able to modify their health plans either by excluding the more expensive, but less distant hospital from their networks or by including financial incentives that encourage physicians and enrollees to use less expensive, but more distant hospitals; and second, that in response to financial incentives in managed care plans, hospital patients are willing to travel to more distant hospitals for acute hospital services (even if these patients have to switch physicians in order to obtain care at more distant hospitals).

With respect to the first assumption, little is known about employers' and MCCs' willingness and ability to modify their health plans in response to anticompetitive behavior on the part of network hospitals. The trend has been toward more, not less, inclusive networks. However, HMOs in California have started to explore the use of tiered provider networks combined with financial incentives to induce enrollees to go to "A-list" hospitals that have agreed to provide services at lower rates than other network hospitals. For example, enrollees in PacifiCare Health System's Select Hospital Plan face no copayments if they receive care from an "A-list" hospital but a copayment ranging from $100–$400 if they receive care at other network hospitals.[66] With regard to the second assumption, empirical evidence suggests that multiple factors influence insured patients' willingness to travel to purchase hospital services,[67] including (1) patient characteristics, such as diagnosis, and thus whether the hospital service is elective or not, (2) consumers' and physicians' perceptions of hospital-specific quality, and (3) hospital characteristics, such as breadth of services and capacity.[68]

Even more to the point, the results of at least four studies suggest that patients are not willing to travel long distances for many hospital services. Two of these studies, while not providing direct tests of the hypothesis that MCCs can steer patients to more distant hospitals, do provide evidence that convenience, measured as distance to the hospital, exerts a very strong influence on hospital choice.[69] Patients appear to be much less likely to choose distant hospitals.

The other two studies provide a more direct test of (and little support for) the hypothesis that managed care increases the size of the geographic market (in terms of travel distance to hospitals). Using patient discharge data from hospitals located in 14 counties in California for the years 1984 and 1993, one study found that HMOs are able to steer patients to slightly more distant hospitals. Between 1984 and 1993 patients insured by HMOs increased their travel distances by about .34 of a mile (compared with other private payers). However, the net effect of HMO penetration on distance traveled was actually negative because HMO penetration was found to reduce travel distances for non-HMO patients.[70]

Similarly, using data on patients discharged from hospitals (excluding births and neonatal discharges) in California in 1985 and 1991, another study found no evidence that travel distances for private patients increased compared with Medicare patients.[71] Since private patients were more likely to be in managed care plans than Medicare patients, the authors conclude that their results do not support the claim that managed care expands the geographic market for hospital services.

We know little about how hospital-physician affiliations and patient-physician loyalties affect patients' hospital choices. There is evidence that some patients do switch providers, but their reasons for these changes are less clear. The results of a 1996–1997 Robert Wood Johnson Foundation survey of 38,000 persons in the United States showed that 13 percent of privately insured individuals changed their usual source of care.[72] Similarly, a survey by the Center for Studying Health

System Change[73] found that of those persons who identified a usual source of care (a physician, nurse, other health professional, or a specific place other than a hospital emergency room), 13 percent changed providers in 1999. More than three-quarters of those who changed their providers did so for reasons unrelated to their health insurance, such as wanting a more convenient provider, unavailability of their provider due to retirement, or personal relocations. Similarly, a 1997 Kaiser/Commonwealth survey of 4,000 adults in the United States found that 31 percent of individuals changing their health insurance plans changed their physicians as well.[74]

MARKETS FOR PHYSICIAN SERVICES

As in markets for hospital services, the geographic boundaries of markets for physician services will depend on the nature of the physician services at issue, the perceptions of patients and referring physicians about physician-specific quality of care, and the willingness and ability of employers and MCCs to modify their health plans in response to anticompetitive behavior on the part of physician organizations. The size of geographic markets for physician services may also vary across urban and rural areas; patients may be willing to travel greater distances in rural areas.

With respect to the nature of the physician services, the relevant issues include whether the physician services are elective or not, how often the services are consumed, and how complex the services are. For example, patients seek the care of primary care physicians on a regular basis (annual examinations and routine care) and thus tend to choose primary care physicians located relatively close to their homes or jobs. This may be especially true for pediatricians, who see their patients frequently. Accordingly, the geographic market for primary care physicians tends to be quite small. Most specialists, however, compete in broader geographic markets. Patients seek the care of most specialists (exceptions include OB/GYNs) on a less regular basis, and thus may be more willing to travel greater distances to obtain the services of specialists. Moreover, because the services of some specialists are sought only in unusual circumstances, patients may not have established relationships with specialists and may be more willing to travel to distant specialists included in managed care networks.

Because there have been many fewer antitrust cases concerning physicians (as compared with hospitals), there has been relatively little analysis of how consumers' and physicians' perceptions of physician-specific quality or employers' and MCCs' willingness to modify their health plans affects patients' willingness to travel to obtain physician services. Further, the lack of public sources of data on where residents of specific areas go to obtain physician services makes it difficult to perform complete E-H tests in markets for physician services. However, if the consolidating physician organizations have data on the addresses of their patients, it may be possible to perform part of the E-H test. Specifically, it may be possible to measure the extent to which persons living outside the city/town travel into the city/town to obtain the physician services in question. With data only from the consolidating physician organizations, however, it is not possible to measure the extent to which local residents currently travel to other geographic areas to obtain the physician services in question. Therefore, it would be especially difficult to predict the extent to which local residents would be willing to travel to other geographic areas in the event that the consolidating physicians attempted to exercise market power.

This inability to calculate both parts of the E-H test for physician services may lead to overestimates of the second-stage geographic market for physician services. As has been shown for hospital markets,[75] if physicians located in cities or larger towns practice in larger groups that offer a wider range of services and consumers perceive these physicians to be offering higher physician-specific quality of care, then one-way migration from the surrounding towns to the more urban physicians will be observed. Based on evidence of this one-way migration, the E-H test will define the geographic market for the urban physicians to include the physicians in the surrounding towns, and this may be a gross overestimate of the geographic market. It is possible that the urban physicians can exercise market power in a smaller geographic area. While rural patients appear to be willing to travel to the urban physicians, most urban patients may not be willing to travel to physicians practicing in the surrounding towns. The problem is there is no patient flow data to measure the extent to which urban patients are willing to travel to the surrounding towns for physician services.

The government and the courts have used E-H tests and alternative methodologies to define geographic markets for physician services. The DOJ in its business review letters regarding proposed consolidations of physician organizations has used county lines, circles, and studies of patient travel patterns to define geographic markets for physician services. For example, in its letter of March 8, 1996, regarding the proposed joint venture of anesthesiologists in California, the geographic market was defined on the basis of county lines—specifically, it was defined as Orange County. In its October 17, 1996 letter regarding the proposed merger of the 16 solo anesthesiologists who were practicing at one hospital in Annapolis, Maryland, the DOJ defined the geographic market using a 25-mile radius around the hospital. However, the DOJ added that under any plausible geographic market definition, the merger did not raise any substantial competitive concern. Yet another approach was taken in the March 19, 1996 letter regarding family practice physicians, internists, and general surgeons in rural, northern Minnesota, where the geographic market was defined to include physicians located as far away as 35 miles. This geographic market definition was based on studies showing that residents of this rural county "commonly travel significant distances to receive primary care and other health care services." However, the DOJ added that in general "geographic markets for primary care services tend to be more localized, often confined to a city and its environs."

As mentioned earlier, few antitrust cases involving physician consolidation have been heard by the courts. In a recent private case involving a challenge to the merger of the two largest physician clinics in Vicksburg, Mississippi, the court allowed the plaintiff to use a one-way E-H test to define the geographic markets for physician services.[76] The court accepted the plaintiff's economic expert's definition of the geographic market for primary care physicians based on patient inflow statistics. This geographic market was defined as the area from which the representative clinics drew 87 percent of their patients, and it included one county and five surrounding zip codes. The expert for the defendants challenged this definition as too narrow and illogical because the area extended 36 miles west but only 17 miles east of Vicksburg. The defendants' expert postulated that if patients were willing to drive 36 miles in one direction, they would be willing to drive 36 miles in all directions. The court rejected the defendants' argument that geographic markets are perfectly round, noting that people's willingness to travel is based on "simple reasons such as highway conditions and the quality of the services available at the end of the road."[77] Similarly, the court in the Marshfield Clinic case disagreed with the plaintiff's use of circles to define geographic markets for physician services: "Compcare [the HMO associated with BC/BS of Wisconsin] draws with a broader brush, drawing a dizzying series of concentric circles around the Clinic's offices and counting the physicians who can serve people living in the circles. It would have been much simpler and we suppose just as good—having in mind the desirability of avoiding a hunt for the snark of delusive exactness—to have treated the counties as the markets."[78]

### MARKETS FOR HEALTH CARE FINANCING

Recent court decisions concerning consolidation in the market for health care financing have focused on the product, rather than the geographic, market definition. As discussed earlier, the courts have been in almost unanimous agreement that the market should be broadly defined as health care financing.[79] Given this product market definition, the relevant geographic market is national, since employers and individuals can purchase indemnity plans from insurance carriers located almost anywhere in the country.

Given the small role now played by indemnity insurance,[80] the product market will most likely be defined more narrowly in future cases (for example, as managed health care financing), and a more narrow geographic market will be called for as well. The main reason for this is that in addition to claims processing and risk bearing, managed care plans provide insured access to a specific network of health care providers. Insurance carriers wanting to sell managed care plans in a particular local market must either employ providers in that local market, contract with providers in that local market, or rent a network of providers in that local market. The network development and management functions of health insurers under managed care tend to shrink the size of relevant geographic markets for managed health care financing.

Interestingly, in a case involving the use of exclusive clauses in contracts between managed care plans and primary care physicians, the district court found the relevant geographic market for health care financing to be limited to the state of New Hampshire. This narrow geographic market is based, in part, on the fact that the managed care plans offered exclusive clauses in contracts with physicians only in New Hampshire. However, the decision suggests at least three types of evidence that may be helpful in determining the geographic market boundaries for managed care plans: where the managed care plans are licensed to do business, where the managed care plans are marketed, and where they recruit their providers. The judge wrote that the "battlefield" is the state of New Hampshire because the managed care plans "are only licensed to do business in New Hampshire. Their recruiting efforts have been directed to primary care physicians and specialists in New Hampshire on a statewide basis. Their marketing efforts have been directed at selling their health care plans to employers and individuals throughout the state of New Hampshire."[81]

## Conclusion

The federal agencies lost four of their last five antitrust challenges to hospital mergers on the basis, at least in part, of issues of market definition. In each case the court sided with the hospital's expert in terms of market definition. These recent market definition controversies boil down to a lack of understanding or appreciation for how managed care and selective contracting have changed health care markets. The parties involved have not fully appreciated who the relevant consumer is under managed care contracting, and accordingly, which market definition methods are most appropriate in health care markets characterized by managed care.

Under managed care contracting, the choice of hospital or physician organization takes place in two successive markets. In the first-stage market the MCC chooses which hospitals or physician organizations will be included in its provider network. In effect, the MCC is the relevant consumer in the first-stage market. In the second-stage market insured enrollees (in consultation with their physicians) make choices among the hospitals or physician organizations in the MCC's network. Therefore, the enrollee is the relevant consumer in the second-stage market. MCCs make their choices among the full set of hospitals and physician organizations, while enrollees make their choices among a more limited set of providers, specifically those providers included in their MCC's provider network.

Hospital and physician prices are determined as part of the negotiations between MCCs and hospitals and physician organizations during the first-stage market. Accordingly, it is the first-stage market that is critically important for antitrust purposes. It is in this first-stage market that hospitals and physician organizations either have or do not have the market power to raise their prices.

Unfortunately, patient flow statistics, currently used to define geographic markets, tell us something about competition and geographic boundaries in the second-stage market, but very little about the critically important first-stage market. Patient flow statistics tell us something about enrollees as the consumer—specifically, how many enrollees are willing and able to travel to more distant hospitals—but very little about MCCs as the consumer in the first-stage market.[82]

Competition and the geographic boundaries of the first-stage market depend on the willingness and ability of MCCs to modify their provider networks in response to anticompetitive behavior on the part of a merged hospital. What determines the geographic boundaries of the first-stage market is how MCCs would respond in the event that the merged hospital raised its prices. More specifically, could MCCs successfully market managed care plans to local employers and their employees if (1) their plans excluded the merged hospital, but included more distant hospitals? Or (2) their plans included the merged hospital, but through financial incentives (higher deductibles or higher copayments) made it more expensive for enrollees to use the merged hospital relative to other hospitals? As more and more information on hospital-specific quality of care becomes available, the answer to the first question will depend increasingly on perceptions of quality differentials across hospitals.

If the answer to this question is yes, then the relevant consumers—local MCCs—have choices in the development of their provider networks, and those more distant hospitals should be included in the merging hospitals' first-stage geographic market. If the answer to this question is no, then those more distant hospitals should not be included.

# 5

# Entry Barriers in
# Health Care Markets

*The lower the barriers to entry, and the shorter the lags of*
*new entry, the less power existing firms have.*
*∼ Seventh Circuit Court, 1986[1]*

THERE IS GENERAL agreement among economists that barriers to entry are a necessary condition for horizontal and vertical consolidation to have anticompetitive effects in health care markets. High market concentration or a small number of competitors in a market alone does not imply that incumbent firms have the ability to restrict output below competitive levels or raise prices above costs.

In the absence of barriers to entry, there should be little concern about long-term anticompetitive effects and little need for antitrust enforcement. If there are no barriers to entry, then even incumbent health care firms with large market shares in concentrated markets will be unable to manipulate their prices to earn excess profits without inducing entry. Accordingly, even in concentrated markets, the threat of entry can provide the incentive for health care firms to keep output and price at competitive levels.

More specifically, if there are no barriers to entry into the market for health care product $X$ (for example, the services of pediatricians) and the incumbent health care firm(s) (for example, a physician organization of pediatricians) raises the prices of $X$ above competitive levels, then the excess profits earned by the incumbent "invites" entry by new competitors. Entry of new competitors will most likely occur in at least one of three ways: (1) established firms in the local market, not currently selling $X$ (for example, a physician organization of internists in the local market) may begin to sell $X$ even though they had not done so in the past; (2) established firms currently selling $X$, but not in the local market (for example, a physician organization of pediatricians located in a distant city) may open a local office and begin to sell $X$ in the local market; and (3) new business may start (for example, pediatricians establishing their first practices after completing their medical education). This entry of additional competitors and the associated increase in the availability of product $X$ defeats the incumbent's attempt to exercise market power.

What constitutes a barrier to entry? Economists disagree on the answer to this question. Basically, the controversy boils down to whether economies of scale represent entry barriers. A firm is said to be realizing economies of scale when it increases production of output and its average costs decline. Technology determines the extent to which firms can realize economies of scale—the extent to which larger firms can produce output at lower average costs than smaller firms.

Economies of scale represent entry barriers using Joe Bain's definition,[2] but not using George Stigler's definition.[3] According to Bain, any factor that allows an incumbent to maintain price above average cost is an entry barrier. Stigler, on the other hand, defines an entry barrier as a cost that must be borne by potential entrants that is not (or has not) been borne by incumbents. Bain's definition, therefore, includes scale economies as potential entry barriers, while Stigler's does not. Despite this lack of agreement over a definition of entry barriers, there is general agreement among economists that the following four factors can play a role in deterring entry: investments that involve sunk costs, absolute cost advantages, pre-entry strategic behaviors by incumbents, and government policies.

## Sunk Costs

Sunk costs are costs that firms cannot recover at the time they exit from the market. As the economists Dennis Carlton and Jeffrey Perloff wrote, "A sunk cost is like spilt milk: once it is sunk, there is no use worrying about it."[4] The costs of medical equipment and buildings are not sunk costs because they can be sold to other buyers, and thus firms can recover the costs of equipment and buildings at the time of exit from the market. There are, however, investments that involve sunk costs in health care markets. These may include physicians' costs of developing a positive reputation and referral partners in local markets, or insurers' costs of developing a local network of providers. Sunk costs can bestow significant advantages on incumbents by increasing the costs of unsuccessful entry attempts, and thus even small sunk costs can deter entry.[5] Sunk costs provide a disincentive to enter the market.

There are reasons to believe that certain aspects of the transformation of the health care industry, specifically (1) greater quality differentiation and quality-based competition and (2) referral patterns increasingly influenced by financial considerations and network membership, are increasing the importance of the sunk costs associated with developing a reputation and referral partners in local markets, and thus are increasing the entry barriers in markets for physician services.

On the other hand, there are at least two factors that reduce the importance of sunk costs in markets for physician services. First, for physicians associated with established practices in other geographic markets, there may be no (or at least lower) sunk costs associated with establishing a reputation in a new geographic market. For example, heart surgeons associated with the Mayo Clinic in Rochester, Minnesota, may not have to incur high marketing costs to gain a positive reputation and establish a new practice in Chicago or Boston because their existing reputation may carry over to new geographic markets. Similarly, physicians' reputations for quality established in one product market may carry over to new product markets. For example, physicians associated with an established general/family practice in the local market may not have to incur sunk costs to enter the local market for pediatricians' services, because their existing reputation in the market for general/family services may carry over to their newly hired or contracted pediatricians.

Unfortunately, there has been very little analysis of sunk costs in health care markets, concerning either their existence or their magnitude. Not much is known about the costs incurred by physicians to develop positive reputations and referral partners in local markets. Further, very little is known about the costs incurred by insurers (and hospitals) in the formation of networks of physicians and hospitals in specific geographic markets, and even less is known about the extent to which these costs of network formation are sunk. Insurers (and hospitals) can develop their own networks, hire firms to develop networks on their behalf,[6] or rent existing networks.[7]

## Absolute Cost Advantages

An incumbent is said to have an absolute cost advantage over a potential entrant when the incumbent can produce a product at lower costs than the potential entrant. In this case the incumbent can raise its prices above its costs (which are lower than potential entrants' costs) and earn a positive profit without inviting entry. An incumbent's cost advantage over potential entrants can arise from a number of factors, including (1) the incumbent's access to and control of superior inputs; (2) the incumbent's ownership of a patent for a superior product or more efficient production technique; (3) some form of first-mover advantage (lower costs associated with being first in the market, for example, if potential entrants face brand loyalty to the first mover and thus potential entrants must incur higher marketing costs); (4) learning-by-doing (lower costs associated with experience in the market, for example, if workers become more skilled and productive with experience); and (5) consumers' imperfect information about quality. When consumers' learning about quality takes place over time (and therefore, consumers have imperfect information about quality), the incumbent has an advantage over subsequent entrants. The incumbent is the standard against which subsequent entrants are judged, and thus it is more difficult and costly for entrants to persuade consumers to invest in learning about their qualities than it was for the incumbent.[8]

## Pre-Entry Strategic Behaviors

Pre-entry strategic behaviors are the actions that incumbent firms take to influence the market environment in ways that may discourage entry and thus increase incumbents' profits. These may include contracts with exclusivity clauses, tying requirements, most-favored nation clauses, and noncompete clauses.[9] Another incumbent strategy that may deter entry in health care markets is overinvesting in capacity (for example, maintaining excess hospital beds beyond the number necessary to meet peak demand). Overinvesting in capacity can signal potential entrants that incumbents are willing and able to respond to new entrants by increasing output. The threat (implied by the holding of the excess capacity) that the incumbent(s) may flood the market with output, which would cause prices and the profitability of entry to fall, may be sufficient to deter entry. Hospital mergers may be a means of acquiring excess capacity in order to be able to price aggressively in the event of entry.

## Government Policies

Health care firms are subject to an amazing number of federal and state regulations. However, for a government regulation to raise entry barriers, it must have a differential impact on incumbents and potential entrants. For example, entry-deterring regulation may actually prohibit additional entry (certificate of need [CON] regulations in markets for hospital services), or it may increase entrants' costs relative to incumbents' costs (a requirement of safer, but more expensive construction).

CON regulations require hospitals to obtain approval from state planning agencies for capital expenditures exceeding state-set thresholds. For example, as of 1999 in Connecticut the following thresholds existed for CON approval: hospital capital investments greater than $1 million, hospital medical equipment expenditures greater than $400,000, and new hospital service expenditures greater than $200,000.[10] Similarly, in Vermont in 1999 the following thresholds existed for CON approval: hospital capital investments greater than $1.5 million, hospital medical equipment expenditures greater than $500,000, and new hospital service expenditures greater than $300,000.[11]

## Potential Entry Barriers in Markets for Physician Services

Economists have tended to characterize markets for physician services as monopolistically competitive (markets with differentiated sellers, but no entry barriers),[12] and empirical evidence based on data collected in the 1970s and 1980s is consistent with this characterization.[13] Further, there is empirical support for the hypothesis that entry by even a small number of physicians into a geographic market is associated with lower prices for physician services in that market.[14]

Also consistent with low entry barriers in markets for physician services is the finding that large buyers or buyer coalitions have the incentive and may have the ability to induce entry even in the presence of significant sunk costs.[15] Large buyers of physician services, such as managed care organizations, employer coalitions involved in direct contracting, or hospitals accepting global capitation contracts, benefit directly from entry-induced lower prices for physician services and thus have the incentive to induce entry into the market for physician services. These buyers may be able to induce entry, despite the presence of sunk costs, by guaranteeing potential physician entrants a market for their services through long-term contracts or vertical integration.

There may, however, be significant entry barriers into markets for physician services under certain conditions, resulting from incumbent physicians' vertical relations (vertical integration, joint ventures, and exclusive deals) with hospitals and health plans[16] and from incumbent physicians' potential influence over who obtains hospital admitting privileges (the authority to admit patients to a particular hospital).

Perhaps with the exception of a physician's own time and technical know-how, the most important inputs into the production of many physician services are the resources obtained at hospitals. For example, to perform many types of surgery physicians require access to hospitals' operating and recovery rooms, specialized equipment, nursing staffs, anesthesiologists, radiologists, and back-up facilities, such as intensive care. If a physician cannot obtain privileges at a certain hospital and a patient desires to receive medical treatment at that hospital, then the physician without privileges will have to refer the patient to another physician who has privileges at the desired hospital. As a result, the physician without privileges loses the opportunity to treat the patient, and thus the opportunity to collect payment for treating the patient. Accordingly, the denial of hospital admitting privileges at certain hospitals can decrease physicians' abilities to compete in local markets for physician services.

Physicians with admitting privileges are usually organized into self-governing medical staffs, which are charged with performing multiple technical functions essential to the operation of a hospital.[17] Medical staffs elect their own officers, appoint committees to oversee physician activities in the hospital, and make recommendations concerning the award, denial, or revocation of admitting privileges to the hospital's governing board. In the past, hospital governing boards rarely did more than acquiesce to their medical staffs' recommendations.[18]

When hospital boards follow the recommendations of their medical staffs, incumbent physicians have the ability to determine which physician entrants will be granted hospital admitting privileges, and under certain conditions, incumbent physicians may have the ability to create an absolute cost advantage for themselves. If qualified potential entrants are denied admitting privileges at the only local hospital or the superior local hospital, then entry into the market for physician services is less likely to occur.[19] Moreover, even if entry occurs, new physicians will be forced to admit their patients at hospitals considered to be less attractive to consumers in terms of location, quality, or price. Therefore, incumbent physicians with admitting privileges at the only local hospital or the superior local hospital may be able to charge prices above their costs, without inducing entry from potential entrants who are unable to obtain similar admitting privileges.

Courts have found hospital medical staffs' control of admitting privileges in certain situations to violate the antitrust laws. In *Weiss v. York Hospital and the Medical and Dental Staff of York Hospital, et al.*,[20] the Court of Appeals upheld the District Court's ruling that the medical staff of York Hospital (the largest provider of inpatient hospital services with a market share of 80 percent and the only provider of numerous tertiary care services in the local market) engaged in a deliberate and covert policy of discrimination against osteopaths[21] in the granting of admitting privileges, in violation of Section 1 of the Sherman Act. Specifically, the court found that the medical staff's unfair, unequal, and unreasonable procedures in reviewing osteopaths' applications for staff privileges[22] were the equivalent of a concerted refusal to deal. The court clearly stated that York Hospital's medical staff was capable of conspiracy under Section 1 since it included physicians with independent medical practices, and thus physicians in competition with one another and capable of conspiring among themselves.[23]

In *Patrick v. Burget et al.*[24] the medical staff of the only hospital in Astoria, Oregon, was found guilty of violating Sections 1 and 2 of the Sherman Act for using hospital peer-review proceedings to reduce competition from Dr. Patrick, a general and vascular surgeon. After Dr. Patrick declined an invitation to join a local group medical practice, the Astoria Clinic, and instead began an independent practice in competition with the surgical practice of the Astoria Clinic, the medical staff of the local hospital voted to recommend the termination of Dr. Patrick's privileges. At that time a majority of the medical staff at the local hospital were employees or partners of the Astoria Clinic.[25]

It is important to remember, however, that hospitals' governing boards, not the physicians on the medical staffs, make the final decisions and thus can constrain the authority of their medical staffs to deny admitting privileges to potential physician entrants.[26] Although hospitals are dependent on their medical staffs for patient admissions, and thus are motivated to keep their medical staffs happy, hospital boards may think twice before yielding authority over medical staff decisions in increasingly competitive markets.[27] Indeed, hospital boards may recognize that the hospitals' and the medical staffs' interests diverge. For example, it may be in hospitals' (but not certain physicians') best interests to reduce the number of specialists on the staff or to use economic credentialing (the application of economic criteria to decisions concerning the appointment of staff and denial of privileges). When hospitals use economic credentialing, the authority of the medical staff to set the criteria for staff appointment and privileges is eroded. On the other hand, hospital boards may recognize that under certain circumstances, entry barriers in markets for physician services can facilitate a hospital's ability to exercise market power, and thus can serve the hospital's interests, as well as physicians' interests. This possibility is discussed further in Chapter 7.

Hospitals' decisions to form physician hospital organizations (PHOs) or purchase physician practices can also change the dynamic of the hospital and medical staff relationship. When physicians become investors in the hospital or employees of the hospital, their financial well-being becomes directly linked to that of the hospital.

The facts of one case, as described in a 1991 FTC complaint,[28] provide an interesting illustration of both the ability of incumbent physicians to delay the entry of rival physicians through boycott threats and influence over admitting privileges, and the constraints placed on this strategy by the divergent interests of the physicians, the hospital, and the public. The FTC charged the physicians on the medical staff of Broward General Medical Center (a major acute care hospital in Florida) with agreeing and threatening to boycott (withhold patient admissions from Broward General) and other anticompetitive practices, such as refusing to process applications for admitting privileges by Cleveland Clinic physicians in order to deter entry by the physicians of the Cleveland Clinic Foundation.

Beginning in 1984 the Cleveland Clinic sought to establish a regional clinic in Northern Broward County, and thus an affiliation with a tertiary care hospital in the area. The new regional clinic was scheduled to open in the spring of 1988. Despite Broward General's initial interest in affiliating with the Cleveland Clinic, in late 1985 (after the medical staff's boycott threats) hospital officials informed the Clinic that further discussions of an affiliation would be futile, and the Clinic terminated negotiations. Between 1986 and 1987 the Cleveland Clinic unsuccessfully sought an affiliation with another hospital, Holy Cross Hospital.

The tide turned in the fall of 1987 when the Cleveland Clinic decided to apply for CON approval to build its own tertiary care hospital in Northern Broward County. Clearly, this would not be in the interests of Broward General Medical Center, and in late 1987 the Chairman of the Board of the hospital encouraged the Cleveland Clinic to explore an affiliation with Broward General. Accordingly, five members of the Clinic's cardiac surgery team applied for staff privileges at Broward General; however, once again the medical staff threatened to leave the hospital, and the Board denied hospital privileges to all five applicants in October of 1988. The Board's decision caused such a public outcry that it reversed its earlier decision. The Board not only granted hospital privileges to the five Cleveland Clinic physicians, but it approved an exclusive contract for cardiac surgery services with the Cleveland Clinic.

Further, in 1989 after its medical staff refused to evaluate the hospital privilege applications of another 35 Cleveland Clinic physicians, the hospital contracted with a panel of outside physicians to evaluate those applications. All 35 physicians received privileges at Broward General. In this case entry was delayed, but not prevented.

## Potential Entry Barriers in Markets for Hospital Services

After 1986, when the federal law requiring state-level CON regulations expired, fifteen states discontinued their CON programs for hospitals.[29] Some states have continued their programs, however, and in those states the CON regulations may (1) prohibit the entry of new hospitals in particular areas, (2) prohibit the acquisition of expensive technologies by existing hospitals, and thus the ability of existing hospitals to expand services, (3) raise potential entrants' costs relative to incumbents, and thus create an absolute cost advantage for incumbents, and (4) since regulatory approvals are not easily transferable, create sunk cost barriers to entry as well.

How effective state CON programs have been and will continue to be in deterring entry by new hospitals and deterring expansion by existing ones is an unsettled empirical issue. A review of the literature found three studies suggesting that CON regulations decreased bed supply, three suggesting that CON regulations had no effect on bed supply, and one suggesting the regulations increased bed supply.[30] The most recent of these studies is based on national data between 1976 and 1993 and found that CON regulations decreased the supply of hospital beds, measured as beds per 1,000 state residents, by approximately 2 percent.[31] However, this study also found that discontinuation of CON programs in some states had no effect on the supply of hospital beds in those states. The bed supply did not surge after the CON programs were discontinued. These conflicting results may be explained by the endogenous nature of state-level decisions to discontinue CON programs for hospitals. CON programs may have been discontinued in those states that had the least effective programs, or in those states where the growth of managed care was exerting a constraint on the bed supply.

The impact of CON regulations on the diffusion of expensive technologies, such as open-heart surgery units and organ transplant units, is also an unsettled issue. A review of the literature suggests that CON regulations deter the expansion of hospitals into cardiac catheterization units, CAT-scan units, MRI units, open-heart surgery units, and cobalt therapy.[32] However, a more recent study suggests that between 1980 and 1993, CON regulations had no effect on the expansion of existing hospitals into new services.[33]

Even if CON laws do not deter entry into markets for hospital services, under certain market conditions there may be entry barriers into markets for hospital services resulting from incumbent hospitals' vertical relations (vertical integration, joint ventures, and exclusive deals) with physicians and health plans.[34]

## Potential Entry Barriers in Markets for Health Care Financing

In 1986 in *Ball Memorial Hospital et al. v. Mutual Hospital Insurance*,[35] the appeals court ruled that entry into the health insurance market is easy because insurers, such as Blue Cross and Blue Shield plans, do not own assets that could block or delay entry by rivals: "The 'productive asset' of the insurance business is money, which may be supplied on a moment's notice, plus the ability to spread risk, which many firms possess and which has no geographic boundary."

Since then, however, the growth of managed care has changed the nature of the health care financing product and thus the conditions of entry into markets for health care financing. The essential "productive assets" of the health care financing business have changed in ways that may raise entry barriers. Managed care has brought together the functions of health care financing and health care delivery, and this has created the potential for barriers to entry into markets for health care financing under certain conditions.

Under managed care, the health care financing business includes at least four functions: two that existed under traditional insurance—risk spreading and claims processing—and two that are associated with managed care—care management (the process of reviewing the appropriateness of service utilization) and network development, contracting, and management (the process of establishing and managing the network of providers).

Certainly, many firms still have the ability to bear risk. In fact, employers and union groups are increasingly becoming self-insured or bearing risk themselves (rather than hiring insurance firms to do so), and providers are increasingly bearing risk as well. The increasing numbers of employers and providers bearing risk suggest that there are still no entry barriers associated with this aspect of the health insurance business. Moreover, the availability of third-party administrators (firms specializing in administrative services, such as claims processing) suggests that the second function of health insurance firms is not a source of entry barriers.

The care management function of health insurers (the development and use of mechanisms to increase the quality of care and reduce the costs) also can be produced and purchased separately from the risk-bearing function. Independent utilization review and case management firms provide care management services.

It is the fourth function of health insurance firms offering managed care plans—the need to provide a local network of hospitals and physicians—that may be a source of entry barriers. While firms in the risk spreading, claims processing, and care management businesses most likely compete in regional, if not national markets, provider networks tend to be more local. The marketability of a health plan in a local area depends, in part, on its local provider network, and thus entry into the market for health care financing in a local area is a function of health insurance firms' abilities to provide networks of health care providers that are attractive to consumers living in that local area.

If incumbent insurers have merged, formed joint ventures, or signed exclusive contracts with local physicians and hospitals, then potential insurer entrants' opportunities to deal with a sufficient number of local providers may be foreclosed. Vertical foreclosure in a local market for health care financing can create entry barriers if three conditions are present: (1) there are entry barriers into the relevant local markets for hospital or physician services; (2) the vertically consolidated provider organizations have large market shares or are the highest-quality or most cost-effective provider organizations in the local market; and (3) the vertically related providers are worth more to incumbent insurers than to potential entrants (for example, learning-by-doing results in the vertically related providers being more productive in incumbent insurers' networks than in potential entrants' networks).[36]

All three of these conditions are required for vertical foreclosure to create entry barriers into markets for health care financing. Absent the first condition, potential entrants into the market for health care financing could recruit new providers into the local area. Absent the second condition, potential entrants could contract with a sufficient number of nonvertically related, high-quality, cost-efficient, incumbent providers in the local market. Absent the third condition, potential entrants would be able to bid the vertically related hospitals and physicians (the superior input in this case) away from incumbent insurers. Vertical foreclosure is discussed further in Chapter 7.

## The Next Step

After the market boundaries and entry barriers have been established, the next step involves distinguishing between practices and arrangements that have net efficiency-enhancing effects and those that have net monopoly power-enhancing effects. Chapter 6 focuses on the issues relevant to making this distinction for horizontal practices and arrangements, while Chapter 7 focuses on those relevant for vertical practices and arrangements—mergers, acquisitions, joint ventures, exclusive dealing agreements, and most favored nation clauses among firms operating in different, but related, product markets.

# 6

# The Effects of Horizontal Consolidation among Hospitals, Physicians, or Insurers

I have asked many providers why they wanted to merge. Although publicly they all invoked the synergies mantra, virtually everyone stated privately that the main reason for merging was to avoid competition and/or obtain market power.
~ David Dranove, 2000[1]

Hospitals in many communities have experienced extensive consolidation, enabling them to exert greater leverage in managed care contract negotiations.
~ Center for Studying Health System Change, 2001[2]

HORIZONTAL MERGERS, acquisitions, and joint ventures can lead to lower prices if they generate efficiencies (cost savings) and encourage more aggressive competition among firms in the market. In other situations, however, horizontal mergers, acquisitions, and joint ventures can result in higher prices by facilitating the exercise of monopoly power. To complicate matters further, it is possible to have both efficiency gains and increases in monopoly power resulting from the same case of consolidation. Whether consumers are better or worse off depends on which effect is stronger.

The antitrust enforcement challenge is to determine which consolidations will be procompetitive (will have net positive impacts on consumers because the efficiency gains are greater than the associated costs) and which consolidations will be anticompetitive (will have net negative impacts on consumers because the increases in firms' market power resulting from the consolidation are greater than the associated benefits). Unfortunately, as with market definition, estimation of efficiency gains and market power enhancements is not an exact science. There are many methodological problems associated with measurement of these concepts. This point was driven home in a recent hospital merger case where the court accepted the efficiencies defense, but acknowledged it would not try to evaluate the magnitude of the efficiency gains of the proposed merger: "Because measuring the efficiencies of a proposed transaction is inherently difficult and because both sides' estimates are clearly based in some measure on speculative self-serving assertions . . . the court finds it neither appropriate nor necessary to engage in a detailed evaluation of the competing views."[3]

In the absence of relevant empirical studies, there are no accepted conventions for back-of-the-envelope estimates of potential efficiency gains.[4] As a result, there can be huge differences between the efficiency estimates of the plaintiff and those of the defendant. For example, in a recent hospital merger case (*U.S. v. Long Island Jewish Medical Center et al.*) the expert witness hired by the merging hospitals estimated the future annual cost saving to be $90 million, while the government's expert witness estimated the future annual saving to be only $6.2 million.[5]

In addition, it is difficult to gauge anticompetitive effects. In markets for heterogeneous products, such as hospital services, physician services, or health care financing, higher prices in one geographic area are not necessarily evidence of hospitals, physicians, or insurers exercising monopoly power in that market. The observation of a positive association between market concentration and prices for physician and hospital services is consistent with at least two hypotheses: (1) physicians and hospitals in more concentrated markets are exercising monopoly power, and (2) physicians and hospitals in more concentrated markets are producing higher-quality care (the opposite case from the medical arms race hypothesis discussed in Chapter 2) and thus more costly and higher-priced services. In markets for health care financing, higher prices are consistent with the scenario that insurers are providing more generous benefits or better service, or insuring a more risky/less healthy and thus more costly to insure group.

In a recent antitrust case involving health care insurers, the judge expressed the opinion that higher prices in health care markets should not be taken as *prima facie* evidence of monopoly power. Judge Posner wrote, "But when dealing with a heterogeneous product or service, such as the full range of medical care, a reasonable finder of fact cannot infer monopoly power just from higher prices—the difference may reflect a higher quality more costly to provide. . . . One HMO may charge higher prices than other HMOs (and Security does charge higher prices) not because it has monopoly power but because it is offering better service than other HMOs in the market."[6]

Rather than reviewing the available methodologies to measure efficiency gains and market power enhancements, I will focus in this chapter on synthesizing the theoretical and empirical literatures on the potential for horizontal consolidation to enhance efficiency and market power. Using both economic theory and empirical research, I will analyze which benefits (efficiency gains) and costs (market power enhancements) of horizontal consolidation are most plausible in health care markets. In this manner, valid claims about efficiency and market power can be distinguished from those that are not. Moreover, an understanding of the potential for both increases in efficiency and increases in market power can facilitate an assessment of the trade-off between the two.

## Evidence and Theory on Consolidation-Specific Efficiency Gains

Horizontal consolidation is said to have a net positive impact, and therefore to make consumers better off, when the consolidated firm lowers its price either because consolidation-induced lower costs are passed on to consumers in the form of lower prices or there are consolidation-induced increases in competition in the post-consolidation market. Increasing competition among all firms increases the likelihood that the cost savings will be passed on to consumers in the form of lower prices. Even if the consolidation-induced lower costs do not result in the firm charging lower prices, these efficiency gains may reduce the likelihood that the firm will increase prices above pre-consolidation levels in the future. However, charging pre-consolidation prices relative to the lower, post-consolidation costs represents the exercise of market power by the consolidated firm.

Consumers are also better off when consolidation facilitates the provision of new products or higher-quality products, and these new or higher-quality products do not confer market power on the consolidated firm.

Consolidation-specific efficiency gains are increases in efficiency that are likely to result from the proposed consolidation and that are unlikely to result in its absence. There are multiple ways to achieve scale economies, and consolidation may not be the best way. For example, rather than consolidating, smaller health care firms may be able to achieve the same economies as larger health care firms by outsourcing certain activities.[7]

Economic theory suggests great potential for horizontal consolidation to lower health care costs and increase health care quality. Specifically, horizontal consolidation in health care markets can be efficiency-enhancing in the following seven ways: (1) by lowering transaction costs—the costs of negotiating, writing, monitoring, and enforcing contracts among physicians, hospitals, insurers, and employers; (2) by allowing the realization of economies of scale in production or administration (administration costs include the capital costs of computer-based information systems to monitor utilization, costs, and quality, and the costs of marketing, financial accounting, and state and federal government reporting); (3) by eliminating excess capacity; (4) by facilitating specialization and its associated increases in experience, skill, and quality of care; (5) by facilitating group risk bearing; (6) by increasing incentives to monitor and improve quality; and (7) by increasing competition among all or some firms in the market. The theory and evidence on each of these potential consolidation-specific efficiency gains will be discussed in this section.

The courts have clearly indicated that potential efficiencies are critically important in health care antitrust cases. In a recent case involving a physician clinic in Wisconsin, the court ruled that the efficiency gains associated with group practice might justify monopoly provision of physician services in rural areas. More specifically, the court stated that physician organizations might be "natural monopolists" in rural areas. In some markets it is efficient for only one firm to produce all of the output (in this example, physician services) because the average costs of producing physician services would be higher if two or more firms produced instead of one. "If an entire county has only 12 physicians, one can hardly expect or want them to set up in competition with each other. We live in the age of technology and specialization in medical services. Physicians practice in groups, in alliances, in networks, utilizing expensive equipment and support. Twelve physicians competing in a county would be competing to provide horse-and-buggy medicine.

Only as part of a large and sophisticated medical enterprise such as the Marshfield Clinic can they practice modern medicine in rural Wisconsin."[8] It is interesting to note that in 1997 (about two years after this court decision) the Marshfield Clinic acquired Wausau Medical Center, a group practice of 73 physicians that is approximately 40 miles from Marshfield.[9]

## *Are Costs Lower in Hospitals That Merge?*

The empirical evidence from the hospital industry supports the hypothesis that hospital mergers reduce the rate of increase in hospital costs. One study using data on 3,500 short-term general hospitals between 1986 and 1994 (during this time period there were 122 mergers) found that hospital costs, measured as expense per outpatient-adjusted admission, increased at a faster rate in nonmerging hospitals compared with merging hospitals.[10] Specifically, hospital costs increased 65.9 percent for merging hospitals and 73.2 percent for nonmerging hospitals (a difference of 7.3 percentage points). However, the cost-saving impact of hospital mergers was reduced in more concentrated hospital markets.

Similarly, a study comparing merging and nonmerging hospitals for an earlier period (1982 to 1989) found the rate of increase in hospital costs was lower for the hospitals involved in the 92 hospital mergers that occurred during this time period than for a control group of nonmerging hospitals.[11]

Consistent with these earlier studies, a more recent study using data on hospital mergers (excluding those in rural areas) between 1989 and 1997 found that hospital costs increased at a slower rate in merging hospitals.[12] Specifically, hospital costs increased 22.5 percent for the merging hospitals and 29.1 percent for the rivals of these merging hospitals. Again, however, the results suggest that merger-associated cost savings are lower in more concentrated markets.

## *Is Quality Higher in Hospitals That Merge?*

While there is some evidence suggesting that hospital mergers are associated with lower hospital costs, there is no empirical evidence suggesting that either hospital consolidation or higher hospital market concentration is associated with higher-quality hospital services. Rather, the recent evidence on the relationship between concentration and quality in the market for hospital services suggests that consolidation has no effect or a negative effect on quality.[13]

Only one study examines quality differences between hospitals that consolidated and those that did not, and its results showed that for patients with heart disease (heart attacks or strokes) admitted to hospitals in California in the 1990s, hospital mergers/acquisitions were associated with no change in quality of hospital care, measured as inpatient mortality rates, and a decrease in quality of hospital care, measured as 90-day readmission rates.[14] During the study period (1992–1995) 21 hospitals in California were involved in mergers, 54 independent hospitals were acquired by hospital systems, and 65 hospitals which already belonged to hospital systems were acquired by other hospital systems.[15]

The results of another study suggest that concentration in the market for hospital services is associated with lower-quality care. Using data on nonrural, elderly Medicare beneficiaries hospitalized for treatment of a new heart attack between 1985 and 1994, this study found that hospitals in more competitive markets provided higher-quality care, measured as lower rates of mortality from acute myocardial infarction, even controlling for differences in hospital capacity across markets. Further, as of 1991 treatment of heart attack patients became significantly less costly in more competitive areas compared with less competitive ones.[16]

Despite the lack of current evidence on consolidation-specific increases in quality, there are still reasons to believe that consolidation among health care firms will be associated with higher quality in the future. The following subsections include discussions of the theoretical reasons for consolidation-specific efficiency gains in the form of both lower costs and higher quality, and, whenever possible, empirical evidence.

## Reductions in Transaction Costs

In theory, horizontal consolidation can reduce transaction costs both within and across geographic markets by reducing the number of contracts that must be negotiated, written, monitored, and enforced. For example, within a geographic market as physicians consolidate into larger groups/networks, it may be less costly for hospitals and insurers to contract with fewer large physician groups/networks, rather than with more numerous solo or small group practices. The hospitals, insurers, and consolidated physicians may be able to realize significant transaction cost savings.

Similarly, as insurers consolidate across geographic markets, employers with employees in multiple geographic markets (and these consolidated insurers) may be able to realize significant transaction cost savings. It may be less costly for employers to contract with one or a few insurers, rather than with different insurers in each geographic market. Likewise, as hospitals or physicians consolidate across geographic markets, insurers with health plans in multiple geographic areas or direct-contracting employers with employees in multiple geographic markets (and these consolidated providers) may be able to realize significant transaction cost savings. It may be less costly for insurers or employers to contract with one or a few provider organizations, rather than with different provider organizations in each geographic market.

Since transaction costs may be quite high in the health care industry,[17] the efficiency gains that result from horizontal consolidation may be large. Unfortunately, there is no empirical research estimating the relationship between transaction costs and consolidation in health care markets.

### Economies of Scale and Scope

It is unfortunate that very little time and energy have gone into estimating the potential for health care firms to realize economies of scope. In theory a hospital could realize economies of scope when it is less costly for one hospital to produce two products (for example, primary care inpatient hospital services and tertiary care inpatient hospital services) than for two or more hospitals (continuing the example, a community hospital providing only primary care inpatient hospital services and a teaching hospital providing only tertiary care inpatient hospital services) to produce those products separately.

On the other hand, a great deal of time and energy has gone into estimating the potential for health care firms to realize economies of scale. This empirical literature suggests that the potential for health care firms to realize economies of scale through consolidation is quite limited, and if the potential exists, most scale economies appear to be exhausted at relatively low levels of output. However, this literature is characterized by methodological and data limitations, and thus its results must be interpreted with caution.

Studies examining hospitals' costs provide inconclusive evidence on scale economies. Some studies show hospital costs increasing as output increases; others show constant or falling costs as output increases.[18] However, the results of a more recent study using data on privately owned hospitals in California in 1992 suggest the existence of scale economies in administration.[19] This study found that non-revenue-producing cost centers, such as hospital administration, medical records, cafeteria, and housekeeping, have the potential to realize substantial economies up to 7,500 discharges (approximately 200 beds), but only minimal scale economies over the range of 7,500 to 15,000 discharges. Anecdotal evidence is also consistent with scale economies in administration. For example, the creation in 1995 of Tenet Healthcare Corporation, the second largest investor-owned hospital chain, through the merger of National Medical Enterprises and American Medical International allowed Tenet to reduce its corporate staff to 618 from a combined pre-merger staff of 1,062.[20]

For physicians, the recent evidence is also mixed.[21] One study using data from 1989 found that self-employed, office-based general internists realize economies of scale. More specifically, the results suggest that internists produce services at lower average costs as their practice volume increases.[22] However, another study using data from office-based general surgeons in 1987 found that scale economies did not exist.[23]

With respect to economies of scale in health care financing, one study based on a sample of HMOs in California between 1986 and 1992 found that HMOs' average costs decline up to 115,000 enrollees and then remain relatively constant as enrollment increases beyond 115,000.[24] Likewise, another study based on a national sample of HMOs between 1988 and 1991 found that all scale economies are realized by 50,000 enrollees.[25] However, a study based on 28 HMOs in Florida ranging in size from just under 1,000 enrollees to over 370,000 enrollees in 1994 suggests that larger HMOs are more technically efficient (able to insure more persons with a given quantity of inputs).[26]

The fact that empirical confirmation of scale economies in the health care industry has been elusive may be explained by the data and methodological problems impeding estimation. It is difficult to measure differences in quality and differences in case mix across health care firms, and these unmeasured variations can bias estimates of scale economies. If larger health care firms produce higher-quality care at correspondingly higher costs, then estimates that do not account for differences in quality of care will underestimate the extent of scale economies. To the extent that patients (or physicians acting as agents for patients) are more likely to choose high-quality providers, size and quality of care will be directly related. On the other hand, to the extent that price and quality are directly related and health plans selectively contract with providers on the basis of price, rather than quality, this bias in estimates of scale economies may be reduced.

Similarly, if larger health care firms treat patients with more complex or difficult to treat problems at correspondingly higher costs, then estimates that do not account for differences in severity of illness will underestimate the extent of scale economies. Since patients with more complex problems are more likely to choose hospitals with the capacity to treat those problems, and larger hospitals are more likely to have this capacity,[27] it is likely that size and severity of illness will be directly related.

Most studies of scale economies in physician practices suffer from two additional problems. The majority of these studies do not account for physician selection into groups (for example, more productive physicians may be more likely to be selected to join larger group practices) or differences in compensation or financial incentives. Some groups share income equally, while others allocate income based on physicians' productivity—payments per service performed and payments for meeting certain utilization targets, immunization targets, or patient satisfaction levels. Physicians are quite responsive to financial incentives. One study found that physicians with compensation contracts based on their individual productivity produced at least 31 percent more office visits than physicians without such incentives.[28] This suggests a major problem with studies that confound the effects of group size and compensation incentives.

Given these methodological and data limitations, the results of the empirical literature on scale economies in health care markets must be interpreted with caution. In fact, scale economies may be quite important in analyzing horizontal consolidation. Economic theory suggests multiple sources of scale economies in health care markets, including spreading fixed costs over additional units of output and economies of massed reserves.

Economies of massed reserves may be realized, for example, with the clinical consolidation of two smaller hospital departments into one larger department. This sort of consolidation may lower average costs by reducing the relative variability of patient demand and with it the need to maintain as much reserve capacity.[29] Nonetheless, consolidation of health care firms is no guarantee that economies of massed reserves will be realized. If the "consolidated" health care firms operate autonomously with little integration of departments, then few benefits of scale economies will be realized.

The increasing importance of managed care, with its emphasis on monitoring, controlling, and reporting health care utilization, costs, and quality, may be increasing the size of the health care firm that can realize all scale economies. It is possible that the new information technologies required to monitor and control health care utilization, costs, and quality—for example, the information infrastructure to manage risk contracts, to credential providers, to implement treatment protocols (critical pathways and practice guidelines), and to profile physicians' utilization patterns—entail significant fixed costs and thus increase the potential for health care firms to realize scale economies. Larger hospitals and physician organizations may be able to spread these costs across more patients and thereby realize lower average costs.

Assuming that the fixed costs of these systems to monitor, control, and report are large, previous research based on data from the 1970s and 1980s underestimates the potential for health care firms to realize scale economies in the 1990s and beyond. However, since it is not clear how large the fixed costs of these systems are, it is difficult to determine how large a provider group/network or insurer must be to achieve these efficiencies.

In addition to economies of scale, horizontal associations among physicians across different specialties may allow for the realization of economies of scope. A physician organization would be realizing economies of scope when it is less costly for that firm to produce two products (for example, annual examinations for children and women) than for two or more firms (continuing the example, a group of pediatricians and another group of OB/GYNs) to produce those products separately.

Unfortunately, there is no direct empirical evidence on economies of scope in multispecialty medical organizations,[30] and there are reasons to fear these organizations may be characterized by diseconomies of scope. James Robinson, an economist, wrote that "in principle, the aggregation of diverse but interdependent activities within one clinical organization [specialized medical group or IPA] can enhance cooperation and minimize conflict between self-interested individuals and otherwise independent entities. But amalgamation also can transfer inside the organization the diversity and disunity, formerly coexisting under the principle that good fences make good neighbors. Multispecialty medical groups are continually challenged by the imperative to mediate the financial and cultural tensions between primary care, which is a high-volume but low-margin business, with specialty care, where the opposite is true. Boundary conflicts among specialties and subspecialties can be numerous and nasty."[31]

## Elimination of Excess Capacity

As demand for inpatient hospital care has decreased, hospital occupancy rates have fallen and many hospitals have found themselves with substantial excess capacity. Hospital consolidation with reallocation or closure of inpatient resources is an efficient response to this decrease in demand and should result in lower hospital costs.

A survey done in the early 1990s of hospital merger "survivors" from the 74 confirmed mergers that occurred in the United States between 1983 and 1988 suggests that more than half of these hospital mergers resulted in substantial reductions of excess capacity.[32] In 41 percent of these mergers acute care capacity was converted to nonacute inpatient uses, such as psychiatric and substance abuse services, rehabilitation, and long-term care. In 17 percent of these mergers the acquired hospitals were closed.

There is anecdotal evidence suggesting that hospital mergers in the 1990s were also associated with reductions in excess capacity. The 1995 merger of two hospitals in Maine (Maine Medical Center and Brighton Medical Center) resulted in the elimination of 150 beds at Brighton, and the conversion of the remaining capacity at Brighton to an outpatient center for day surgery and drop-in treatment.[33] In January 1997, Tenet Healthcare purchased OrNda Health and six months later closed one of the acquired hospitals with an average daily census running at less than 30 percent.[34]

However, for reasons other than economic efficiency, not all hospital mergers are associated with reductions in excess capacity. Using data from 1982 to 1996 for St. Louis and data from 1989 to 1996 for Philadelphia, one study found that merged hospitals consolidated administrative services, such as marketing, finance, public relations, and human resources, but not clinical services or hospital beds considered inefficient and redundant to capacity elsewhere in the hospital system.[35] Hospital system leaders in the two cities reported that consolidation of specialized clinical services is strongly resisted by senior medical staff trying to protect their "fiefdoms."[36]

Similarly, a recent case study of the health care system in Cleveland found plenty of hospital merger activity by the two largest hospital systems, the Cleveland Clinic and the University Hospitals Health System, but no attempt to eliminate the "considerable excess hospital capacity" or consolidate services across hospitals. "Instead, hospital mergers appear to have propped up otherwise vulnerable hospitals and contributed to the expansion of highly specialized services."[37]

There is anecdotal evidence suggesting that consolidation of health care insurers may eliminate excess capacity. The merger of Aetna and U.S. Healthcare resulted in the closure of half of the merged companies' claim processing centers and the elimination of approximately 4,000 jobs in its health division.[38]

## Economies of Experience Due to Increased Patient Volume

Independent of the issue of scale economies, horizontal associations among hospitals or among physicians that allow hospitals or physicians to treat more patients may result in experience economies, and thus higher-quality care. In fact, a recent review of empirical literature by the Institute of Medicine found an association between higher volume and better outcome in three-quarters of the 88 studies reviewed.[39] Hospitals and physicians performing higher volumes of specific procedures tended to do so with better patient outcomes.

Many of these studies have been based on cross-sectional data. For example, using data on patients with hip fractures in 1982, one study found that patients in hospitals that performed more femur fracture reductions had better outcomes, measured as in-hospital mortality and length of stay.[40] Likewise, using data on patients receiving coronary artery bypass surgery in New York state in 1989, another study found that the patients of high-volume surgeons (annual bypass volumes of 180 or more) in high-volume hospitals (annual bypass volumes of 700 or more) had lower risk-adjusted mortality rates (2.67 percent in comparison to 4.29 percent for other bypass operations).[41] Similarly, using 1989 data on patients undergoing percutaneous transluminal coronary angioplasty (PTCA), a procedure used to treat coronary artery disease, another study found that hospitals and physicians performing higher volumes of PTCAs are associated with better outcomes.[42]

A problem with these studies based on cross-sectional data, however, is that their results are consistent with two different hypotheses. With only one year of data it is difficult to tell whether higher volumes led to better outcomes because "practice makes perfect," or whether better outcomes were related to higher volumes because patients seek care from physicians and hospitals with reputations for better outcomes.

Fortunately, there are studies based on longitudinal data and fixed-effects models that can sort out this issue of causality. One study analyzes eight years of data on a national sample of 500 community hospitals and finds that higher volumes are associated with better outcomes because practice makes perfect.[43] Specifically, the results show that for three out of five groups of hospital admissions (acute myocardial infarction, inguinal hernia repair, and acute respiratory distress syndrome in neonates),[44] increases in volume within hospitals lead to better patient outcomes, measured as lower adjusted mortality. Another study analyzes six years of data (1994–1999) on Medicare patients receiving six types of cardiovascular procedures and eight types of cancer resections and finds that adjusted-mortality rates (rates of death before hospital discharge or within 30 days after the procedure) decrease as hospital volume (average number of each surgical procedure performed per year at a given hospital) increases for all 14 types of procedures.[45] Accordingly, to the extent that horizontal consolidation facilitates higher volumes of particular hospital services at the consolidated hospital, horizontal consolidation may improve health care quality.

## Group Risk Bearing

As described previously, physicians and hospitals increasingly are bearing the population health risk, or the risk related to the frequency of medical problems and the costs of treating those problems. It is more efficient for large groups/networks of providers to bear this risk than it is for individual or small groups/networks of providers. Large provider groups/networks can pool risk to take advantage of the law of large numbers, whereas small groups/networks or individual physicians face the potential of large losses due to high-cost outliers. One option available to small groups or individual providers is the purchase of stop-loss insurance or threshold protection. With stop-loss insurance, expenses against a provider's pool are no longer deducted after a certain threshold has been reached. However, the expense of the stop-loss insurance raises individual or small group providers' costs.

Accordingly, another potential efficiency consideration for antitrust policy is that consolidation among providers may facilitate more efficient risk bearing, as it reduces the variance in medical treatment utilization and thus lowers the costs of risk bearing. Similarly, consolidation of health insurers may facilitate more efficient risk bearing because it allows for the spreading of the population health risk across additional patients and possibly across additional geographic markets.

## Shared Reputations

Physicians practicing in groups or hospitals belonging to multi-hospital systems develop a shared reputation. Each physician of the group shares the group's reputation, and likewise each hospital of the multihospital system shares the system's reputation. Further, the reputation of a group or system can be disseminated via brand names to consumers. Brand names, such as Mayo for physicians, "Memorial-Care: The Standard of Excellence in Health Care" for hospitals,[46] and BlueSelect and BlueCare for insurers, in combination with standardization of quality, convey information about quality to consumers in multiple geographic markets. The fact that a physician is a member of a certain physician organization may provide consumers with information on the quality of care provided by that physician. This is similar to the information conveyed by brand names such as McDonalds (hamburgers), Merrill Lynch (financial services), or H&R Block (tax services).

This provides an incentive for the providers in the organization to standardize quality within their organization by (1) allowing only those providers who provide a similar or higher level of quality of care to join the organization; (2) removing incompetent physicians or low-quality hospitals; and (3) establishing peer review or continuously monitoring and controlling the quality provided by each member of the organization.

The shared reputation incentive of hospital systems and physician organizations to standardize and increase quality may turn out to be one of the most important efficiency gains associated with horizontal consolidation in health care markets. Increased incentives to implement the system-wide changes that will facilitate higher quality across hospital systems or physician organizations are greatly needed. As the physicians Lucian Leape, Donald Berwick, and David Bates explain, health care quality, especially the reduction of medical errors and patient safety, is primarily a systems problem. Health care organizations need to change their systems; in particular, "better systems must be developed to prevent errors and equally important, better systems must be developed to ensure that clinicians provide the effective care they intend to provide."[47]

There is some evidence that physicians practicing in groups and IPAs attempt to standardize and control the quality of care provided by member physicians. Evidence from 131 large multispecialty groups in 1987 and 1988 shows that about three-quarters of these groups had formal procedures to deal with individual physicians doing a poor job in terms of quality of care.[48] Likewise, evidence based on a survey of 94 capitated physician organizations in California in the winter of 1993–94 suggests that one-half to two-thirds of physician organizations have quality assurance programs to monitor underprovision of preventive services.[49] The results of a survey of IPAs in California in 1996 showed that 21 of 53 IPAs had terminated a contract with a physician in the last year, and the most commonly cited reasons for termination were concerns about quality of care (64 percent) and patient satisfaction (55 percent).[50]

There is also anecdotal evidence that hospital systems are trying to standardize and improve the quality of care across member hospitals. For example, Memorial Health Services, a four-hospital system in southern California, has developed clinical pathways and variance tracking tools to be used in all four of its hospitals in order to standardize care across the hospitals.[51]

Increasing standardization of quality within hospital systems and physician organizations and dissemination of this quality information via brand names and report cards will increase consumers' knowledge about the differences between providers and thus may increase quality competition by increasing consumers' willingness to switch providers to obtain higher quality.

## Increased Competition

Finally, if consolidation among hospitals, physicians, or insurers results in significant efficiency gains, then these efficiency gains may increase competition among all competitors in the market(s). For example, the consolidated firm may be able to lower its costs and prices or increase its quality, and thereby stimulate price and quality competition among rivals or decrease the ability of rivals to coordinate their conduct.

## Evidence and Theory on the Anticompetitive Effects of Horizontal Consolidation

The downside of horizontal consolidation is that it can facilitate the exercise of market power to the detriment of consumers. This can occur in at least three ways. First, in any given health care market, as the number of firms decreases and firm size increases (and thus market concentration increases), the likelihood of coordination or collusion among firms increases. Horizontal consolidation increases the likelihood that the consolidated firm and its competitors will recognize their mutual interdependence and thus will jointly coordinate their prices, outputs, markets, or other choices.

The one study that directly tests whether hospital mergers increase coordination among all hospitals in the geographic market found no evidence of merger-induced price increases among the rivals of the merging hospitals. More specifically, using data on approximately 3,500 short-term general hospitals in the United States between 1986 and 1994, this study found no significant differences between the price increases[52] of the non-merging hospitals in markets with merging hospitals (the group of hospitals with increased opportunity for coordination) and the price increases of the hospitals in markets without merger activity.[53] During the period of this study, however, hospital mergers were most likely to occur in less concentrated markets, and mergers in such markets are not expected to increase hospitals' potential for coordination and the exercise of market power.

The second way consolidation can facilitate the exercise of monopoly power is by increasing the consolidated firm's ability to directly exercise market power. The one study that directly tests this hypothesis found evidence that hospital mergers in concentrated markets increase the merged hospitals' market power.[54] Using data on approximately 3,500 short-term general hospitals in the United States between 1986 and 1994 and looking at concentrated markets only, this study found the average increase in price for merged hospitals was 1.4 percentage points higher than the average increase in price for nonmerging hospitals (including nonmerging hospitals in concentrated markets with merging hospitals and all hospitals in concentrated markets without merging hospitals). If one looks at both more and less concentrated markets, however, merged hospitals appear to have had smaller percentage price increases between 1986 and 1994. Specifically, this study showed that the average increase in price between 1986 and 1994 was 75.5 percent for nonmerging hospitals, or approximately 7 percentage points higher than the 68.4 percent increase for merging hospitals. However, as mentioned earlier, during this time period hospitals were more likely to merge in less concentrated markets.

Finally, horizontal consolidation in one product market (for example, physician services) may decrease competition in other product markets, such as markets for hospital services or health care financing. The empirical evidence on horizontal consolidation in one market decreasing competition in another market is reviewed in Chapter 7.

An example of a large physician organization using its power to decrease competition in another market (in this case the market for health care financing) is provided by the FTC's 1997 complaint charging the Mesa County Physicians IPA, comprising approximately 85 percent of the physicians in private practice around Grand Junction, Colorado, with fixing the prices of physician services and collectively refusing to deal with certain managed care plans, specifically those plans that could engender competition among physicians or that would use more aggressive utilization management programs.[55] There was an implicit exclusive agreement in the sense that members were encouraged to deal with payers only through the IPA or on terms the IPA had approved. The complaint charged that competition in the market for health care financing was harmed because potential entrants into this market were unable to contract with a sufficient number of physicians in Mesa County to enter the local market for health care financing. The IPA accepted a consent order that prohibits it from acting as the exclusive bargaining agent for its members and orchestrating collective refusals to deal.

## Concentration and Price

The vast majority of empirical studies on the relationship between health care prices and market concentration use data from markets for hospital services. Although these studies have used differing product and geographic market definitions and differing research methods, the consistency of their results is striking. Since the introduction of selective contracting between insurers and hospitals in the mid-1980s, increased concentration in markets for hospital services has been associated with higher prices for those services.

At least seven empirical studies provide support for the hypothesis that hospital prices are higher in more concentrated markets.[56] These studies suggest that concentration in the market for hospital services increases hospitals' bargaining power and results in smaller discounts from nonprofit and for-profit hospitals' list prices. For example, one study found that Blue Cross of Indiana PPO paid higher prices to hospitals located in more concentrated hospital markets (counties with fewer hospitals).[57] Similarly, another study found that Blue Cross of California PPO paid higher per diem prices for medical/surgical services to hospitals located in more concentrated markets in 1987.[58] A third study found that between 1988 and 1992 the fee-for-services plans of approximately 70 self-insured firms obtained smaller price discounts for inpatient episodes of appendectomy from hospitals located in more concentrated markets.[59]

Unfortunately, because of the difficulties involved with measuring

quality in health care markets, none of these studies of the relationship
between market concentration and price in markets for hospital services control for differences in quality across hospitals. There is one
study that controls for differences in costs,[60] however, and its findings
are consistent with the other research. This study found that in 1988
the markup of price (the average price for a market basket of inpatient
treatments for all private payers) over costs was higher in more concentrated hospital markets in California. Further, the results of this study
suggest that large hospitals (more than 300 beds) and hospitals offering
high-tech services, such as open heart surgery or transplant services,
have significant market power.

In regard to physician services, there is little empirical research on
the relationship between concentration and price. Physician consolidation, and thus concentration in markets for physician services, is a relatively recent phenomenon.

The number of local physician organizations (groups, IPAs, and so
on) and the number of organizations each local physician participates
in will determine, at least in part, the extent of price competition in
that local market. When physicians belong to multiple IPAs, local IPAs
will be relatively homogeneous, and managed care plans will be able to
negotiate price more aggressively with IPAs. The managed care plans
can credibly threaten not to contract with one IPA because that does
not mean the managed care plans' enrollees will be denied access to the
physicians of that IPA. When physicians belong to only one physician
organization, managed care plans cannot negotiate as aggressively, if
their enrollees value access to the physicians of that organization.

On a related topic, there is some evidence suggesting that selective
contracting reduces physicians' abilities to price above costs. Specifically, one study using national data found that between 1990 and
1992 the ratio of physician fees to costs[61] was increasing (an increasing
ratio suggests increasing monopoly power), while after 1992 the ratio
of physician fees to costs was decreasing (a decreasing ratio suggests
decreasing monopoly power) for hospital-based primary care physicians and for both hospital-based and office-based specialists.[62] These
results are consistent with the hypothesis that selective contracting increased price competition among physicians in the 1990s and thus led
to a convergence of prices and costs.

As with markets for physician services, there is little empirical evidence on the competitive conduct of health insurers in concentrated markets characterized by the presence of managed care organizations. Consolidation in the market for health care financing and antitrust challenges to this consolidation are a relatively recent phenomenon. Very little is known about health insurers' potential to raise prices above competitive levels or to lower quality below competitive levels in concentrated markets.

The empirical analyses completed before the growth of managed care suggest that traditional Blue Cross/Blue Shield plans were able to exercise market power.[63] However, it is unclear whether Blue Cross/Blue Shield plans (or, for that matter, any plan) would be able to raise prices above costs in markets where there is significant competition from other MCCs.

Two recent papers have examined the competitive conduct of HMOs, and both are consistent with the hypothesis that competition in the market for health care financing reduces prices. The first paper found that between 1988 and 1991 the private (non-Medicare and non-Medicaid) premiums set by HMOs were lower in markets with more HMOs.[64] The second paper, using national data on non-Medicaid HMOs between 1985 and 1993, found that HMOs in the most competitive markets, measured as the number of HMOs in the market, had the lowest private premiums.[65] However, this paper also found that HMO mergers (which tend to reduce the number of HMOs in a market) were not associated with higher or lower HMO premiums. Unfortunately, both papers include information only on HMOs, not on other insurers that compete with them, and thus it is difficult to interpret these results.

## Conclusion

Economic theory and empirical research suggest that horizontal health care consolidations have the potential both to increase efficiency (lower costs and increase quality) and to enhance market power (increase prices). Thus, whether a particular merger, acquisition, or joint venture between hospitals, physicians, or insurers will make consumers better off depends on whether the efficiency or the market-power-enhancing effect predominates, and this, in turn, depends on factors particular to the market and firms involved.

Given the potential for horizontal consolidation in health care markets to enhance market power, health care consumers will be better off if federal and state agencies continue (despite these agencies' recent defeats in the courts) to challenge those horizontal consolidations that appear most likely to greatly enhance the market power of hospitals, physician organizations, or insurers.

# 7

# The Effects of Vertical Consolidation in Health Care Markets

> Vertical merger policy is in a transitional period. . . . During the 1970s and 1980s, vertical merger enforcement policy fell dormant in the wake of Chicago School arguments that vertical integration was most likely procompetitive or competitively neutral. Recently, though, government enforcement agencies began scrutinizing mergers with significant vertical elements.
>
> ∼ Michael H. Riordan, 1998[1]

VERTICAL CONSOLIDATION IN health care markets (consolidation between health care firms operating in different, but related, product markets, such as insurers and physicians, insurers and hospitals, or hospitals and physicians) comes in many forms and can have both pro-competitive and anticompetitive impacts. Accordingly, like horizontal consolidation, vertical consolidation among insurers, hospitals, and physicians can have significant implications for the well-being of health care consumers.

Vertical consolidations among health care firms can lead to lower prices if they generate efficiencies (cost savings) and encourage more aggressive competition among firms in the market. In other situations, however, vertical consolidations can lead to higher prices by facilitating the exercise of monopoly power. It is possible to have both efficiency gains and increases in monopoly power resulting from the same case of vertical consolidation. Whether consumers are better or worse off depends on which effect is stronger.

Analyses of the welfare effects of vertical consolidation are further complicated by three factors. First, there is considerable theoretical debate concerning whether and when vertical consolidation in health care markets facilitates the exercise of market power. Second, there is

161

virtually no empirical research providing evidence of the impacts of vertical consolidation in health care markets. The major exception is an unpublished study of physician-hospital integration in three states between 1994 and 1998.[2] Third, when health care firms consolidate vertically, individual competitors—physician organizations, hospitals, or insurers—are often hurt (for example, individual competitors may lose customers or even be driven out of business). Complications arise because individual competitors can be hurt both in cases where vertical consolidation decreases competition and in cases where it enhances (or at least does not lessen) competition. Harmed competitors are likely to raise antitrust challenges to the vertical consolidation in either case; however, the antitrust laws were designed to protect competition, not individual competitors.

In *Doctor's Hospital of Jefferson Inc. v. Southeast Medical Alliance, Inc.*,[3] for example, one hospital challenged its termination from a PPO that simultaneously began to contract with the hospital's competitor. The court correctly granted summary judgment on the grounds that the plaintiff failed to establish injury to competition. Vertical foreclosure of this sort is common, and the evidence presented, such as the large number of competitors in the market for health care financing and the fact that the terminated hospital was still a preferred provider at six other PPOs, suggested no anticompetitive effect.

Given the many complications involved in distinguishing the procompetitive vertical consolidations from the anticompetitive ones, it is not surprising that there are many unsettled antitrust policy issues concerning vertical consolidation among health care firms. Consistent with these unsettled antitrust policy issues, the DOJ and FTC have established "antitrust safety zones" for horizontal provider arrangements, such as hospital mergers and physician network joint ventures, but not for vertical provider arrangements. These safety zones describe a subset of the provider arrangements that the federal agencies are unlikely to challenge under the antitrust laws. Specifically, the agencies stated: "Because multiprovider networks involve a large variety of structures and relationships among many different types of health care providers, and new arrangements are continually developing, the Agencies are unable to establish a meaningful safety zone for these entities."[4]

As in the previous chapter on horizontal consolidations, I will focus in this chapter on synthesizing the theoretical and empirical literatures on the potential for vertical consolidation to enhance efficiency and market power. The analyses, based on both economic theory and empirical research, will show which benefits (efficiency gains) and costs (market power enhancements) of vertical consolidation are most plausible in health care markets. My hope is that this synthesis will facilitate the antitrust enforcement process of determining which vertical consolidations will be procompetitive (will have net positive impacts on consumers because the efficiency gains are greater than the associated costs) and which ones will be anticompetitive (will have net negative impacts on consumers because the increases in firms' market power resulting from the consolidation are greater than the associated benefits).

## Types of Vertical Consolidation

The types of vertical consolidation found in health care markets range from vertical integration (mergers and acquisitions) to nonexclusive vertical contracts, with exclusive dealing contracts, tying restrictions, joint ventures, and most-favored nation (MFN) clauses falling somewhere in the middle. Vertical integration, exclusive dealing contracts, and tying restrictions (under certain circumstances) present the greatest concern for anticompetitive behavior.

Vertical integration involves ownership—for example, a hospital or an insurer merging with or acquiring a physician organization.[5] Most old-style closed-panel HMOs are perfect examples of vertical integration. Although there are still numerous examples of this sort of integration in health care, its prevalence in the future is unclear. As discussed in Chapter 1, many vertically integrated providers are selling their insurance plans, and many vertically integrated insurers are selling their provider organizations. Likewise, many hospitals are selling their physician practices.

Exclusive dealing contracts are often thought of as integration through contract rather than through ownership. Their competitive impact may be quite similar to vertical integration because under exclusive dealing contracts at least one of the parties in the exchange agrees to trade only with the other. Under a hospital-physician exclusive contract, for example, the hospital may give certain physicians the right to be the only providers of the contracted services at that hospital.

This is called a one-sided exclusive contract because the exclusivity is binding on the hospital, but not the physicians, who are free to practice at other hospitals. If, in addition, the physicians agree to practice solely at the contracting hospital or to refer all patients to that facility, then the contract is called a two-sided exclusive contract.

Under certain circumstances one- and two-sided exclusive contracts can foreclose rivals from the market, decrease competition, and facilitate the exercise of market power. In particular, when hospital markets are characterized by few competing hospitals, this type of single-sided exclusive contract may decrease competition in the market for physician services.[6] Moreover, this sort of double-sided exclusive contract may decrease competition in two markets (the markets for physician and hospital services) by limiting the ability of competing hospitals to obtain sufficient numbers of patient admissions.

The actual competitive effect of exclusive dealing arrangements depends critically on the nature of the contract. The key factors are the degree of formal or implicit exclusivity (the extent to which the contract requires network members either to sell or to buy services only from other network members or the extent to which unwritten agreements prevent network members from contracting with other physicians or hospitals), the duration of the contract, the penalties for breach of the contract, and the proportion of the local hospital and physician services markets involved in the contract. Increasing any of these factors increases the likelihood that the exclusive contract will decrease competition and consumer welfare.

Exclusive contracts between hospitals and hospital-based physicians, such as radiologists, anesthesiologists, pathologists, and emergency room physicians, are quite common. An American Hospital Association survey found that 73 percent of hospitals had exclusive contracts with physicians in 1984.[7] More recently, hospitals have been contracting with cardiologists, internists, obstetricians, and thoracic surgeons on an exclusive basis.[8]

Exclusive arrangements between insurers and providers are not common,[9] and two states (Minnesota and New Hampshire) actually prohibit these sorts of contracts between HMOs and providers.[10] In 1997 the California Department of Corporations banned the use of exclusive provider contracts by PacifiCare.[11]

Tying restrictions require that buyers purchase two separate (but often complementary) products from particular sellers.[12] As a condition of the sale of one of these two products, called the tying good, the seller of the tying good requires the buyer to purchase the tied good from a seller of the tying good seller's choice. In the health care industry, tying restrictions might require MCCs to purchase physician and hospital services, two separate but complementary products, from particular hospital systems and physician organizations.[13] For example, a dominant hospital system's decision (and written contract) to enter risk-sharing contracts with only one local physician organization effectively imposes a tying restriction on MCCs. MCCs wanting to contract and share risk with the dominant hospital system would have to contract with the tied physician organization as well. In this case hospital services are the tying good and physician services are the tied good. Under certain conditions, for example when the hospital system (or seller of the tying product) has appreciable economic power to impose the tie and thereby force unwanted purchase of the tied product,[14] this sort of tying restriction has the potential to decrease competition in the market for the tied good (physician services) by eliminating other physician organizations' abilities to compete for risk contracts with the dominant hospital system.

Tying may be anticompetitive because it is an effective way for the dominant hospital system to affect the market structure of the tied good market.[15] Specifically, rival physician organizations may be foreclosed from sufficient sales because of the tying restriction, and thus their continued operation may become unprofitable. These sellers of the tied good are denied the scale necessary to survive in the market.

Likewise, a dominant physician organization's decision (and written contract) to enter risk-sharing contracts with only one local hospital system effectively imposes a tying restriction. MCCs entering into risk-sharing agreements with the dominant physician organization would have to contract with the tied hospital as well. In this case physician services are the tying good and hospital services are the tied good. Again under certain conditions, this restriction has the potential to decrease competition in the market for the tied good (hospital services) by eliminating other hospitals' abilities to compete for risk contracts with the dominant physician organization.

Vertical joint ventures involve collaboration and partial integration among providers and insurers or hospitals and physicians. For example, a physician organization and an insurer may form a joint venture to offer a new HMO. Or a physician organization and a hospital may form a joint venture to open an ambulatory surgery center, outpatient cancer treatment center, pain management clinic, cardiac catheterization lab, imaging center, or outpatient physical therapy/sports medicine facility. These sorts of joint ventures between hospitals and physicians seem to be increasing in number.[16]

PHOs and management service organizations (MSOs) often take the form of joint ventures between hospitals and physicians. In many cases the PHO is jointly owned and operated by a hospital(s) and its affiliated physicians. PHOs enable hospitals and physicians to contract with managed care plans to provide both physician and hospital services. An MSO is similar to a PHO, but it has evolved into an organization that provides more services to physicians, such as billing and collection services and utilization management services. An example of a hospital-physician joint venture involving many hospitals and physicians is the joint venture between Caregroup, a Boston-based system of six hospitals and its approximately 2,000 physicians, and Lahey Clinic, a system of three hospitals and its approximately 800 physicians.[17] By 1998, approximately 54 percent of acute care hospitals in the United States had PHOs or MSOs.[18]

Most-favored nation (MFN) clauses are vertical contractual agreements concerning prices. MFN clauses specify that the seller (for example, a hospital or physician organization) will not charge the contracting insurer more than the lowest price the seller charges any other buyer. If the seller offers another buyer a lower price, then the seller must offer the same lower price to the contracting insurer with the MFN clause. The prevalence of MFN clauses in contracts between insurers and hospitals or physicians is not known; however, in 1995 Washington became the first state to ban the use of these clauses in contracts between health care providers and health plans.[19]

## Efficiency Gains Specific to Vertical Consolidation

Vertical consolidation between health care firms can be efficiency-enhancing in many of the same ways as horizontal consolidation between health care firms. For example, vertical consolidation may allow for the realization of both transactional economies (lower costs due to reductions in transaction costs) and economies of scope (lower costs due to more efficient joint production of two or more products).

In addition, economic theory suggests that vertical consolidation between health care firms can be efficiency-enhancing in at least two other ways: (1) by correcting problems caused by misaligned incentives (externalities), and (2) by eliminating the double monopoly markup that can occur when both insurers and providers have market power. Issues of the alignment of incentives are particularly salient in health care markets, given the difficulty of contracting for and assuring quality.

## Internalization of Externalities or Improved Alignment of Incentives

In health care markets, positive production externalities can result in hospitals and physicians providing services of lesser quality than is socially optimal. A positive production externality is said to occur when the actions of a producer (a physician or hospital) confer a benefit on a party not directly involved in the market transaction. For example, when a physician who contracts nonexclusively to provide services to the enrollees of a managed health plan is faced with a treatment decision that affects the quality of care received by a patient (the physician and patient are directly involved in the market transaction), the physician will consider the benefits of providing higher quality to the patient and to him/herself (improved reputation and additional profits for the physician), but may not consider the benefits of providing higher quality to the managed health plan (improved reputation and additional profits for the owners of the health plan). As a result of this externality, physicians underestimate the total benefits (the benefits received by patients, physicians, and owners of managed health plans) of providing higher-quality care, and physicians may forgo some opportunities to increase quality that are in society's best interests.

Vertical integration of insurers and providers or exclusive contracts between insurers and providers may induce physicians to take into account the total benefits (including the benefits to the owners of the managed health plans, in addition to the benefits to patients and themselves) of providing higher-quality care to patients. Thus, vertical associations between insurers and providers may eliminate this externality and result in physicians and hospitals providing higher-quality care.

Likewise, vertical integration or exclusive contracts between hospitals and physicians may induce physicians to consider the impact of their treatment decisions on hospitals' reputations. Clearly, physicians' treatment decisions concerning hospitalized patients have an impact on both physicians' and hospitals' reputations. When hospitals and physicians are not vertically associated, however, the physician may only take his/her reputation for quality into account when making important decisions concerning quality of care. If hospitals and physicians are vertically integrated or physicians have signed exclusive contracts with hospitals, then physicians will be more likely to take hospitals' reputations into account when making these sorts of decisions. As a result, vertical associations between hospitals and physicians may result in higher quality of care.[20]

Another example is health insurers, who make multiple decisions that affect both their reputations and profits and health care providers' profits—decisions about benefit design (which health care services are covered and how much is covered—visit limits or expenditure limits), provider network inclusiveness (which hospitals and physicians are included in the network), and marketing. When an insurer is not vertically integrated or exclusively contracted with certain providers, that insurer will select its benefit design, network inclusiveness, and marketing strategy based on estimates of what will maximize its profit, not taking into account the impact on those providers' profits. However, a more generous benefit design, a less inclusive network, or additional marketing may result in additional profits for those providers (sometimes at the expense of those providers' competitors). Vertical integration or exclusive contracts between insurers and providers can internalize this externality.

## Elimination of the Double Monopoly Markup

In the absence of vertical integration, providers with market power contract with insurers at prices that include monopoly markups over the providers' costs, and then insurers with market power turn around and charge premiums that include monopoly markups over insurers' costs. Since insurers' costs include the higher costs of contracting with providers with market power, there is a double markup and insurance prices are higher.

With vertical integration between providers and insurers, costs are marked up only once, and insurance prices will be lower. Therefore, vertical integration (but not necessarily exclusive contracts) between insurers and providers can increase efficiency and reduce insurance prices when both insurers and providers have market power.

## Anticompetitive Effects Specific to Vertical Consolidation

Economists are still debating the competitive effects of vertical consolidation, and so far there is little agreement. Some economists, often grouped under the label "the Chicago School," argue that vertical consolidation is competitively neutral or has procompetitive effects,[21] while others, known as "the post-Chicago School," argue that vertical consolidation can be anticompetitive under certain conditions.

The theory and conclusions of the Chicago School, however, depend on assumptions that are inapplicable to health care markets. In particular, it has been shown that the Chicago School conclusion of a "single monopoly profit"—the notion that vertical mergers cannot increase a monopolist's profits further[22]—is critically sensitive to the assumptions of a fixed-proportions technology (the requirement that inputs into the production process be used in a fixed ratio to one another so that substitution between inputs is not possible), perfect competition in the input market (for example, the market for hospital services), and monopoly in the output market with prohibitive barriers to entry.[23] The models of the post-Chicago School do not depend on these same restrictive assumptions, and thus are more applicable to health care markets.

Nevertheless, much can be learned from Chicago School thinking, especially in regard to the competitive effects of exclusive dealing contracts. Both parties to an exclusive deal must benefit from it, and accordingly, it is less likely that exclusive dealing contracts will have anticompetitive effects.[24] For example, why would a physician organization be willing to sign an exclusive dealing contract that limited its physicians' abilities to admit patients to other hospitals, when the net effect of this exclusive dealing contract was to decrease competition in the market for hospital services, raise prices for hospital services, and therefore reduce demand for the services of the physicians[25] and reduce the physician organization's profits? To induce the physician organization to sign this sort of exclusive dealing contract, the hospital would have to compensate the physicians for lost profits, potentially rendering the anticompetitive exclusive deal unprofitable for the hospital.

## Vertical Consolidation and Post-Chicago School Thinking

Post-Chicago School theories suggest that in health care markets characterized by entry barriers, the anticompetitive impacts of vertical integration and exclusive contracts derive from (1) the potential for vertically-consolidated firms to raise rivals' costs and/or foreclose rivals' access to a necessary market, and (2) the potential for vertical consolidation to confer market power by facilitating horizontal coordination or collusion.[26]

In the following subsections, the four possible cases of vertical consolidation between hospitals, physician organizations, and insurers (illustrated in Figure 1) are described, and the conditions under which each of these cases has the potential to be anticompetitive are analyzed. A discussion of most-favored nation clauses follows.

### HOSPITAL-PHYSICIAN CONSOLIDATION THAT INHIBITS OTHER PHYSICIANS' ACCESS TO HOSPITALS

In 1995 the DOJ challenged the behavior of a monopoly hospital and its medical staff in Danbury, Connecticut, as having anticompetitive impacts in the markets for physician and hospital services.[27] The DOJ and the state attorney general alleged that the only acute care hospital in Danbury limited the size and mix of its medical staff (thereby inhibiting other physicians' access to the only acute care hospital in Danbury) in order to restrain competition in the market for physician services and coerce physicians to use its outpatient facilities. According to the complaint, both the threat of losing hospital admitting privileges and the "generous" physician fees negotiated by HealthCare Partners, a jointly owned corporation with the Danbury Area IPA (which included over 98 percent of the physicians on the hospitals' medical staff), provided the incentive for physicians to increase their use of Danbury Hospital's outpatient surgery facilities, and thus inhibit competition in markets for hospital services. The defendants consented to abide by the Final Judgment without trial, and accordingly not to fix prices or restrain competition.

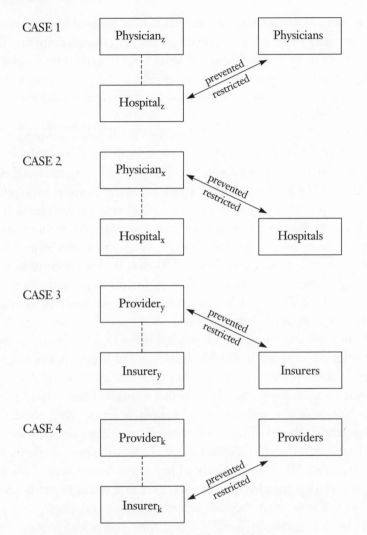

*Figure 1* Four possible cases of vertical consolidation

In general, the case of physician organization$_z$ and hospital$_z$ merging, forming a joint venture (for example, a PHO), or signing an exclusive dealing contract (specifying that physician organization$_z$ will be the sole supplier of certain physician services at that hospital) can be anticompetitive under certain conditions. This sort of vertical consolidation has the potential to be anticompetitive—specifically, to reduce competition in the local market for physician services and thus to allow the vertically-consolidated physicians to exercise market power—when there are entry barriers in the local market for hospital services and (1) the vertically-consolidated hospital is the only hospital in the local market or (2) the vertically-consolidated hospital is the highest-quality provider or the most cost-effective provider of hospital services in the local market and the vertically-consolidated hospital can maintain that position over time.

Assuming entry barriers in the market for hospital services, if the vertically-consolidated hospital is the sole supplier of hospital services and the vertically-consolidated hospital/physician organization does not allow other physicians to treat patients at this hospital, rival physicians and potential physician entrants are effectively foreclosed from the local market for physician services. For example, without access to the local hospital's operating rooms, surgeons would be unable to perform inpatient surgeries locally, and thus their abilities to operate profitable practices in the local market for physician services would be diminished. This increases the ability of the vertically-consolidated physicians to exercise market power.

If the vertically-consolidated hospital is the highest-quality or most cost-effective hospital in the local market and the vertically-consolidated hospital/physician organization does not allow other physicians to treat patients at this hospital (so the vertically-consolidated physicians have access to and control of a superior input), rival physicians' and potential physician entrants' costs of providing physician services can be raised or their abilities to provide high-quality physician services lowered. Nonvertically-related physicians (and potential entrants into the market for physician services) are at a competitive disadvantage in the sense that they are forced to admit and treat patients at lower-quality hospitals (holding travel time and price constant, consumers prefer higher-quality hospitals) or higher-cost hospitals (holding quality and travel time constant, consumers—managed care plans —prefer lower-priced hospitals). Facing less formidable competitors in the market for physician services, the vertically-consolidated firm gains the market power to sell physician services at prices above its costs.

Competition in the market for physician services will not necessarily be lessened if rival physicians and potential physician entrants can gain access to new sources of high-quality, low-cost hospital services. This is exactly why monopoly provision of hospital services or monopoly provision of the highest-quality or lowest-cost hospital services in combination with entry barriers into the market for hospital services are necessary conditions for anticompetitive effects to result from physician organization$_z$'s acquisition of, joint venture with, or exclusive dealing contract with hospital$_z$.

The Chicago School critique raises the issue of why a hospital would sign an exclusive dealing contract specifying that it could not contract with other physicians, if the net effect of the exclusive deal was to raise the prices of physician services and possibly decrease the hospital's profits. Clearly, a hospital's willingness to sign this sort of exclusive contract depends on the hospital being made better off, as well. For the physicians to exercise market power and the hospital to be better off, simultaneously, requires an arrangement by which the physicians share their anticompetitive gain with the hospital.[28]

The necessity of such side payments to induce a hospital's participation in an anticompetitive exclusive deal, however, reduces the probability that the exclusive deals found in practice are anticompetitive. "We expect to see exclusive contracts only when the hospital is both willing and able to 'give away the store.'"[29] However, it has also been suggested that physicians may coerce hospitals into accepting these sorts of exclusive contracts.[30]

The Chicago School critique does not apply in the cases of vertical integration and joint ventures because the hospital (as part of the vertically integrated firm or joint venture) can share the benefits of enhanced market power in the market for physician services. This provides an incentive for hospitals to allow their medical staffs to control admitting privileges.

HOSPITAL-PHYSICIAN CONSOLIDATION THAT INHIBITS
OTHER HOSPITALS' ACCESS TO PHYSICIANS

In 1996 the DOJ challenged as being anticompetitive a PHO in Baton Rouge, Louisiana, a vertical joint venture between Woman's Hospital (the largest provider of inpatient obstetrical services in the area) and its medical staff (representing approximately 90 percent of the OB/GYNs in the area). The terms of the PHO contract required physicians to refer all patients covered by PHO contracts only to other PHO physicians and to Woman's Hospital.[31] Woman's Hospital and its medical staff formed this PHO after General Health Inc. (the operator of a tertiary care hospital in the area) announced plans to open a new hospital with five to six dedicated OB/GYN beds in the Baton Rouge area. The DOJ challenged the PHO because its intent was to inhibit the hospital entrant's access to local physicians and prevent entry by this potential new rival, and thus reduce competition in the market for hospital services.[32]

Chicago School thinking raises the question of why the OB/GYNs on the medical staff of Woman's Hospital were willing to participate if the net effect of the exclusive joint venture was to reduce competition in the market for hospital services. The answer to this question was found in the physician fee schedule developed by the PHO, which included fees that were substantially higher than the fees managed care plans were then paying OB/GYNs under individual contracts. These higher than competitive fees provided the OB/GYNs on the medical staff of Woman's Hospital with the incentive to participate in the PHO and to agree to the terms of the PHO contract, such as referring all patients covered by PHO contracts only to other PHO physicians and to Woman's Hospital.

The case did not go to court. Instead, the defendants consented to a Final Judgment in which they were enjoined from various activities, including negotiating on behalf of competing physicians, owning or contracting with an organization in which the participating physicians constitute more than 30 percent of the physicians in any relevant market, and discouraging physicians from dealing with rival hospitals.

In another recent case, *HTI Health Services v. Quorum Health Group*,[33] one hospital in Vicksburg, Mississippi (a town with two hospitals and two large physician groups) challenged the proposed merger between one of the two large physician groups in Vicksburg and a physician-owned integrated delivery system that included the other large physician group and the other hospital in Vicksburg. The challenge was based, in part, on the argument that allowing one hospital to own both physician groups would foreclose the other hospital from a sufficient base of customers. The vertically integrated physicians would become postmerger equity shareholders in the integrated delivery system, and thus would have the incentive to shift their patient admissions to the vertically integrated hospital. The court allowed the merger. Interestingly, these two hospitals are no longer competitors in the market for hospital services. As of November 1998, both hospitals became part of a joint venture to build a larger hospital to replace the two smaller hospitals in Vicksburg.[34]

In general, the case of hospital$_x$ and physician organization$_x$ merging, forming a joint venture, or signing an exclusive dealing contract specifying that physician organization$_x$ cannot treat patients at other hospitals (thereby foreclosing rival hospitals and potential hospital entrants from the patients of these physicians)[35] has the potential to be anticompetitive under certain conditions. Specifically, this sort of vertical consolidation has the potential to decrease competition in the local market for hospital services, and thus to allow the vertically-consolidated hospital to exercise market power, when (1) the vertically-consolidated physicians have a large market share or provide (and will continue to provide) the highest-quality or most cost-effective physician services in the local market (and the vertically-related physicians are worth more to hospital$_x$ than to other hospitals or potential entrants because, for example, learning-by-doing results in the vertically-related physicians being more productive at hospital$_x$), and (2) there are entry barriers into the market for physician services. Without entry barriers in the market for physician services, competition in the market for hospital services will not be reduced because rival hospitals and potential entrants into the market for hospital services will be able to recruit a sufficient number of physicians from other areas to practice at their institutions.[36] In what follows, entry barriers in the market for physician services are assumed.

In the case of physicians who admit patients to hospitals, as opposed to the case of hospital-based physicians (such as anesthesiologists and radiologists who provide services to patients admitted by other physicians), if the vertically-consolidated physicians have a large market share and treat their patients exclusively at hospital$_x$, then this vertical consolidation may foreclose rival hospitals and potential hospital entrants from a sufficient base of customers. With fewer physicians to admit patients, nonvertically-consolidated hospitals (and potential entrants into the market for hospital services) may be at a competitive disadvantage in the sense that they may be forced to reduce their outputs of hospital services, thereby incurring higher average costs (assuming scale economies) and having to charge higher prices (for example, higher per diem rates). It is also possible that forcing rival hospitals to reduce their outputs will decrease rival hospitals' abilities to compete on the basis of quality (assuming practice makes perfect). Facing less formidable competitors in the market for hospital services, the vertically-consolidated firm gains the market power to sell hospital services at prices above its (relatively lower) costs.

Even if the physicians associated with physician organization$_x$ continue to admit patients at rival hospitals, such admissions may involve sicker and more costly-to-treat patients. This too would put rival hospitals at a competitive disadvantage, forcing them to sell at higher prices (in order to cover their higher costs), and allowing the vertically-consolidated firm to sell hospital services at prices above its (relatively lower) costs.

When physician organization$_x$ includes the highest-quality or most cost-effective physicians, nonvertically-consolidated hospitals are at a competitive disadvantage in the sense that the vertical consolidation forces rival hospitals and potential entrants to deal with lower-quality or less cost-effective physicians. A hospital's reputation for quality is closely tied to the reputations of the physicians on its medical staff. Again, facing less formidable competitors (hospitals with higher costs or reputations for lower quality), hospital$_x$ gains market power.

As already emphasized, entry barriers into markets for physician services are a necessary condition for hospitals' use of these vertical consolidation strategies to increase their market power in markets for hospital services. One implication of this is that entry barriers in markets for physician services may be in both the physicians' and the hospital's best interests. Accordingly, a vertically-consolidated hospital may be willing to give the vertically-consolidated physicians authority over admitting privileges because, as discussed in Chapter 5, the physicians on a hospital's medical staff may be able to use their authority over hospital staffing policies to effectively deter entry into markets for physician services. Since only physicians with admitting privileges can admit patients and use the hospital's resources to treat patients, lack of admitting privileges at the only local hospital or the superior local hospital could put potential physician entrants at a severe disadvantage, and thus deter entry into the market for physician services. By giving these physicians control of admitting privileges, the hospital may be creating an entry barrier into the market for physician services and thus creating the condition necessary for vertical consolidation to enhance its own market power.

In *Blue Cross and Blue Shield of Wisconsin v. Marshfield Clinic,*[37] BC/BS charged that the vertical integration of the Marshfield Clinic (a clinic employing approximately 400 physicians and contracting with another 900 physicians on a nonexclusive basis) and its HMO foreclosed BC/BS from access to the physicians of the Marshfield Clinic and thus reduced competition in the market for HMOs.[38] The Court of Appeals, however, ruled that the vertical integration of the Marshfield Clinic and its HMO did not result in anticompetitive vertical foreclosure in the market for HMOs (in large part because the court ruled there is not a separate market for HMOs).

In general, the case of insurer$_y$ merging, forming a joint venture, or signing an exclusive contract with provider$_y$ specifying that provider$_y$ will treat only those patients insured by insurer$_y$ (thereby foreclosing other insurers' access to provider$_y$)[39] has the potential to be anticompetitive, specifically to decrease competition in the market for health care financing and thus to allow insurer$_y$ to exercise market power under certain conditions.[40] First, the vertically-related provider must have a large market share or must be (and continue to be) the highest-quality or the most cost-effective provider in the local market (and provider$_y$ must be worth more to insurer$_y$ than to rival insurers and potential entrants). Second, there must be entry barriers in the market for provider$_y$'s services.

Under these conditions, vertical consolidation by reducing the abilities of nonvertically-related insurers to compete can be anticompetitive. Rival insurers and potential entrants into the market for insurance are at a competitive disadvantage in the sense that eliminating rival insurers' opportunities to contract with the most cost-effective provider(s) raises their costs, and eliminating rival insurers' opportunities to contract with the largest or highest-quality provider(s) reduces their abilities to market their health plans. Holding price constant, consumers will prefer health plans with insured access to the highest-quality providers, and holding quality constant, consumers will prefer the lowest-priced health plans. With rivals and potential entrants at a competitive disadvantage, insurer$_y$ gains the market power to raise its prices above its costs.

Even if provider$_y$ continues to contract with rival insurers and potential entrants into the market for insurance, provider-insurer mergers and joint ventures still have the potential to be anticompetitive. Provider$_y$ may continue to contract with other insurers, but at prices above the internal prices at which it implicitly sells to itself. This sort of strategy to raise rivals' costs can be anticompetitive if (1) there are entry barriers into the market for provider$_y$'s services and (2) nonvertically-consolidated incumbent providers are unable (possibly due to permanent capacity constraints) or unwilling (possibly due to the tendency for vertical consolidation to facilitate horizontal collusion on price) to contract with nonvertically-consolidated insurers at prices as low as the internal prices at which the vertically-consolidated firm implicitly sells to itself. In this case, nonvertically-consolidated insurers are at a competitive disadvantage in the sense that they have to raise their insurance prices to cover their higher input costs, and insurer$_y$ gains the market power to raise its insurance prices above its costs.

Despite the court's decision in the Marshfield case, the conditions for anticompetitive vertical foreclosure in the market for insurance may have been present. Although Marshfield Clinic did not have a particularly large market share, there was evidence that its physicians offered the highest-quality services in the local market. Both parties of the dispute acknowledged Marshfield's unsurpassed reputation for quality.[41] Moreover, barriers to entry may have been present in the local market for physician services. There was evidence presented at trial that only Marshfield physicians had hospital admitting privileges at the dominant local hospital. To the extent that control over which physicians obtain admitting privileges at the dominant or highest-quality local hospital creates entry barriers into the market for physician services, the two requirements for anticompetitive vertical foreclosure in the market for insurance may have been present in the Marshfield case. Interestingly, in January 1999 (about four years after the Court of Appeals ruling in the Marshfield Clinic case) the Marshfield Clinic signed a contract with BC/BS of Wisconsin to provide physician services to enrollees of BC/BS.[42] No information, however, is available on the contracted prices established between Marshfield Clinic and BC/BS of

Wisconsin (nor is there information on the internal prices at which Marshfield Clinic implicitly sells to its HMO), and thus this new contract implies little about the monopoly power of Marshfield Clinic's HMO.

In *U.S. Healthcare, Inc. v. Healthsource, Inc.*,[43] although it was not exactly an insurer-provider exclusive dealing case, one HMO asserted that another HMO had foreclosed it from the market by offering to pay physicians higher capitation payments if they agreed not to contract with other HMOs. On the basis of multiple factors, including the fact that only 25 percent of the primary care physicians in the local market were under exclusive contracts, the short duration of the contracts (initially 100 days, but later shortened to 30 days), and the magnitude of the financial incentive, the court ruled that the pay differentials offered to physicians could not foreclose a rival HMO from the market.[44]

Another case with related but not exactly insurer-provider exclusive dealing issues[45] is *Reazin v. Blue Cross and Blue Shield of Kansas, Inc.*[46] A BC/BS memorandum that was sent to all hospitals in Kansas, suggesting that BC/BS would punish hospitals for participating in other health plans, was introduced as evidence. In effect, BC/BS sought implicit exclusive deals with these hospitals. A federal court jury found BC/BS guilty of conspiring with hospitals to stifle development of competing managed care plans and exercising market power to raise prices. In addition, the jury determined that BC/BS's threat of punishment against hospitals participating in competing managed care plans (the implicit exclusive deal) was intended to decrease competition in the market for health care financing.[47]

## INSURER-PROVIDER CONSOLIDATION THAT INHIBITS OTHER PROVIDERS' ACCESS TO INSURERS

This sort of exclusive contracting is also called selective contracting. The courts have looked favorably on insurers' selective contracting choices where procompetitive justifications are present.[48] For example, in *Capital Imaging Associates v. Mohawk Valley Medical Associates*[49] an HMO had contracted for MRI services with only one of the two radiology groups in the area, and the excluded radiology group brought an antitrust suit. The court found, however, that the HMO lacked market power since it had only 2.3 percent of all HMO enrollees and there were 53 HMOs operating in the area. The extent to which the plaintiff was foreclosed from the market was minimal, and therefore there was no significant anticompetitive impact.

In general, the case of insurer$_k$ merging, forming a joint venture, or signing an exclusive contract with provider$_k$ specifying that provider$_k$ will be the only provider to treat the enrollees of insurer$_k$ (thereby foreclosing other providers' access to the enrollees of insurer$_k$)[50] has the potential to be anticompetitive under certain conditions. Specifically, this sort of vertical consolidation can decrease competition in the markets for hospital and physician services, and thus allow provider$_k$ to exercise market power, when (1) there are entry barriers in the market for insurance and (2) the vertically-consolidated insurer has a large market share.

Under these conditions the vertical consolidation can be anticompetitive by reducing the ability of nonvertically-related providers to compete. Rival providers (and potential entrants into the market for hospital or physician services) are at a competitive disadvantage in the sense that eliminating rival providers' opportunities to contract with insurer$_k$ may exclude rival providers from a sufficient customer base. If the vertically-consolidated insurer does not contract with rival providers, those providers may be forced to reduce their outputs and incur higher average costs. This makes rival providers less formidable competitors (their costs and prices will be higher) and may allow the vertically-consolidated firm to increase its provider prices above the competitive level.

## Most-Favored Nation Clauses

Until 1997 the courts consistently allowed the use of MFN clauses.[51] In *U.S. v. Delta Dental of Rhode Island*, however, the Court for the first time rejected an insurer's argument that most MFN clauses are *per se* legal and agreed with the DOJ that under certain market conditions MFN clauses may have anticompetitive effects. Specifically, the DOJ argued that Delta's use of MFN clauses had the effect of excluding potential entrants, such as PPOs that work by negotiating discounted fees with selected dentists, from the market for dental insurance in Rhode Island. However, the courts have yet to fully analyze MFN clauses as unreasonable vertical restraints.[52]

Prior to 1997 the courts upheld MFN clauses with "virtually no analysis" of when an MFN might be anticompetitive,[53] and extremely broad statements in support of insurers' use of MFN clauses accompanied some of these decisions. For example, in *Ocean State Physicians Health Plan v. Blue Cross & Blue Shield of R.I.*[54] the district court judge wrote: "As a naked proposition, it would seem silly to argue that a policy to pay the same amount for the same service is anticompetitive, even on the part of one who has market power. This, it would seem, is what competition should be all about."[55] Similarly, in *Blue Cross & Blue Shield United v. Marshfield Clinic*[56] Judge Posner characterized MFN clauses as "the sort of conduct that the antitrust laws seek to encourage."[57]

In the *Ocean State* case, an HMO called Ocean State challenged BC/BS's use of a most-favored nation clause in its contracts with physicians as anticompetitive under Section 2 of the Sherman Act. Ocean State argued that BC/BS's MFN clause was intended to decrease competition in the market for health care financing, specifically to weaken Ocean State by inducing physicians to resign from Ocean State. In fact, 350 of Ocean State's 1,200 physicians did resign after BC/BS's implementation of the MFN clause.[58] BC/BS argued that its MFN clause was intended to lower its costs, specifically to ensure that BC/BS did not pay physicians more for particular physician services than those physicians received from Ocean State or other insurers. Both the District Court and the Court of Appeals sided with BC/BS and ruled that MFN clauses tend to increase rather than decrease competition.

In *Blue Cross & Blue Shield United of Wisconsin v. Marshfield Clinic*, BC/BS charged the Marshfield Clinic and its HMO (Security) with enforcing MFN clauses in Security's contracts with physicians in an attempt to monopolize the market for HMOs. BC/BS argued that Security's enforcement of MFN clauses excluded potential entrants into the HMO market. In fact, BC/BS's HMO had attempted to contract with the physicians of the Marshfield Clinic, but was refused. The court sided with the Marshfield Clinic, in large part because there was no evidence of a separate market for HMOs, and the market share of Security HMO was quite small in the broader market of health care financing.

Although the court's decision in the *Marshfield Clinic* case appears to be defensible based on the facts,[59] the issue of under what market conditions MFN clauses may be anticompetitive was left unsettled. Economists argue that under certain conditions, the use of MFN clauses by insurers with large market shares, such as BC/BS of Rhode Island, can be a mechanism to raise rival insurers' costs, and thus to achieve or maintain market power.[60] In general, the anticompetitive concerns associated with MFN clauses include decreasing price competition in the market for the seller's services, foreclosing entry of other insurers into the market for health care financing, and facilitating the exercise of market power by the contracting insurer with the MFN clause.

With respect to the *Ocean State* case, Jonathan Baker, an economist, wrote: "BC/BS may have achieved market power if the [MFN] contract provision caused so many doctors to terminate their affiliations with the rival HMO that Ocean State fell below a minimum efficient scale of production."[61] There is no evidence, however, that BC/BS's MFN contract provision reduced Ocean State's ability to compete in the market for insurance. In fact, between 1986 (the year when BC/BS began using the MFN clause in its contracts with physicians) and 1990 the enrollment of Ocean State increased by 59 percent.[62] Again this implies little about the anticompetitive potential of MFN clauses as there is also no evidence that BC/BS was enforcing its MFN contract provisions. It appears that although BC/BS of Rhode Island won the legal right to use MFN clauses in its physicians' contracts, the physicians were unaware of the policy until 1998 when the insurer began to "spell out" the MFN policy because a new state law required health care firms to be more explicit about their policies in contracts.[63] Apparently, hospitals in Rhode Island have had MFN clauses in their contracts for many years, but the clauses have been largely unenforced.

In addition to the argument that MFN clauses may raise rival insurers' costs, economists argue that the use of MFN clauses by insurers may be anticompetitive when these clauses facilitate horizontal pricing coordination among competing sellers of health care services. After providers have agreed to such clauses, they have little incentive to reduce their prices. In fact, as part of provider-owned health plans, providers may use MFN clauses to reduce price competition in the market for their services.

Although the courts allowed MFN clauses until 1997, between 1994 and 1996 the DOJ and the FTC challenged the MFN clauses in two other (in addition to Delta Dental of Rhode Island)[64] state-wide dental insurance plans (Delta Dental Plan of Arizona[65] and Oregon Dental

Service),[66] as well as a national vision care insurer (Vision Service Plan [VSP]) and a state-wide pharmacy network (RxCare of Tennessee), as unreasonable vertical restraints. The cases against Delta Dental Plan of Arizona and Oregon Dental Services were settled out of court, with the dental plans agreeing to discontinue the use of MFN clauses in their contracts with providers. The DOJ's settlement agreement with VSP enjoined VSP from continuing to use MFN clauses in its contracts with optometrists. Likewise, the FTC and RxCare of Tennessee entered into a consent order that stopped RxCare's use of MFN clauses.

In 1998 the DOJ challenged the most-favored rate clauses in Medical Mutual of Ohio's (formerly known as Blue Cross and Blue Shield of Ohio) contracts with hospitals. In this case the government alleged that these most-favored rate clauses violated antitrust law because they actually required hospitals to charge other insurers 15 to 30 percent more than they charged Medical Mutual. Medical Mutual filed a consent decree one day after the DOJ lawsuit was filed.[67]

## Conclusion

Economic theory suggests that vertical health care mergers, acquisitions, joint ventures, and contracts have the potential to both increase efficiency (lower costs and increase quality) and enhance market power (increase prices). As discussed throughout this chapter, the net procompetitive or anticompetitive impact of a particular vertical consolidation depends on multiple factors, and these factors vary across markets and firms. Thus it must be determined for each individual case whether a particular vertical consolidation among health care firms will make consumers better or worse off. We can hope that the courts will take off their Chicago School blinders and analyze vertical consolidations in health care (and other) markets on a case-by-case basis.

# Conclusion

The right mix of regulation and competition is not easily determined. What
works for one industry may not work for another. What works well at
one point in time may not work well at another. Thus, when antitrust
principles are applied to markets that are—perhaps of necessity—
partially regulated, the application must be done with care.

~ Almarin Phillips, 1994[1]

CONSISTENT AND CAREFUL enforcement of our antitrust laws is essential
for healthy competition in markets for hospital and physician services.
Consistent antitrust enforcement is necessary to send a loud and clear
message to physicians and hospitals that the exercise of monopoly
power will not be tolerated. Consistent enforcement requires that enforcers have the authority to challenge, without exception, all violations of our antitrust laws. Therefore, legislative proposals that would
weaken either federal or state agencies' abilities to enforce the antitrust
laws in health care markets, such as proposals to grant physicians an exemption from the *per se* rule against price fixing, should be rejected.

Careful enforcement of our antitrust laws is necessary to guarantee
that antitrust enforcement activity will not discourage the growth of
new and better (more efficient) forms of health care organization.
Careful enforcement requires that antitrust enforcers, especially the
judges litigating antitrust cases, be knowledgeable about economics.
Economic theory and empirical analyses facilitate antitrust enforcers'
abilities to draw the line between health care consolidations that will
make consumers better off, and thus should be allowed, and those that
will make consumers worse off, and thus should be challenged.

Short of this, there are built-in safeguards against overly aggressive
enforcement agencies.[2] If a federal or state agency errs and challenges
a health care consolidation that will likely have a net efficiency-
enhancing impact, the courts can and (as history shows) will decide
against the federal or state agency. However, only a retrospective study

on how these mergers played out could show whether the courts' decisions were in the public interest. Unfortunately, these sorts of studies are rarely available.[3]

In summary, where competition is feasible and in the public interest, enforcement of the antitrust laws can help keep this competition healthy. Consistent and careful enforcement of the antitrust laws is the linchpin of a real commitment to competition in health care markets.

Health care competition and enforcement of the antitrust laws, however, may not always be feasible or in the public interest. In local markets currently characterized by natural monopoly conditions,[4] for example, the public interest may be served by allowing only one large hospital or only one large physician organization to supply all necessary hospital or physician services. Under natural monopoly conditions, a monopoly hospital or physician organization can supply services at lower costs than two or more hospitals or physician organizations.

Little empirical research has addressed the issue of whether hospitals or physician organizations are characterized by natural monopoly conditions. Economic theory, however, has clearly demonstrated that subadditivity of the firm's cost function is the factor determining whether a multiproduct firm is a natural monopoly.[5] Subadditivity, which is a function of both economies of scale and scope, means that the production of combinations of products is accomplished at the least cost by one firm. Hospitals and physician organizations, like electric utilities (with peak and off-peak power) and telephone companies (local services, long-distance services, and 800 services), are multiproduct firms.

An important implication of this subadditivity requirement is that economies of scale are neither a necessary nor a sufficient condition for a multiproduct firm to be a natural monopoly. The reason for this is that the lower costs associated with scale economies can be canceled out by the higher costs associated with diseconomies of scope. Thus, documentation of new sources of potential scale economies in the health care industry, such as those resulting from the fixed costs associated with information technologies required to monitor and control health care utilization, costs, and quality, does not provide sufficient evidence of natural monopolies in rural markets for hospital or physician services. In general, evidence of both scale and scope economies is required.

It is also important to note that in health care markets it may be evidence of economies of experience, rather than those of scale and scope, that drives future governmental decisions to allow one hospital or one physician organization to supply the entire market. As discussed in Chapter 6, economies of experience occur when as a result of physicians and hospitals performing higher volumes of specific procedures, such as coronary artery bypass graft surgery, patient outcomes improve.

## Public Policies for Dealing with Natural Monopolies

This section is at best an introduction to the very complicated issues involved with public and private policies for dealing with natural monopolies. A more complete analysis of policies to deal with natural monopolies in health care markets would require a book-length project.

If a decision were made to allow one hospital or physician organization to supply the entire market, effectively there would be no competition and the monopolist would be able to charge monopoly prices (in the absence of government intervention). In this situation where competition is not possible, enforcement of the antitrust laws makes little sense. Antitrust enforcement policies are not the best tools to facilitate low prices and high quality in markets characterized by natural monopoly.

Fortunately, governments have alternative tools to address the negative aspects of allowing one hospital or one physician organization to supply the market, or more specifically, to address the problem that unregulated, private monopolists tend to charge monopoly prices. The policy dilemma is that under natural monopoly conditions, allowing an unregulated monopolist to supply the entire market involves a trade-off—lower costs (production efficiency) but higher prices (allocative inefficiency). Can consumers get the benefits of least-cost production, which under natural monopoly conditions requires only one hospital or physician organization in the market, without suffering from monopoly prices?

To address this trade-off there are basically two policy tools—public utility regulation and public enterprise policy—neither of which has been applied to markets for physician services. However, under the state action immunity doctrine a weak variant of public utility regulation is being tried in hospital markets in some states. Moreover, public ownership of hospitals (not necessarily those hospitals characterized as natural monopolies) by federal, state, and local governments has a long history in the United States. In 1999 the federal government owned and operated 264 hospitals (173 of which were operated by the Department of Veterans Affairs), and state and local governments owned and operated 1,197 community hospitals.[6]

Full-blown public utility regulation involves granting legal monopoly status to one supplier (believed to operate under natural monopoly conditions) and then subjecting that supplier to government (regulatory agency) regulation of its prices, qualities, and service availability, including preventing the monopolist from discontinuing any services or denying services to particular customers. As this definition suggests, in many ways public utility regulation is different from price regulation of firms in competitive markets, as has been tried by some states in markets for hospital services. Examples of industries subject to public utility regulation in the United States include natural gas, water, and electric utilities, local telecommunications, and transportation authorities (canals, railroads, and local transit systems). Interestingly, in recent years deregulation has allowed some competition in the transmission of natural gas and in the generation and distribution of electricity.

While the issue of whether hospitals and physician organizations in certain markets are natural monopolies is beyond the scope of this book, there are similarities (and differences) between the industries currently subject to public utility regulation and the hospital and physician services industries. Like hospitals and physician organizations, the industries currently subject to public utility regulation offer products considered to be vital or indispensable. Also like hospitals and physician organizations, many of these industries supply a product that cannot be stored (must be generated/produced as it is needed) and thus require excess capacity to meet periods of peak demand. But, unlike hospitals and physician organizations, these other industries supply a product that requires consumer-to-consumer or consumer-to-supplier connections by wire, pipeline, waterway, pavement, or rail.

Public utility regulation is not without its shortcomings. The problems associated with this type of regulation include the fact that regulators are often prevented from implementing their preferred policies because of informational constraints (for example, regulators often have less information about costs and other relevant variables than the regulated firm), transactional constraints (for example, regulatory contracts are often incomplete due to the costs of writing, monitoring, and enforcing them), and administrative and political constraints (for example, laws and codes of regulation often limit the regulatory instruments).[7] In addition, these regulations often induce inefficiencies in production by distorting the regulated firm's incentives away from cost minimization; for example, since returns are based on the rate base (value of capital assets) under rate-of-return regulation, the regulated firm has incentives to expand its rate base by substituting capital for labor beyond the point that would minimize costs in the absence of regulation.

Public enterprise policy involves government ownership and operation of a natural monopoly. Examples in the United States include the U.S. Postal Service and Amtrak, the government-owned passenger railroad service. Public enterprise policy is also not without its problems. The empirical literature suggests that, like regulated private utilities, public utilities tend to overcapitalize (possibly to garner political support by avoiding shortages, such as blackouts), and that regulated privately-owned utilities tend to achieve greater production efficiency than publicly-owned utilities.[8]

## State Action Immunity Doctrine in Markets for Hospital Services

Despite the lack of theoretical and empirical evidence of natural monopoly conditions in the hospital industry, under the state action immunity doctrine some states have experimented with allowing certain hospitals to merge—effectively creating "state-blessed monopolies," at least in the short run.

State action immunity doctrine holds that activities approved and monitored by the state are exempt from federal antitrust laws. The resultant policy—a very watered-down version of public utility regulation—trades long-term hospital antitrust exemptions for hospitals' promises to pass merger-related cost savings on to consumers and some short-term restrictions on (not long-term regulation of) monopoly hospitals' business practices. Hospitals often accept some restrictions on their short-run operations, such as temporary price freezes or temporary limits on their profit margins, in exchange for the green

light to merge. For example, since 1996 Benefis Healthcare has operated the state-authorized monopoly hospital in Great Falls, Montana,
under Montana's state action immunity doctrine. In return for exemption from federal antitrust scrutiny, the merged hospital agreed to earn
no greater than a 6 percent profit margin, to base price increases on increases in the hospital component of the U.S. Labor Department's
Producer Price Index, to generate a minimum of $86 million in cost re-
ductions and to give these savings to the community over a ten-year
period, to maintain current service offerings, and to deal fairly with insurers and providers.[9]

With respect to making decisions about the allocation of society's
scarce health care resources, one can think of these sorts of applications
of the state action immunity doctrine as substitutions of packages of
state restrictions for packages of competitive market forces assisted by
antitrust enforcement policies. This substitution can be in the public
interest only when it is possible for the package of state restrictions to
do a better job of allocating health care resources than competitive
market forces assisted by antitrust enforcement policies. This is possible, at least in theory, when the merged hospital is a natural monopoly.

When the package of state restrictions cannot do a better job, using
the state action immunity doctrine to exempt hospitals or physician organizations from federal antitrust review may result in a minefield of
inefficiencies that may harm consumers. When the merged hospital is
not a natural monopoly, there is little to gain in the form of production
efficiencies, but much to lose in the form of allocative inefficiencies. It
is not clear what will happen when the short-term restrictions eventu-
ally expire, but there is plenty of evidence suggesting that monopoly
hospitals can and do exercise monopoly power to the detriment of consumers.

There is also anecdotal evidence indicating that the short-term restrictions placed on "state-blessed monopoly hospitals" under the state
action immunity doctrine are not always effectively enforced. For example, a recently filed antitrust suit suggests that it was a mistake to
allow the formation of a "state-blessed monopoly hospital" in north
central Pennsylvania in 1994. In August 2000, the 150,000-member
HealthAmerica of Pennsylvania HMO filed an antitrust lawsuit against
Susquehanna Health System (consisting of the three hospitals allowed
to merge into the "state-blessed monopoly" in 1994) and the 101-

member Susquehanna Physicians Services. The suit alleges the defendants have jointly exercised their market power to charge "exorbitant prices."[10] This example suggests that the current policy of using state oversight (which may or may not be effective) of hospitals (which may or may not be natural monopolies) is not serving the public interest.

## The Usefulness of Competitive Market Forces

The types of problems described above can be avoided by allowing competitive market forces to do their thing, especially in markets that are currently working reasonably well and that are expected to continue to do so (at least with a little help from antitrust friends).

We can hope that the federal and state agencies' recent defeats in the courts will not make the antitrust enforcement agencies "gun-shy" about challenging future health care consolidations. If the antitrust enforcement agencies are currently taking a break from challenging mergers in the health care industry,[11] let us hope it is only a short break. As this book suggests, competitive markets for hospital and physician services are in the public interest in most cases, and in order to maintain this healthy competition, it is essential to have consistent and careful health care antitrust enforcement.

Notes

Index

# Notes

## Introduction

1. Further, the U.S. health care system is characterized by relatively poor health outcomes by certain measures. For example, infant mortality rates are higher in the United States than in other developed countries. In 2001 the rate of deaths of children under one year of age per 1,000 live births was 6.8 in the United States, but only 3.9 in Japan and 4.4 in the Netherlands *(Statistical Abstract of the United States, 2001)*.

2. In the language of economists, the link between competition and an optimal allocation of scarce resources (one that maximizes social welfare) is fairly direct in most industries.

3. A firm that simultaneously raises price and quality is not necessarily exercising monopoly power. If higher-quality products are more expensive to produce, then higher-quality products selling at higher prices (relative to lower-quality products) is evidence that markets are working well.

4. Robert H. Landes and Richard A. Posner, "Market Power in Antitrust Cases," *Harvard Law Review* 94 (1981): 937–977.

5. *American Medical Association v. United States*, 317 U.S. 519 (1943).

6. Frank R. Kennedy, "The American Medical Association: Power, Purpose, and Politics in Organized Medicine," *Yale Law Journal* 63 (1954): 936–1022.

7. *Group Health Cooperative of Puget Sound v. King County Medical Society*, 39 Wash.2d 586 (1951).

8. Kennedy, "American Medical Association."

9. Ibid.

10. 895 F.2d 352 (1990).

11. *Arizona v. Maricopa Medical Society*, 102 S. Ct. 2466 (1982).

12. 114 F.T.C. 783 (1991).

13. 118 F.T.C. 1130 (1994).

14. The Department of Justice (DOJ) was also active in 2002. In December

193

the DOJ charged an IPA in Asheville, North Carolina, with restraining competition by adopting a uniform fee schedule governing the prices of its participating physicians.

15. 106 FTC 361.

16. *U.S. v. Rockford Memorial Corporation*, 717 F. Supp. 1251 and 898 F.2d 1278.

17. The federal government still regulates the prices that hospitals and physicians can charge for services provided through the Medicare program.

18. John E. McDonough, *Interest, Ideas, and Deregulation: The Fate of Hospital Rate Setting* (Ann Arbor: University of Michigan Press, 1997), Table 2.1.

19. Ibid., p. 207.

20. *New York Times*, January 13, 1999, A1.

21. Robert F. Leibenluft, "Antitrust Enforcement and Hospital Mergers: A Closer Look," paper presented at the First Friday Forum of the Alliance for Health, Grand Rapids, Michigan, June 5, 1998.

22. Natalie Marjancik, "Risky Business: Proposed Reform of the Antitrust Laws as Applied to Health Care Provider Networks," *American Journal of Law and Medicine* 24 (1998).

23. Robert E. Bloch, "State Action Immunity as a Defense in an Antitrust Health Care Context: What Works and What Doesn't," in *Antitrust Developments in Evolving Health Care Markets*, ed. Howard Feller (Chicago: American Bar Association, 1996).

24. The merging hospitals are located in Joplin, Missouri, Dubuque, Iowa, Grand Rapids, Michigan, Long Island, New York, and Poplar Bluff, Missouri.

25. Thomas Leary, FTC Commissioner, said: "The problem is many judges can't get it through their heads that not-for-profits doing good work can violate antitrust law." *Modern Healthcare* (November 6, 2000): 4.

26. Thomas L. Greaney, "Night Landings on an Aircraft Carrier: Hospital Mergers and Antitrust Law," *American Journal of Law and Medicine* 23 (1997): 191.

27. Thomas L. Greaney, "The FTC's Report on Competition Policy: Implications for Hospital Mergers," paper presented at the National Health Lawyers Association Antitrust in the Healthcare Field Meeting, Washington, D.C., 1997.

28. While there is agreement on this point, there is a lack of professional consensus among economists on the issue of how vigorously the antitrust laws should be enforced. Richard Posner wrote, "A perfectly respectable economist might be an antitrust 'hawk,' another equally respectable economist a 'dove.'" Richard Posner, "The Law and Economics of the Economic Expert Witness," *Journal of Economic Perspectives* 13 (1999): 91–99.

29. Robert H. Bork, *The Antitrust Paradox: A Policy at War with Itself* (New York: Basic Books, 1978), p. 90.

30. Michael Chernew, "General Equilibrium and Marketability in the Health Care Industry," *Journal of Health Politics, Policy and Law* 26 (2001): 885–897.

31. Greaney, "Night Landings on an Aircraft Carrier."

## 1. The Transformation of the Health Care System

1. Charles D. Weller, "Antitrust and Health Care: Provider Controlled Health Plans and the *Maricopa* Decision," *American Journal of Law and Medicine* 8 (1982).

2. John D. Blum, "The Evolution of Physician Credentialing and Managed Care Selective Contracting," *American Journal of Law and Medicine* 22 (1996).

3. *OECD Health Data 2002*, 4th ed., table 10. Available at *www.oecd.org*.

4. Ibid.

5. It was assumed that physicians' professional ethics would ensure quality of care.

6. John E. Wennberg, Jean Freeman, Roxanne Shelton, and Thomas Bubolz, "Hospital Use and Mortality among Medicare Beneficiaries in Boston and New Haven," *New England Journal of Medicine* 321 (1989): 1168–1173.

7. James C. Robinson, *The Corporate Practice of Medicine: Competition and Innovation in Physician Organization* (Berkeley: University of California Press, 1999): 10–11.

8. *Wall Street Journal*, July 7, 1999, A22.

9. Section 1122 investment regulation established the denial of Medicare and Medicaid cost reimbursement to hospitals expanding capacity without prior approval by local planning agencies.

10. For example, the 1986 Emergency Medical Treatment and Active Labor Act.

11. For estimates of the welfare losses associated with various government regulations, see Robert W. Hahn, "Government Analysis of the Benefits and Costs of Regulation," *Journal of Economic Perspectives* 12 (1998), Table 1.

12. Walter Adams and James W. Brock, "The Sherman Act and the Economic Power Problem," in *The Antitrust Impulse: An Economic, Historical, and Legal Analysis*, ed. Theodore P. Kovaleff (Armonk, N.Y.: M. E. Sharpe, 1994), vol. 1, p. 513.

13. William L. Roper, "Regulating Quality and Clinical Practice," in *Regulating Managed Care: Theory, Practice, and Future Options*, ed. Stuart H. Altman, Uwe E. Reinhardt, and David Shactman (San Francisco: Jossey-Bass, 1999).

14. H. E. Frech, "Physician Fees and Price Controls," in *American Health Care: Government, Market Processes, and the Public Interest*, ed. Roger Feldman (New Brunswick: Transaction, 2000), p. 360.

15. John J. Antel, Robert L. Ohsfeldt, and Edmund R. Becker, "State Regulation and Hospital Costs," *Review of Economics and Statistics* 77 (1995): 416–422.

16. Winnie C. Yip, "Physician Response to Medicare Fee Reductions: Changes in the Volume of Coronary Artery Bypass Graft (CABG) Surgeries in the Medicare and Private Sectors," *Journal of Health Economics* 17 (1998): 675–699.

17. Reuben Kessel, "Price Discrimination in Medicine," *Journal of Law and Economics* 1 (1958): 20–53; Thomas Moore, "The Purpose of Licensing," *Journal of Law and Economics* 4 (1961): 93–117.

18. Kenneth J. Arrow, "Social Responsibility and Economic Efficiency," *Public Policy* 21 (1973): 310.

19. Dennis W. Carlton and Jeffrey M. Perloff, *Modern Industrial Organization* (New York: HarperCollins, 1994).

20. Erwin A. Blackstone and Joseph P. Fuhr, "Hospital Mergers: The Shift from Federal Antitrust Enforcement to State Regulation," *Journal of Health Law* 33 (2000): 103–127.

21. H. E. Frech, *Competition and Monopoly in Medical Care* (Washington, D.C.: AEI Press, 1996), p. 151.

22. John J. Miles, *Health Care and Antitrust Law: Principles and Practice* (Deerfield, Ill.: Clark, Boardman, and Callaghan, 1993), p. 1.

23. Malcolm B. Coate, Richard S. Higgins, and Fred S. McChesney, "Bureaucracy and Politics in FTC Merger Challenges," *Journal of Law and Economics* 33 (1990): 463–482.

24. Barbara A. Ryan, "Hospital Regulation and Antitrust Paradoxical Policies," in *American Health Care*, ed. Feldman, pp. 191–192.

25. William Encinosa, "The Economics of Regulatory Mandates on the HMO Market," *Journal of Health Economics* 20 (2001): 85–107.

26. Ibid.

27. Fred J. Hellinger, "Regulating the Financial Incentives Facing Physicians in Managed Care Plans," *American Journal of Managed Care* 4 (1998): 663–674.

28. Robert L. Ohsfeldt, Michael A. Morrisey, Leonard Nelson, and Victoria Johnson, "The Spread of State Any Willing Provider Laws," *HSR: Health Services Research* 33 (1998): 1537–1562.

29. Mark V. Pauly and Marc L. Berger, "Why Should Managed Care Be Regulated?" in *Regulating Managed Care*, ed. Altman, Reinhardt, and Shactman.

30. Robert Langreth, "Do Your Homework: How to Learn about Your Doctor—Before You Pick One," *Wall Street Journal*, October 19, 1998, R13.

31. Phillip Areeda, "Antitrust Policy," in *American Economic Policy in the 1980s*, ed. Martin Feldstein (Chicago: University of Chicago Press, 1994), p. 575.

32. Thomas Rice, "Macro- Versus Microregulation," in *Regulating Managed Care*, ed. Altman, Reinhardt, and Shactman, pp. 77–78.

33. H. E. Frech and Lee R. Mobley, "Health Insurance: Designing Products to Reduce Costs," in *Industry Studies*, ed. Larry L. Duetsch (Armonk, N.Y.: M. E. Sharpe, 1998), p. 216. The court case was *Griesman v. Newcomb Hospital*, 40 N.J. 384, 192 A.2d 817.

34. Clark C. Havighurst, "American Health Care and the Law—We Need to Talk," *Health Affairs* 19 (2000): 91.

35. Charles D. Weller, "Antitrust and Health Care: Provider Controlled Health Plans and the *Maricopa* Decision," *American Journal of Law and Medicine* 8 (1982).

36. Mark D. Whitener, "Antitrust, Medicare Reform and Health Care Competition," paper presented at The American Enterprise Institute for Public Policy Research, Washington, D.C., December 5, 1995.

37. Thomas L. Greaney, "Managed Competition, Integrated Delivery Systems and Antitrust," *Cornell Law Review* 79 (1994): 1525.

38. Peter J. Hammer, "Questioning Traditional Antitrust Presumptions: Price and Non-Price Competition in Hospital Markets," *University of Michigan Law Review* 32 (1999): 752.

39. *Arizona v. Maricopa County Medical Society*, 457 U.S. 332, 102 S. Ct. 2466, 73 L. Ed. 2nd 48, 1982 U.S. LEXIS 5, 50 U.S.L. W 4687, 1982-2 Trade Cas. (CCH) P64, 792.

40. *Wall Street Journal*, July 7, 1999, A22.

41. The application of these technological innovations to the health care industry, however, has been slowed by a lack of standardization across existing information systems, and concerns about both the confidentiality of health care information and the accuracy and completeness of the information stored within these systems. William L. Roper and Charles M. Cutler, "Health Plan Accountability and Reporting: Issues and Challenges," *Health Affairs* 17 (1998): 152–155.

42. This increase in scientific evidence is due in part to the Agency for Health

Care Policy and Research (AHCPR). The AHCPR has funded outcomes and effectiveness research on many common clinical conditions and treatments, including localized breast cancer, pelvic inflammatory disease, pediatric asthma, dialysis care, cardiac arrhythmia, depression, prostate disease, acute myocardial infarction, back pain, biliary tract disease, cataracts, childbirth, diabetes, hip fracture repair, osteoarthritis, ischemic heart disease, low birth weight, and stroke prevention. Kathleen McCormick, Mary A. Cummings, and Chris Kovner, "The Role of the Agency for Health Care Policy and Research in Improving Outcomes of Care," *Outcomes Measurement and Management* 32 (1997): 521–542.

43. "Diagnostic guidelines are targeted at evaluating patients with particular symptoms (such as chest pain) for the presence of diseases that would benefit from interventions (such as angina or esophagitis). They are also used to guide the screening of asymptomatic populations for early stages of disease (to detect, for example, hypertension or diabetes). . . . Management guidelines cover the evaluation and treatment of patients who are known to have certain conditions. Examples are guidelines dealing with low back pain or benign prostatic hypertrophy. . . . Service guidelines are organized around particular diagnostic and therapeutic procedures (such as chest X-ray, colonoscopy, appendectomy, or administration of hepatitis vaccine), presenting appropriate and inappropriate indications for their use." Physician Payment Review Commission, *Annual Report to Congress* (Washington, D.C., 1992), p. 214.

44. Michael L. Millenson, *Demanding Medical Excellence: Doctors and Accountability in the Information Age* (Chicago: University of Chicago Press, 1997), p. 348.

45. David Blumenthal, "The Future of Quality Measurement and Management in a Transforming Health Care System," *JAMA* 278 (1997): 1623.

46. Linda Prager, "Health Plan to Go National with Physician Profiling," *American Medical News* 41 (1998): 8.

47. National Committee on Quality Assurance, *The State of Managed Care Quality, 1999* (Washington, D.C., 1999).

48. Lawrence P. Casalino, "The Unintended Consequences of Measuring Quality on the Quality of Medical Care," *New England Journal of Medicine* 341 (1998): 1148.

49. J. Duncan Moore, "Real Results: Pa. Report Gives Consumers Outcomes Data They Can Use," *Modern Healthcare* 28 (1998): 46.

50. Julie A. Rainwater, Patrick S. Romano, and Deirdre M. Antonius, "The California Hospital Outcomes Project: How Useful Is California's Report Card for Quality Improvement," *Journal on Quality Improvement* 24 (1998): 31–39.

51. Jack A. Meyer, Elliot K. Wicks, Lise S. Rybowski, and Michael J. Perry, "Report on Report Cards: Initiatives of Health Coalitions and State Government Employers to Report on Health Plan Performance and Use of Financial Incentives" (Washington, D.C.: Economic and Social Research Institute, 1998).

52. Risk adjustment is necessary because patients' health outcomes are a function of multiple factors, including some that are under providers' control (the quality of care provided) and some that are not (random chance and patients' risk factors, such as age or severity of illness).

53. Edward Hannan, Harold Kilburn, Michael Racz, et al., "Improving the Outcomes of Coronary Artery Bypass Surgery in New York State," *JAMA* 271 (1994): 761–766.

54. David Dranove, Daniel Kessler, Mark McClellan, and Mark Satterthwaite,

"Is More Information Better? The Effects of 'Report Cards' on Health Care Providers," NBER working paper no. 8697 (2002).

55. See, for example, *www.healthgrades.com.*

56. See, for example, the National Guideline Clearinghouse *(www.guideline .gov)* and the National Library of Medicine *(www.nlm.nih.gov).*

57. Jon Gabel, Larry Levitt, Holve, et al., *Health Affairs* 21 (2002): 148; Academy for Health Services Research and Health Policy, *The Challenge of Managed Care Regulation: Making Markets Work?* (Washington, D.C., August 2001).

58. Eric R. Wagner, "Types of Managed Care Organizations," in *Essentials of Managed Care,* 2nd ed., ed. Peter Kongstvedt (Gaithersburg, Md.: Aspen, 1997).

59. *Modern Healthcare* (December 23, 2002): 24.

60. Bureau of Labor Statistics, "Employee Benefits in Small Private Industry Establishments, 1996" (Washington, D.C.: U.S. Department of Labor, 1998): 98–240.

61. Bureau of Labor Statistics, "Employee Benefits in Medium and Large Private Establishments, 1997" (Washington, D.C.: U.S. Department of Labor, 1999).

62. Statistics from the American Medical Association's Socioeconomic Monitoring System Survey in *American Medical News,* March 9, 1998; and Center for Studying Health System Change, "Tracking Report," 5 (November 2002).

63. *Modern Healthcare* (December 23, 2002): 24.

64. Providers are bearing more risk as a result of public policy as well. For example, in 1983 the federal government shifted some of the risk of treating Medicare patients to hospitals through its Medicare Prospective Payment System (PPS). Since 1983 reimbursement to hospitals has been based on a system of regulated prices for episodes of treatment of specific diagnoses rather than a system of reimbursement based on actual costs of treatment. Accordingly, hospitals are at risk for deviations in treatment costs above these regulated prices. However, the PPS system does not shift full risk to hospitals because reimbursements to hospitals can vary with the number of hospital services delivered. Hospital reimbursement varies with number of services delivered because some DRGs are defined by procedure (for example, patients with the diagnosis of ischemic heart disease who receive cardiac catheterization, a bypass operation, or an angioplasty are placed in a different DRG than those who do not, and thus hospitals are reimbursed at a higher rate if they perform these procedures). In addition, hospitals receive outlier payments for patients whose costs of hospital care are particularly high. Joseph P. Newhouse, "Risk Adjustment: Where Are We Now?" *Inquiry* 35 (1998): 122–131.

65. Some of the risk that costs of treatment will exceed fixed prospective rates can be managed, and some cannot. Health care providers can affect some of the risk by changing the efficiency and quality of their services. In fact, some providers hire firms specializing in risk management to manage their risk. For example, firms such as PhyMatrix and MainStreet Practice Management provide risk management services to IPAs. Other risks of unexpectedly high treatment costs that are borne by providers under certain risk-shifting reimbursement systems, such as the risk that patients will contract illnesses that are particularly expensive to treat, are beyond providers' control.

66. Center for Studying Health System Change, "Tracking Report."

67. *Modern Healthcare* (June 29, 1998): 4.

68. The current trend, however, appears to be away from global capitation. *Modern Healthcare* (September 6, 1999): 52–57.

69. *Managed Care Week* (June 29, 1998): 3.

70. Center for Studying Health System Change, "Community Report: Greenville, S.C." (Spring 1999).

71. Center for Studying Health System Change, Issue Brief no. 21 (September 1999).

72. John E. Kralewski, Terence D. Wingert, and Bryan E. Dowd, "Managed Care, Provider Consolidation, and Health Care Costs in the Twin Cities," *Journal of Medical Practice Management* 12 (1996): 61–71.

73. James C. Robinson and Lawrence P. Casalino, "Vertical Integration and Organizational Networks in Health Care," *Health Affairs* (Spring 1996): 7–22.

74. Alison E. Cuellar and Paul J. Gertler, "Strategic Integration of Hospitals and Physicians" (School of Public Health, Columbia University, May 1, 2002, photocopy).

75. By 1996 approximately 22 percent of community hospitals had an ownership interest in an HMO, and 31 percent had an ownership interest in a PPO. American Hospital Association, *Hospital Statistics, 1998 Edition* (Chicago: Healthcare Source). Similarly, physicians owned approximately 3 percent of all health plans by 1996. American Association of Health Plans, *Profile of Health Plans and Utilization Review Organizations, 1997–1998 Edition* (Washington, D.C.).

76. *Modern Healthcare* (December 24, 2001): 28.

77. American Hospital Association Resource Center, statistics by fax transmission on February 28, 2002.

78. *Modern Healthcare* (January 31, 2000): 32–33.

79. *Modern Healthcare* (June 15, 1998): 65.

80. *American Medical News* (November 17, 1997): 9.

81. *Modern Healthcare* (April 13, 1998): 14.

82. *Modern Healthcare* (July 22, 1996): 8 and (March 10, 1997): 22; *Managed Care Week* (January 5, 1998): 8.

83. *Modern Healthcare* (April 20, 1998): 114.

84. Reports of Irving Levin Associates of New Canaan, Connecticut, as reported in *Modern Healthcare*, February 26, 1996; March 10, 1997; February 2, 1998; and January 25, 1999.

85. Center for Studying Health System Change, Issue Brief no. 38 (May 2001).

86. *Modern Healthcare* (December 23–30, 1996): 37 and (January 11, 1999): 48.

87. *Modern Healthcare* (January 14, 2002): 22.

88. *Modern Healthcare* (February 22, 1999): 76.

89. Center for Studying Health System Change, "Community Report: Cleveland, Ohio" (Fall 2000).

90. *Modern Healthcare* (December 23, 2002): 14.

91. Janet M. Corrigan, Jill S. Eden, Marsha R. Gold, and Jeremy D. Pickreign, "Trends Toward a National Health Care Marketplace," *Inquiry* 34 (1997): 11–28.

92. *Modern Healthcare* (December 23, 2002): 14.

93. *Modern Healthcare* (January 12, 1998): 40.

94. *Wall Street Journal*, December 14, 1998.

95. Corrigan et al., "Trends Toward a National Health Care Marketplace."

96. American Medical Association, *Physician Socioeconomic Statistics 2000–2002*, Table 60.

97. *Modern Healthcare* (April 12, 1999): 36.

98. American Medical Association, *Physician Socioeconomic Statistics 2000–2002*, Table 60.

99. Estimates by Albert Holloway of the IPA Association of America as reported in *Modern Healthcare* (August 5, 1996): 86.

100. *Modern Healthcare* (June 29, 1998): 72.

101. *Modern Healthcare* (December 1, 1997): 70.

102. *American Medical News* (October 13, 1997): 14.

103. *Wall Street Journal*, November 11, 1998, A4.

104. *Wall Street Journal*, December 16, 1998.

105. *Modern Healthcare* (April 9, 2001): 12.

106. *Modern Healthcare* (December 24, 2001): 28.

107. *Managed Care Week* (July 27, 1998): 2–3, and phone call with executive at Capp Care, December 23, 1998.

108. *Managed Care Week* (July 27, 1998): 2–3.

109. Ibid.

110. *Modern Healthcare* (September 9, 2002): 15.

111. President's Advisory Commission on Consumer Protection and Quality in the Health Care Industry, *Quality First: Better Health Care for All Americans* (Washington, D.C.: U.S. Government Printing Office, 1997).

112. Atlantic Information Services, *Strategic Report on Managed Care Plans in 40 Metropolitan Areas* (Washington, D.C., 4th Quarter 1998).

113. *Modern Healthcare* (September 14, 1998): 56.

114. Jon Gabel, "Ten Ways HMOs Have Changed during the 1990s," *Health Affairs* 16 (1997): 134–145.

115. Linda Prager, "Health Plan Releases Report Cards on Doctor Groups," *American Medical News* 41 (1998): 6.

116. Rhoda Rundle, "PacifiCare Offers Medical-Quality Index," *Wall Street Journal*, August 31, 1998, B6.

117. "Without the test to monitor glucose, diabetic patients can go blind, suffer strokes or have heart attacks, require amputations or endure kidney failure requiring transplants or dialysis." Thomas M. Burton, "An HMO Checks Up on Its Doctors' Care and Is Disturbed Itself," *Wall Street Journal*, July 8, 1998, A1 and A8.

118. *Managed Care Week* (January 26, 1998): 5.

119. *Digest of Managed Health Care* (March 1998): 18.

120. *Managed Care Outlook* (April 9, 1999): 5.

121. *Wall Street Journal*, January 15, 2002, B12, and Center for Studying Health System Change, "Tracking Report."

122. Kevin Grumbach, Janet Coffman, Karen Vranizan, Noelle Blick, and Edward H. O'Neil, "Independent Practice Association Physician Groups in California," *Health Affairs* 17 (1998): 227–237.

123. Larry Stevens, "Quality-Based Physician Pay Gets Off to a Slow Start," *Healthcare Leadership Review* 17 (1998): 4.

124. Ibid.

125. *Capitation Management Report* 5 (November 1998): 166–167.

126. *Modern Healthcare* (March 2, 1998): 74.

127. Ibid.

128. *Modern Healthcare* (September 9, 1996): 24.

129. More specifically, they are developing clinical pathways and variance tracking tools to be used to standardize care across the four hospitals. *Data Strategies and Benchmarks: The Monthly Advisor for Health Care Executives* 2 (March 1998): 37–42.

130. As better measures of quality develop, selective contracting on the basis of price and quality is more likely to occur.

131. *Modern Healthcare* (September 14, 1998): 60; and Kralewski, Wingert, and Dowd, "Managed Care, Provider Consolidation."

132. Robert A. Berenson, "Beyond Competition," *Health Affairs* 16 (1997): 175.

133. Atlantic Information Services, *Strategic Report on Managed Care Plans*, 5.

134. Ibid.

135. Kralewski, Wingert, and Dowd, "Managed Care, Provider Consolidation"; and Robinson and Casalino, "Vertical Integration and Organizational Networks."

136. The related and very important question of the wisdom of promoting managed care and other forms of competition in public insurance programs, such as Medicare and Medicaid (a federal-state health insurance program for persons in need, including children, the elderly, the blind, and the disabled), is beyond the scope of this book.

137. See Kenneth J. Arrow, "Uncertainty and the Welfare Economics of Medical Care," *American Economic Review* 53 (1963): 941.

138. However, given the radical transformation occurring in health care markets, these ambiguities are not that surprising. By changing the nature of health care competition, the transformation has both created some of the ambiguities and eliminated the policy (as opposed to the historical) relevance of many empirical papers based on data predating the transformation. Accordingly, the pre- and post-1990s literature is often reviewed separately.

139. One could argue that the theory of the second best—as outlined in R. J. Lipsey and K. Lancaster, "The General Theory of the Second Best," *Review of Economic Studies* 24 (1956–1957): 11–32—implies that enforcement of the antitrust laws in health care markets is never good public policy. The theory of the second best suggests that government interventions, such as antitrust enforcement policies, to make markets more competitive may not make consumers better off. If two or more causes of market failure are present in the market (for example, it is both very difficult for consumers to learn about the quality of sellers' products *and* sellers face entry barriers), then fixing one condition (in this example, providing consumers with more information on the quality of sellers' products *or* eliminating entry barriers) will not necessarily bring us closer to realizing the benefits of market competition. However, as Robert Bork suggests, one must disregard the theory of the second best because its acceptance would require repeal of the antitrust laws: "The legislative decision to promote competition rules out the adoption of the theory [of the second best] as the general rule of antitrust, since its adoption would require repeal of the laws in their entirety, and the theory provides no criteria that could be applied by a court to the decision of individual cases." Robert H. Bork, *The Antitrust Paradox: A Policy at War with Itself* (New York: Basic Books, 1978), p. 113.

## 2. The Current Treatment: A Strong Dose of Competition

1. Robert Pitofsky, "Thoughts on Leveling the Playing Field in Health Care Markets," National Health Lawyers Association Twentieth Annual Program on Antitrust in the Health Care Field, Washington, D.C., February 13, 1997.

2. David Dranove, *The Economic Evolution of American Health Care* (Princeton, N.J.: Princeton University Press, 2000).

3. Timothy J. Muris, "Everything Old Is New Again: Health Care and Competition in the 21st Century," 7th Annual Competition in Health Care Forum, Chicago, November 7, 2002.

4. Dranove, Shanley, and White call this the change from "patient-driven competition" to "payer-driven competition." David Dranove, Mark Shanley, and William White, "Price and Concentration in Hospital Markets: The Switch from Patient-Driven to Payer-Driven Competition," *Journal of Law and Economics* 36 (1993): 179–204.

5. Center for Studying Health System Change, Washington, D.C., Issue Brief 27 (2000).

6. Lawrence P. Casalino, "Canaries in a Coal Mine: Physician Groups and Competition," *Health Affairs* 20 (2001): 97–108.

7. What do economists mean by a price-sensitive consumer? Economic theory of consumer behavior suggests that a consumer will continue to purchase additional units of a product until the additional benefit to the consumer from consuming an additional unit of that product is just equal to the price of the product. One implication of this theory is that when the price of product X decreases, consumers will purchase more X. Likewise, when the price of product X increases, consumers will purchase less X, *ceteris paribus*. In other words, consumers alter their purchase decisions in response to price changes.

8. A market is characterized by natural monopoly if a single-product firm's long-run average cost curve declines for all outputs. In this case, allowing one single-product firm to operate as a monopoly minimizes costs. A multiproduct firm is considered a natural monopoly if that firm's cost function is subadditive. In this case, one multiproduct firm can produce all combinations of those outputs at least cost, and thus allowing it to operate as a monopoly minimizes costs.

9. See Joseph P. Newhouse and Insurance Experiment Group, *Free for All? Lessons from the RAND Health Insurance Experiment* (Cambridge, Mass.: Harvard University Press, 1993).

10. More recent estimates based on data from the early 1990s and a different methodological approach suggest that insured health care consumers may be somewhat more responsive to price. Specifically, these estimates suggest that if the price of medical care increased by 10 percent, the quantity of medical care demanded by consumers would decrease by approximately 6 to 8 percent. Matthew J. Eichner, "The Demand for Medical Care: What People Pay Does Matter," *American Economic Review* 88 (1998): 117–121. This method uses the price variation associated with some individuals (or their family members) spending more than their deductibles and thus facing a marginal price of 20 percent for additional health care services, and other individuals facing a marginal price of 100 percent because they (or their family members) have not met their deductibles.

11. Willard G. Manning, Joseph P. Newhouse, Naihua Duan, Emmett B.

Keeler, Arleen Leibowitz, and M. Susan Marquis, "Health Insurance and the Demand for Medical Care: Evidence from a Randomized Experiment," *American Economic Review* 77 (1987): 251–277.

12. Some evidence of this is provided by a study that found hospitals' prices played an important role in HMOs' selection of hospitals for tertiary care services in 1995. See Kevin A. Schulman, L. Elizabeth Rubenstein, Damon M. Seils, Melissa Harris, Jack Hadley, and Jose J. Escarce, "Quality Assessment in Contracting for Tertiary Care Services by HMOs: A Case Study of Three Markets," *Journal on Quality Improvement* 23 (1997): 117–127.

13. Jack Zwanziger and Glenn A. Melnick, "The Effects of Hospital Competition and the Medicare PPS Program on Hospital Cost Behavior in California," *Journal of Health Economics* 7 (1988): 301–320; Emmett B. Keeler, Glenn Melnick, and Jack Zwanziger, "The Changing Effects on Non-Profit and For-Profit Hospital Pricing Behavior," *Journal of Health Economics* 18 (1999): 69–86; Dranove, Shanley, and White, "Price and Concentration in Hospital Markets."

14. Further, federal subsidization of health insurance through the federal tax system may lead to consumers purchasing too much health insurance.

15. For example, if a consumer has an insurance plan with no deductible and a 20 percent coinsurance rate, then that consumer pays only 20 percent of his/her medical bills for covered services. If a hospital's costs and prices increase by $100, the insured consumer's bill increases by only $20 per day.

16. In addition to health insurance, individuals are often covered by sick leave and disability insurance, and thus insurance affects more than the out-of-pocket price of health care goods and services. Sick leave and disability insurance affect the income of the insured, and thus the opportunity cost of the insured individual's time in the event of sickness. Peter Zweifel and Willard G. Manning, "Moral Hazard and Consumer Incentives in Health Care," in *Handbook of Health Economics*, ed. Anthony J. Culyer and Joseph P. Newhouse (New York: Elsevier, 2000).

17. See the results of Victor R. Fuchs, "Economics, Values, and Health Care Reform," *American Economic Review* 86 (March 1996): 1–24.

18. For a thorough review of the theory and evidence on physician-induced demand, see Thomas G. McGuire, "Physician Agency," in *Handbook of Health Economics*, ed. Culyer and Newhouse.

19. David M. Cutler, "A Guide to Health Care Reform," *Journal of Economic Perspectives* 8 (1994): 13–29.

20. David Bates, Deborah L. Boyle, and Eve Rittenberg, "What Proportion of Common Diagnostic Tests Appear Redundant?" *American Journal of Medicine* 104 (1998): 361–368.

21. Mark McClellan and Joseph P. Newhouse, "The Marginal Costs and Benefits of Medical Technology: A Panel Instrumental Variables Approach," *Journal of Econometrics* 77 (1997): 39–64.

22. Robert H. Lee, "Monitoring Physicians: A Bargaining Model of Medical Group Practice," *Journal of Health Economics* 9 (1990): 463–481.

23. See, for example, *oncolink.com* operated by the University of Pennsylvania Cancer Center; *nimh.nih.gov* by the National Institute of Mental Health and *guideline.gov/index.asp* by the Agency for Health Care Policy and Research; and *WebMD.com* and *Drkoop.com*.

24. One study using insurance claims data from a large private insurance car-

rier in 1984 and 1985 found that utilization review reduced hospital admissions by 12.3 percent and inpatient days by 8 percent. Paul J. Feldstein, Thomas M. Wickizer, and John R. C. Wheeler, "Private Cost Containment: The Effects of Utilization Review Programs on Health Care Use and Expenditures," *New England Journal of Medicine* 318 (1988): 1310–1314.

25. Using data from 56 Blue Cross and Blue Shield plans, one study found that preadmission certification, concurrent review, and retrospective review programs were associated with lower hospital admissions and fewer inpatient days between 1980 and 1988. Richard M. Scheffler, Sean D. Sullivan, and Timothy Haochung Ko, "The Impact of Blue Cross and Blue Shield Plan Utilization Management Programs, 1980–1988," *Inquiry* 28 (1991): 263–275.

26. Physician profiling is a method of comparing utilization, cost, or quality across physicians. Each physician's practice pattern is compared to a norm, such as the average of other physicians in the organization, or to a standard set by a practice guideline. For these comparisons to be meaningful, practice patterns must be adjusted for differences in case mix and severity of illness. For example, results from the Medical Outcomes Study (reported by Richard Kravitz et al., "Differences in the Mix of Patients Among Medical Specialties and Systems of Care: Results from the Medical Outcomes Study," *JAMA* 267 [1992]: 1617–1623) suggest that patients of cardiologists have worse functional status (the extent to which physical or mental disorders interfere with performance of usual activities) and more chronic diagnoses than patients of general internists, and that these case-mix and severity of illness characteristics are associated with differences in hospitalization rates, physician visit rates, and rates of prescription drug use.

27. Marsha Gold and Robert Hurley, "The Role of Managed Care 'Products' in Managed Care Plans," *Inquiry* 34 (1997): 29–37.

28. Eve A. Kerr, Brian S. Mittiman, Ron D. Hays, Albert L. Siu, Barbara Leake, and Robert Brook, "Managed Care and Capitation in California: How Do Physicians at Financial Risk Control Their Own Utilization?" *Annals of Internal Medicine* 123 (1995): 500–504.

29. Kathleen McCormick, Mary A. Cummings, and Chris Kovner, "The Role of the Agency for Health Care Policy and Research in Improving Outcomes of Care," *Outcomes Measurement and Management* 32 (1997): 521–542.

30. *Modern Healthcare* (March 29, 1999): 50.

31. Scott Hensley, "Recognizing Quality: Disease Management Protocols at Core of Pa. System's Award-Winning Approach," *Modern Healthcare* (February 2, 1998): 31.

32. It is interesting to note that simultaneously mortality fell to 28 percent from 36 percent. *Modern Healthcare* (March 16, 1998): 84.

33. Robinson and Luft found this result for hospitals in the 1970s: James C. Robinson and Harold Luft, "The Impact of Hospital Market Structure on Patient Volume, Average Length of Stay, and the Cost of Care," *Journal of Health Economics* 4 (1985): 333–356. Hospitals with more competitors had higher costs and more medical equipment. Robinson, Garnick, and McPhee found this result for hospitals in the early 1980s: James C. Robinson, D. Garnick, and S. McPhee, "Market and Regulatory Influences on the Availability of Coronary Angioplasty and Bypass Surgery in U.S. Hospitals," *New England Journal of Medicine* 317 (1987): 85–90. Dranove, Shanley, and Simon found this result using data on hospital markets in

California in 1983: David Dranove, Mark Shanley, and Carol Simon, "Is Hospital Competition Socially Wasteful?" *Rand Journal of Economics* 23 (1992): 247–262. Specifically, hospitals were more likely to offer diagnostic and emergency services in more competitive markets; however, the level of competition did not appear to have a statistically significant effect on hospitals' probabilities of offering cardiology services, deliveries, neonatology services, pediatric services, CT scans, radiation therapy, or radioisotope therapy. Another study found that increases in the percentage of neighboring hospitals (within a 15 mile radius) offering mammography services and cardiac catheterization services were associated with higher probabilities that a hospital offered that particular service in 1972. Yet in less competitive hospital markets, hospitals were more likely to offer 24-hour emergency services. Harold S. Luft, James C. Robinson, Deborah W. Garnick, Susan C. Maerki, and Stephen J. McPhee, "The Role of Specialized Clinical Services in Competition among Hospitals," *Inquiry* 23 (1986): 83–94.

34. Peter J. Hammer, "Questioning Traditional Antitrust Presumptions: Price and Non-Price Competition in Hospital Markets," *University of Michigan Law Review* 32 (1999): 727–783.

35. Laurence C. Baker and Martin L. Brown, "The Effect of Managed Care on Health Care Providers: Evidence from Mammography," *RAND Journal of Economics* 30 (1999): 351–374.

36. Laurence C. Baker, "Managed Care and Technology Adoption in Health Care: Evidence from Magnetic Resonance Imaging," *Journal of Health Economics* 20 (2001): 395–421.

37. Laurence Baker and Joanne Spetz, "Managed Care and Medical Technology Growth," NBER working paper no. 6894, Cambridge, Mass., 1999.

38. Y. S. Chan and H. Leland, "Prices and Qualities in Markets with Costly Information," *Review of Economic Studies* 49 (1982): 499–516; R. Cooper and T. W. Ross, "Prices, Product Qualities and Asymmetric Information: The Competitive Case," *Review of Economic Studies* 51 (1984): 197–207.

39. David Dranove and Mark A. Satterthwaite, "Monopolistic Competition When Price and Quality Are Imperfectly Observable," *RAND Journal of Economics* 23 (1992): 518–534.

40. Akerlof showed that the used car market will not work well when consumers cannot tell the difference between used cars in good condition and "lemons." George A. Akerlof, "The Market for 'Lemons': Quality Uncertainty and the Market Mechanism," *Quarterly Journal of Economics* 84 (1970): 488–500.

41. Defining health care quality is especially complicated because insurers, employers, patients, hospitals, and physicians may each define quality differently.

42. Mark Chassin, "Assessing Strategies for Quality Improvement," *Health Affairs* 16 (1997): 151–161.

43. Robert H. Brook, "Managed Care Is Not the Problem, Quality Is," *JAMA* 278 (1997): 1612–1614.

44. Mark A. Schuster, Elizabeth A. McGlynn, and Robert H. Brook, "How Good Is the Quality of Health Care in the United States?" *Milbank Quarterly* 76 (1998): 517–563.

45. Institute of Medicine, *To Err Is Human: Building a Safer Health System* (Washington, D.C.: National Academy Press, 1999).

46. General Accounting Office, *Cancer Treatment 1975–1985: The Use of*

*Breakthrough Treatments for Seven Types of Cancer* (Washington, D.C.: U.S. General Accounting Office, 1988), p. 4.

47. Edward F. Ellerbeck et al., "Quality of Care for Medicare Patients with Acute Myocardial Infarction," *JAMA* 273 (1995): 1509–1514.

48. Stephen B. Soumerai, Thomas McLaughlin, Ellen Hertzmark, et al., "Adverse Outcomes of Underuse of Beta-Blockers in Elderly Survivors of Acute Myocardial Infarction," *JAMA* 277 (1997): 115–121.

49. Kevin Volpp and Joel Waldfogel, "Competition and the Quality of Hospital Care: Heart Attack Mortality after the Onset of Price Competition in New Jersey," May 18, 1998, photocopy.

50. Center for Studying Health System Change, Issue Brief no. 28 (March 2000).

51. Ibid.

52. Randall P. Ellis, "Creaming, Skimping and Dumping: Provider Competition on the Intensive And Extensive Margins," *Journal of Health Economics* 17 (1998): 537–555.

53. Joseph P. Newhouse, "Risk Adjustment: Where Are We Now?" *Inquiry* 35 (1998): 122–131.

54. Eve A. Kerr, Brian S. Mittman, Ron D. Hays, Barbara Leake, and Robert Brook, "Quality Assurance in Capitated Physician Groups," *JAMA* 276 (1996): 1236–1239.

55. A. Wolinsky, "Prices as Signals of Product Quality," *Review of Economic Studies* 50 (1983): 647–658; Carl Shapiro, "Premiums for High Quality Products as Returns to Reputations," *Quarterly Journal of Economics* 98 (1983): 659–679.

56. There is empirical evidence of this in health care markets. The results of one study suggest that private-practice social workers in Massachusetts with established reputations for high-quality care charge higher prices. Deborah Haas-Wilson, "Consumer Information and Providers' Reputations: An Empirical Test in the Market for Psychotherapy," *Journal of Health Economics* 9 (1990): 321–333.

57. One study found that higher quality is provided in teaching, larger, more urban hospitals: Emmett Keeler, Lisa Rubenstein, Katherine Kahn, et al., "Hospital Characteristics and Quality of Care," *JAMA* 268 (1992): 1709–1714. The results of another study examining 89,851 patient discharges between 1991 and 1993 from 30 hospitals in Ohio suggested that (after adjusting for severity of illness) patients treated in major teaching hospitals had 19 percent lower odds of dying than patients treated in nonteaching hospitals: Gary E. Rosenthal, Dwain L. Harper, Linda M. Quinn, and Gregory S. Cooper, "Severity-Adjusted Mortality and Length of Stay in Teaching and Nonteaching Hospitals," *JAMA* 278 (1997): 485–490. Further, the risk-adjusted length of stay was 9 percent lower among patients in major teaching hospitals relative to nonteaching hospitals. Another study found that Medicare patients hospitalized with congestive heart failure and pneumonia in four states between 1991 and 1992 received higher-quality care in teaching hospitals compared to nonteaching hospitals: John Z. Ayanian, Joel S. Weissman, Scott Chasan-Taber, and Arnold M. Epstein, "Quality of Care for Two Common Illnesses in Teaching and Nonteaching Hospitals," *Health Affairs* 17 (1998): 194–205.

58. Harold S. Luft, Deborah W. Garnick, David H. Mark, Deborah J. Peltz-

man, Ciaran S. Phibbs, Erik Lichtenberg, and Stephen J. McPhee, "Does Quality Influence Choice of Hospital?" *JAMA* 263 (1990): 2899–2906.

59. Mark McClellan and Douglas Staiger, "The Quality of Health Care Providers," NBER working paper no. 7327 (1999).

60. However, health plan participation is voluntary, and only about 33 percent of plans reported HEDIS measures to the NCQA in 1997. Donna O. Farley, Elizabeth A. McGlynn, and David Klein, "Assessing Quality in Managed Care: Health Plan Reporting of HEDIS Performance Measures," Policy Brief of the Commonwealth Fund (September 1998).

61. *State Initiatives in Health Care Reform* 25 (January 1998): 6–8.

62. Jack A. Meyer, Elliot K. Wicks, Lise S. Rybowski, and Michael J. Perry, "Report on Report Cards: Initiatives of Health Coalitions and State Government Employers to Report on Health Plan Performance and Use of Financial Incentives" (Washington, D.C.: Economic and Social Research Institute, 1998).

63. For additional information, see *www.thcic.state.tx.us/publications.htm#hmo*.

64. For multiple case studies see L. McCormack, J. Garfinkel, J. Schnaier, A. Lee, and J. Sangl, "Consumer Information Development and Use," *Health Care Financing Review* 18 (1996): 15–30.

65. An example of the information available on the Internet: the Association of State Medical Board Executive Directors publishes information on physicians' education, malpractice judgments, and disciplinary histories on their Web site, *www.docboard.org* (site visited on July 13, 2001).

66. Julie A. Rainwater, Patrick S. Romano, and Deirdre M. Antonius, "The California Hospital Outcomes Project: How Useful Is California's Report Card for Quality Improvement," *Journal on Quality Improvement* 24 (1998): 31–39.

67. Edward L. Hannan, Cathy C. Stone, Theodore L. Biddle, and Barbara A. DeBuono, "Public Release of Cardiac Surgery Outcomes Data in New York: What Do New York State Cardiologists Think of It?" *American Heart Journal* 134 (1997): 1120–1128.

68. *American Medical News*, December 1, 1997, 5; *Wall Street Journal*, September 17, 1997, B6.

69. Meyer, Wicks, Rybowski, and Perry, "Report on Report Cards."

70. *Wall Street Journal*, August 23, 1999, A1, A8.

71. *Wall Street Journal*, January 17, 2002, B2. Information is posted on the group's Web site, *www.leapfroggroup.org*.

72. Center for Studying Health System Change, "Tracking Report," no. 5 (November 2002).

73. David Eddy, "Performance Measurement: Problems and Solutions," *Health Affairs* 17 (1998): 7–25.

74. California Office of Statewide Health Planning and Development, *Report of the California Hospital Outcomes Project: Hospital Specific Detailed Statistical Tables* (Sacramento, Calif.: OSHPD, 1996).

75. Lisa I. Iezzoni, "The Risks of Risk Adjustment," *JAMA* 278 (1997): 1600–1607.

76. For example, the information about health plans in the Quality Compass is self-reported.

77. National Committee on Quality Assurance, *The State of Managed Care Quality, 1999* (Washington, D.C., 1999).

78. Deborah Haas-Wilson, "The Relationships between the Dimensions of Health Care Quality and Price: The Case of Eye Care," *Medical Care* 32 (1994): 175–182; Michael Chernew and Dennis P. Scanlon, "Health Plan Report Cards and Insurance Choice," *Inquiry* 35 (1998): 9–22.

79. Jon R. Gabel, Kelly A. Hunt, and Kimberly Hurst, "When Employers Choose Health Plans: Do NCQA Accreditation and HEDIS Data Count?" (New York: The CommonWealth Fund, September 1998).

80. James Maxwell, Peter Temin, and Corey Watts, "Corporate Health Care Purchasing among Fortune 500 Firms," *Health Affairs* 20 (2001): 181–188.

81. Evidence from the federal government is provided in Gerard J. Wedig and Ming Tai-Seale, "The Effect of Report Cards on Consumer Choice in the Health Insurance Market," *Journal of Health Economics* 21 (2002): 1031–1048. Evidence from the Buyers Health Care Action Group is provided in Schultz, Call, Feldman, and Christianson, "Impact of Performance Information on Health Care Choices," *HSR: Health Services Research* 36 (2001): 509–530. Evidence from General Motors is provided in Dennis P. Scanlon, Michael Chernew, Catherine McLaughlin, and Gary Solon, "The Impact of Health Plan Report Cards on Managed Care Enrollment," *Journal of Health Economics* 21 (2002): 19–41.

82. In 1998 General Motors, Ford Motor Co., Chrysler Corp., and the UAW began development of a common health plan report card to rank quality across the plans offered to Big Three employees. Joseph B. White, "Business Plan: Big Employers Are Starting to Design Their Own Report Cards on Competing HMOs," *Wall Street Journal*, October 19, 1998, R18.

83. Meyer, Wicks, Rybowski, and Perry, "Report on Report Cards."

84. *Managed Care Week* (October 19, 1998): 4.

85. Ibid.

86. Scanlon, Chernew, McLaughlin, and Solon, "The Impact of Health Plan Report Cards."

87. *Managed Care Week* (March 9, 1998): 6.

88. Chernew and Scanlon, "Health Plan Report Cards."

89. Judith H. Hibbard and Jacquelyn J. Jewett, "Will Quality Report Cards Help Consumers?" *Health Affairs* 16 (1997): 218–228.

90. Meyer, Wicks, Rybowski, and Perry, "Report on Report Cards."

91. Council on Ethical and Judicial Affairs, *Code of Medical Ethics* (Chicago: American Medical Association, 1996).

92. *Wall Street Journal*, April 30, 2002, A3.

93. Lars C. Erickson, David Torchiana, Eric C. Schneider, Jane Newburger, and Edward Hannan, "The Relationship between Managed Care Insurance and Use of Lower-Mortality Hospitals for CABG Surgery," *JAMA* 283 (2000).

94. Schulman et al., "Quality Assessment in Contracting."

95. Michael Chernew, Dennis Scanlon, and Rod Hayward, "Insurance Type and Choice of Hospital for Coronary Artery Bypass Graft Surgery," *HSR: Health Services Research* 33 (1998): 447–466.

96. Jose J. Escarce, R. Lawrence Van Horn, Mark V. Pauly, Sankey V. Williams, Judy A. Shea, and Wei Chen, "Health Maintenance Organizations and Hospital Quality of Care for Coronary Artery Bypass Surgery," *Medical Care Research and Review* 56 (1999): 340–362.

97. Mark V. Pauly, *Doctors and Their Workshops: Economic Models of Physician Behavior* (Chicago: University of Chicago Press, 1980).

98. David Orentlicher, "The Role of Professional Self-Regulation," in *Regulation of the Healthcare Professions*, ed. Timothy S. Jost (Chicago: Health Administration Press, 1997).

99. American Medical Association, *Code of Medical Ethics* (Chicago, 1994 edition), p. 93.

100. *Wall Street Journal*, July 21, 1999, B7.

101. Michael L. Millenson, *Demanding Medical Excellence: Doctors and Accountability in the Information Age* (Chicago: University of Chicago Press, 1997).

102. Ibid.

103. Gabel, Hunt, and Hurst, "When Employers Choose Health Plans."

104. Mary Chris Jaklevic, "Fewer Docs Punished," *Modern Healthcare* 28 (1998): 14.

105. Two states, Texas and Missouri, passed laws in 1997 to extend malpractice liability to health plans. In Texas health plans are now liable for damage caused to plan enrollees as a result of treatment decisions or failure to exercise a degree of care under ordinary prudence: *Managed Care Week* (February 23, 1998). In 1999 California passed a law allowing HMO enrollees to sue their HMOs: *Modern Healthcare* (October 4, 1999).

106. William M. Sage, "Enterprise Liability and the Emerging Managed Health Care System," *Law and Contemporary Problems* 60 (1997): 159–210.

107. The evidence is reviewed in Patricia M. Danzon, "Liability for Medical Malpractice," *Journal of Economic Perspectives* 5 (1991): 51–69. She suggests that these patterns are consistent with the malpractice system inducing physicians to be more careful and with the malpractice system resulting in an efficient increase in physician specialization.

108. William M. Sage, "Enterprise Liability," 166.

109. M. Rothchild and Joseph Stiglitz, "Equilibrium in Competitive Insurance Markets: An Essay on the Economics of Imperfect Information," *Quarterly Journal of Economics* 90 (1976): 629–649; David M. Cutler and Sarah J. Reber, "Paying for Health Insurance: The Trade-off between Competition and Adverse Selection," *Quarterly Journal of Economics* (May 1998): 433–466.

110. Using data from the Group Insurance Commission of Massachusetts (which offers a generous indemnity plan and 10 more stringent HMOs) for 1994 and 1995, one study estimated that 38 percent of the higher costs of the indemnity plan relative to the HMOs can be explained by differences in the demographics of those insured in the two types of insurance plans. Daniel Altman, David M. Cutler, and Richard J. Zeckhauser, "Adverse Selection and Adverse Retention," *American Economic Review* 88 (1998): 122–126. Moreover, their results suggest that adverse selection by individuals (more specifically, lower-risk individuals moving out of the indemnity plan to HMOs) resulted in a 1 percent increase in the indemnity plan's average costs and a 1 percent decrease in HMOs' average costs in 1995.

111. David Cutler suggests that as our knowledge of the biomedical link between genetics and health increases, insurers will become increasingly skilled at predicting who will incur high health care costs and thus increasingly able to sort individuals on the basis of their expected health care costs. In the future, DNA tests at birth may provide estimates of the probability that an individual will contract particular diseases. David M. Cutler, "Public Policy for Health Care," NBER working paper no. 5591 (Cambridge, Mass.: National Bureau of Economic Research, 1996).

112. John Cochrane, "Time Consistent Health Insurance," *Journal of Political Economy* (June 1995): 445–473.

113. Fred J. Hellinger, "Selection Bias in HMOs and PPOs: A Review of the Evidence," *Inquiry* 32 (1995): 135–142.

114. Gerald Riley, Cynthia Tudor, Yen-pin Chiang, and Melvin Ingber, "Health Status of Medicare Enrollees in HMOs and Fee-for-Service in 1994," *Health Care Financing Review* 17 (1996).

115. Altman, Cutler, and Zeckhauser, "Adverse Selection and Adverse Retention."

116. Cutler and Reber, "Paying for Health Insurance."

117. *Modern Healthcare* (March 16, 1998): 54.

118. *Modern Healthcare* (March 23, 1998): 8.

119. Sherry Glied, Jane Sisk, Sheila Gorman, and Michael Ganz, "Selection, Marketing, and Medicaid Managed Care," NBER working paper no. 6164 (Cambridge, Mass.: National Bureau of Economic Research, 1997).

120. Joseph P. Newhouse, "Reimbursing Health Plans and Health Providers: Efficiency in Production Versus Selection," *Journal of Economic Literature* 34 (1996): 1236–1263.

### 3. Antitrust Policy in Health Care Markets

1. *United States v. Topco Associates Inc.*, 1972.

2. Many states have antitrust laws as well.

3. See Richard Posner, *Antitrust Law: An Economic Perspective* (Chicago: University of Chicago Press, 1976); and Robert H. Bork, *The Antitrust Paradox: A Policy at War with Itself* (New York: Basic Books, 1978).

4. The President appoints the Assistant Attorney General, who heads the Antitrust Division of the Department of Justice and the five Commissioners who constitute the FTC. However, the Senate must confirm FTC Commissioners, and no more than three Commissioners can be from the same political party.

5. State attorneys general also enforce their state's antitrust laws.

6. Peter J. Hammer and William M. Sage, "Antitrust, Health Care Quality, and the Courts," *Columbia Law Review* 102 (2002).

7. Natalie Marjancik, "Risky Business: Proposed Reform of the Antitrust Laws as Applied to Health Care Provider Networks," *American Journal of Law and Medicine* 24 (1998).

8. Market share is used as a proxy for market power. The degree of market share required as a minimum to support an attempted monopolization claim is not set in stone; however, most courts recognize that a market share of 70 percent or greater sustains a monopolization claim.

9. For a review of these cases see Bryan A. Liang, "An Overview and Analysis of Challenges to Medical Exclusive Contracts," *Journal of Legal Medicine* 18 (1997): 1–45.

10. 466 U.S. 2 (1984).

11. 861 F.2d 1440 (9th Cir. 1988).

12. The Supreme Court has stated that *per se* rules are created to reduce litigation costs and to increase business certainty about illegal behavior.

13. John J. Miles, *Health Care and Antitrust Law: Principles and Practice* (Deerfield, Ill.: Clark, Boardman, and Callaghan, 1993).

14. Ibid.

15. Kevin E. Grady and Douglas C. Ross, "A Primer on Antitrust Fundamentals," in *Antitrust Developments in Evolving Health Care Markets*, ed. Howard Feller (American Bar Association, 1996).

16. *State of New York v. Saint Francis Hospital, Vassar Brothers Hospital and Mid-Hudson Health*, U.S. District Court for the Southern District of New York (April 10, 2000).

17. 94-5566 (December 5, 1994).

18. *Arizona v. Maricopa Medical Society*, 102 S. Ct. 2466 (1982).

19. Roscoe B. Starek, "Reinventing Health Care Antitrust Enforcement," prepared remarks before the Antitrust Common Ground Conference, Nashville, Tennessee, May 17, 1996.

20. Crim. No. W9CR114 (W.D. Tex., December 15, 1995).

21. *U.S. v. American Society of Anesthesiologists*, 473 F. Supp. 147 (S.D.N.Y. 1979).

22. The plaintiffs in *Marshfield* later suffered summary judgment on this claim because they could not demonstrate damages resulting from the market allocation scheme. However, another set of plaintiffs brought suit on a similar theory and survived summary judgment (*Rozema v. Marshfield Clinic*, 977 F. Supp. 1362 [W.D. Wis. 1997]).

23. Jonathan B. Baker, "Two Sherman Act Section 1 Dilemmas: Parallel Pricing, the Oligopoly Problem, and Contemporary Economic Theory," *Antitrust Law Journal* 38 (1993): 143–219.

24. Alexis Jacquemin and Margaret E. Slade, "Cartels, Collusion, and Horizontal Merger," in *Handbook of Industrial Organization, Volume 1*, ed. Richard Schmalensee and Robert D. Willig (Elsevier Science Publishers, 1989).

25. Posner, *Antitrust Law*, p. 160.

26. As amended in 1950 with the passage of the Celler-Kefauver Amendment.

27. Concentration is often used as a proxy for market power for two main reasons: first, market concentration is much easier to measure than market power, and second, both theoretical and empirical research has established a direct relationship between market concentration and firms' willingness and abilities to exercise market power.

28. Timothy F. Bresnahan, "Empirical Studies of Industries with Market Power," in *Handbook of Industrial Organization, Volume 2*, ed. Richard Schmalensee and Robert D. Willig (New York: North-Holland, 1989), p. 1052.

29. George A. Hay and Daniel Kelley, "An Empirical Survey of Price-Fixing Conspiracies," *Journal of Law and Economics* 17 (1974): 13–38.

30. There is evidence that managed care plans and employers are willing to contract with specialized organizations on this basis for managed behavioral health (mental health/substance abuse) and for HIV patients, while diabetes and cancer carve-outs have not caught on with managed care organizations or employers. David Blumenthal and Melinda Beeuwkes Buntin, "Carve Outs: Definition, Experience, and Choice among Candidate Conditions," *The American Journal of Managed Care* 4 (1998): 45–57.

31. A very relevant issue is to what extent merger-specific cost savings will be passed through to consumers in the form of lower prices.

32. Federal Trade Commission, *Anticipating the 21st Century: Competition Policy in the New High-Tech Global Marketplace* (Washington, D.C., 1996), chap. 2.

33. It is rare to find something about which economists are in agreement.

34. Richard Posner, "The Social Costs of Monopoly and Regulation," *Journal of Political Economy* 83 (1975): 807–827.

35. *Modern Healthcare* (December 7, 1998): 4.

36. Quality is usually measured on a scale from high to low, while product differentiation is measured on the basis of differences between product characteristics, such as color, size, or location. For example, hospital quality can be measured as high or low mortality rates, while differentiation in the market for hospital services can be measured as differences in the provision of specialized hospital services or differences across hospitals' medical staffs.

37. See David Levhari and Yoram Peles, "Market Structure, Quality and Durability," *Bell Journal of Economics* 4 (1973): 235–248; and Keith B. Leffler, "Ambiguous Changes in Product Quality," *American Economic Review* 72 (1982): 956–967.

38. For a discussion of this issue see Paul L. Joskow, "Editorial: Reimbursement Policy, Cost Containment, and Nonprice Competition," *Journal of Health Economics* 2 (1983): 167–174.

39. G. W. Douglas and J. C. Miller, "Quality Competition, Industry Equilibrium, and Efficiency in the Price-Constrained Airline Market," *American Economic Review* 64 (1974): 657–669; Richard Schmalensee, "Comparative Static Properties of Regulated Airline Oligopolies," *Bell Journal of Economics* 10 (1977): 472–482.

40. Theory suggests that monopolistically competitive markets may produce more or less than the optimal product variety. See Michael Spence, "Product Selection, Fixed Costs, and Monopolistic Competition," *Review of Economic Studies* 43 (1976): 217–235; and Kevin Lancaster, *Variety, Equity, and Efficiency* (New York: Columbia University Press, 1979).

41. Spence, "Product Selection."

42. This evidence is reviewed in Chapter 2 in the section on the medical arms race.

43. William M. Sage and Peter J. Hammer, "Competing on Quality of Care: The Need to Develop a Competition Policy for Health Care Markets," *Journal of Law Reform* 32 (1999): 1069–1118.

44. Ibid.

45. Kenneth J. Arrow, "Economic Welfare and the Allocation of Resources for Innovation," in *Essays in the Theory of Risk-Bearing* (Amsterdam: North-Holland, 1976).

46. Joseph Schumpeter, *Capitalism, Socialism, and Democracy* (New York and London: Harper & Brothers, 1942).

47. Zoltan J. Acs and David B. Audretsch, "Innovation, Market Structure, and Firm Size," *Review of Economics and Statistics* 69 (1987): 567–574.

48. Jonathan B. Baker, "Fringe Firms and Incentives to Innovate," *Antitrust Law Journal* 63 (1995): 621–641.

49. Wesley M. Cohen and Richard C. Levin, "Empirical Studies on Innovation and Market Structure," in *Handbook of Industrial Organization, Volume 2*, ed. Schmalensee and Willig, p. 1078.

50. Annetine Gelijns, Joshua Graff Zivin, and Richard R. Nelson, "Uncertainty and Technological Change in Medicine," *Journal of Health Politics, Policy and Law* 26 (2001): 913–924.

51. Ibid.

52. Darren E. Zinner, "Medical R&D at the Turn of the Millennium," *Health Affairs* (2001).

53. Peter J. Neumann and Eileen A. Sandberg, "Trends in Health Care R&D and Technological Innovation," *Health Affairs* 17 (1998): 111–119.

54. Annetine Gelijns and Nathan Rosenberg, "The Dynamics of Technological Change in Medicine," *Health Affairs* (Summer 1994): 28–46.

55. Gelijns, Zivin, and Nelson, "Uncertainty and Technological Change."

56. Gelijns and Rosenberg, "Dynamics of Technological Change."

57. Neumann and Sandberg, "Trends in Health Care R&D."

58. H. E. Frech and Lee R. Mobley, "Health Insurance: Designing Products to Reduce Costs," in *Industry Studies*, ed. Larry L. Duetsch (Armonk, N.Y.: M. E. Sharpe, 1998).

59. Manuel Trajtenberg, *Economic Analysis of Product Innovation: The Case of CT Scanners* (Cambridge, Mass.: Harvard University Press, 1990), p. 50.

60. Anthony J. Dennis, "Hospitals, Physicians, and Health Insurers: Guarding against Implied Agreements in the Health Care Context," *Washington University Law Quarterly* 71 (1993): 115–149.

61. Foreman and Keeler argue that accreditation, licensing, and malpractice liability standards combine to enforce a singe level of care for all patients regardless of ability to pay. Stephen E. Foreman and Theodore E. Keeler, "Regulation, Competition and Cross-subsidization in Hospital Care: Lessons from the Economics of Regulation," University of California at Berkeley working paper no. 95–236, 1995.

62. Peter J. Cunningham, Joy M. Grossman, Robert F. St. Peter, and Cara S. Lesser, "Managed Care and Physicians' Provision of Charity Care," *JAMA* 281 (1999): 1087–1092.

63. Center for Studying Health System Change, "Tracking Report," no. 6 (December 2002).

64. *Modern Healthcare By the Numbers* (December 23, 2002): 12.

65. Center for Studying Health System Change, "Tracking Report," no. 6.

66. Jonathan Gruber, "The Effect of Competitive Pressure on Charity: Hospital Responses to Price Shopping in California," *Journal of Health Economics* 38 (1994): 183–212.

67. Ibid., pp. 204–205.

68. Joyce Mann, Glenn Melnick, Anil Bamezai, and Jack Zwanziger, "Uncompensated Care: Hospitals' Responses to Fiscal Pressures," *Health Affairs* (Spring 1995): 263–270.

69. Cunningham et al., "Managed Care and Physicians' Provision."

70. Mark V. Pauly, "A Primer on Competition in Medical Markets," in *Health Care in America*, ed. H. E. Frech III (San Francisco: Pacific Research Institute for Public Policy, 1988).

71. *FTC v. Butterworth Health Corporation and Blodgett Memorial Medical Center,* 1996-2 Trade Cases 71, 571; 1996 QL 570479 (W.D. Michigan, September 26, 1996).

72. No. 95-5015-CV-SW-1, 1995 WL 462226 (W.D. Mo., June 5, 1995), at 7.

73. Only one empirical study suggests otherwise: William J. Lynk, "Nonprofit Hospital Mergers and the Exercise of Market Power," *Journal of Law and Economics* 38 (1995): 437–461. Using data on California hospitals in 1989, Lynk found that

mergers between nonprofit hospitals resulted in lower rather than higher prices. Presumably, the merging nonprofit hospitals realized cost efficiencies and passed those efficiencies on to consumers in the form of lower prices. William J. Lynk and Lynette R. Neumann, "Price and Profit," *Journal of Health Economics* 18 (1999): 99–116.

74. Emmett B. Keeler, Glenn Melnick, and Jack Zwanziger, "The Changing Effects on Non-Profit and For-Profit Hospital Pricing Behavior," *Journal of Health Economics* 18 (1999): 69–86.

75. John Simpson and Richard Shin, "Do Nonprofit Hospitals Exercise Market Power?" *International Journal of the Economics of Business* 5 (1998): 141–157; David Dranove and Richard Ludwick, "Competition and Pricing by Nonprofit Hospitals: A Reassessment of Lynk's Analysis," *Journal of Health Economics* 18 (1999): 87–98.

76. The reason is that the class includes most university-affiliated teaching hospitals. The typical nonprofit community hospital conducts little or no research and teaching. M. Gregg Bloche, "Should Government Intervene to Protect Nonprofits?" *Health Affairs* 17 (1998): 7–25.

77. A review of studies pertaining to acute care hospitals concluded that "regardless of the types of quality measures studied (for example, qualifications of staff physicians, staff physician subjective evaluation of services, postoperative mortality rates), there are no clear differences between nonprofit and for-profit hospitals." Richard G. Frank and David S. Salkever, "Nonprofit Organizations in the Health Sector," *Journal of Economic Perspectives* 8 (1994): 131.

78. Frank A. Sloan, "Not-for-Profit Ownership and Hospital Behavior," in *Handbook of Health Economics*, ed. Culyer and Newhouse (2000).

79. Ibid., p. 1165.

80. American Hospital Association, *Hospital Statistics* (2001), and *Modern Healthcare By the Numbers* (December 23, 2002): 12.

81. These guidelines were introduced in September 1993, and then revised in September 1994 and August 1996.

82. Gregory J. Werden, "Demand Elasticities in Antitrust Analysis," U.S. Department of Justice, Economic Analysis Group Discussion Paper no. EAG 96-11, Washington, D.C., November 29, 1996.

83. When demand is inelastic, consumers are less sensitive to price increases so that if a firm increases its price by 5 percent, it will lose less than 5 percent of its customers and the firm's revenue and profit will increase.

84. Werden, "Demand Elasticities," p. 34.

85. Robert F. Leibenluft, "Antitrust Enforcement and Hospital Mergers: A Closer Look," paper presented at the First Friday Forum of the Alliance for Health, Grand Rapids, Michigan, June 5, 1998.

86. Most of the action with respect to MCC consolidation has been at the state level. In addition to antitrust enforcement by state attorneys general, state departments of insurance often have approval or enforcement authority under their state insurance holding company system laws. For example, in Massachusetts the attorney general did not challenge the combination of Harvard Community Health Plan and Pilgrim Health Care, but imposed a series of conduct and community benefit remedies. In Missouri, the Department of Insurance allowed the acquisition of MetraHealth by United HealthCare, subject to the condition that the

merged firm divest MetLife HMO of St. Louis. In 1998 the Insurance Commissioner of Montana approved, subject to certain conditions, the merger of two of the largest insurers in the state, Blue Cross and Blue Shield of Montana and Yellowstone Community Health Plan (*Modern Healthcare*, November 16, 1998: 14). The conditions included the stipulation that the merged health insurance firm's contracts with providers may not prohibit or discourage those providers from contracting with other insurers.

87. Marjancik, "Risky Business."

88. FTC advisory opinion concerning the Phoenix Medical Network, Inc. (May 19, 1998).

89. However, the FTC did acknowledge that the network could have significant anticompetitive impacts if it operates as an exclusive network (if participating physicians refuse to contract with payers or other networks independently), or if the network's operation facilitates collusion among participating physicians.

90. Department of Justice Business Review Letter re: Vermont Physicians Clinic (July 30, 1997).

91. Department of Justice Business Review Letter re: First Priority Health System (November 3, 1997).

92. Thomas E. Kauper, "The Justice Department and the Antitrust Laws: Law Enforcer or Regulator?" in Kovaleff, ed., *The Antitrust Impulse: An Economic, Historical, and Legal Analysis* (Armonk, N.Y.: M. E. Sharpe, 1994).

93. Kevin E. Grady, "Overview of Government Policy Statements on Healthcare," paper presented at the National Health Lawyers Association Antitrust in the Healthcare Field Meeting, February 12–14, 1997.

94. *Modern Healthcare* (October 29, 2001): 14–15.

95. Jack Zwanziger, Glenn Melnick, and Kathleen M. Eyre, "Hospitals and Antitrust: Defining Markets, Setting Standards," *Journal of Health Politics, Policy, and Law* 19 (1994): 423–447; David Dranove, "Market Definition in Antitrust Analysis and Application to Health Care," in *Managed Care and Changing Health Care Markets*, ed. Michael A. Morrisey (Washington, D.C.: AEI Press, 1998).

96. William G. Kopit and Tanya B. Vanderbilt, "Unique Issues in the Analysis of Non-Profit Hospital Mergers," *Washburn Law Journal* 35 (1996): 254–271.

## 4. Market Definition in Health Care Antitrust Cases

1. *U.S. Healthcare, Inc., et al. v. Healthsource, Inc., et al.*, 986 F.2d 589, 598 (1st Cir. 1993).

2. *FTC v. Freeman Hospital*, 911 F. Supp. 1213, 1227 (W.D. Mo. 1995).

3. *FTC v. Freeman Hospital*, 69 F.3d 270 (8th Cir. 1995).

4. *U.S. v. Mercy Health Services*, 902 F. Supp. 978 (N.D. Iowa 1995).

5. 107 F.3d 632 (8th Cir. 1997).

6. *FTC v. Tenet Healthcare Corp., et al.*, 186 F.3d 1045 (8th Cir. 1999).

7. *U.S. v. Long Island Jewish Medical Center*, No. CV 97-3412 (ADS) (E.D.N.Y., October 23, 1997).

8. Gregory Vistnes, "Hospital Mergers and Two-Stage Competition," *Antitrust Law Journal* 67 (2000): 671–692.

9. Ibid., p. 672.

10. Some economists argue that it would be better to use estimates of own

elasticities of demand: "Using own elasticities of demand to delineate markets, the question posed is whether a given group of products and area constitute a market. That is the question that must ultimately be addressed when market delineation is used for antitrust analysis. Using cross elasticities to delineate markets, the question posed is whether one given product is in the same market with another, and posing this question not only tends to obscure the ultimate issue, but also necessarily evokes a fundamentally flawed pairwise analysis." Gregory J. Werden, "Demand Elasticities in Antitrust Analysis," U.S. Department of Justice, Economic Analysis Group Discussion Paper no. EAG 96-11, November 29, 1996, p. 43.

11. 370 U.S. 294 (1962). However, *Brown Shoe* has been called "a somewhat rudderless standard" because the Supreme Court did not establish how high an estimate of the cross-price elasticity is required to include a potential substitute in the product market of the consolidating firms. James A. Keyte, "Market Definition and Differentiated Products: The Need for a Workable Standard," *Antitrust Law Journal* 63 (1995): 699.

12. David Dranove and William D. White, "Competition, Managed Care and the Evolving Structure of the U.S. Hospital Industry: A Historical Perspective," photocopy, 1998.

13. David Dranove, "Market Definition in Antitrust Analysis and Application to Health Care," in *Managed Care and Changing Health Care Markets*, ed. Michael A. Morrisey (Washington, D.C.: AEI Press, 1998); David Dranove and William D. White, "Emerging Issues in the Antitrust Definition of Healthcare Markets," *Health Economics* 7 (1998).

14. Dranove, "Market Definition in Antitrust Analysis," notes that managed care networks always include at least one local hospital offering tertiary services.

15. The empirical evidence from the 1990s does not suggest that MCCs were steering enrollees to higher-volume hospitals. For example, one study found that cancer patients (with breast, colorectal, and gynecological cancers) in managed care plans in Massachusetts in 1995 tended to be treated at hospitals that performed few of these types of surgeries. Sarah Feldman and David A. Scharfstein, "Quality Differences in Managed Care and Fee-for-Service," NBER Working Paper no. 6523, Cambridge, Mass., 1998.

16. 370 U.S. 294, 325 (1962).

17. *U.S. v. Mercy Health* Services, 902 F. Supp. 968 (N.D. Iowa 1995); *FTC v. Freeman Hospital*, 911 F. Supp. 1213, 1227 (W.D. Mo. 1995); *FTC v. University Health Inc.*, 938 F.2d 1206, 1211 (11th Cir. 1991); *U.S. v. Rockford Memorial Corp.*, 898 F.2d 1278, 1284 (7th Cir. 1990).

18. *FTC v. Butterworth Health Corp.*, 946 F. Supp. 1285 (W.D. Mich. 1996). The FTC characterized general acute care inpatient hospital services as "a common host of distinct services and capabilities that are necessary to meet the surgical, medical, and other needs of inpatients, e.g., operating rooms, anesthesia, intensive care capabilities, 24-hour nursing care, lodging, and pharmaceuticals" (at 1290).

19. *United States v. Carilion Health System*, Civil Action No. 88-0249-R, U.S. District Court for the Western District of Virginia, 707 F. Supp. 840.

20. *Jefferson Parish Hospital District No. 2 v. Hyde*, 466 U.S. 2 (1984) and *Oltz v. St. Peter's Community Hospital*, 861 F.2d 1440 (1988).

21. Kevin A. Schulman, L. Elizabeth Rubenstein, Damon M. Seils, Melissa Harris, Jack Hadley, and Jose J. Escarce, "Quality Assessment in Contracting for

Tertiary Care Services by HMOs: A Case Study of Three Markets," *Journal on Quality Improvement* 23 (1997): 117–127.

22. For example, performing cardiac catheterization (a radiological study of blood flows in the heart) requires radiological scanners, specialized monitoring devices, dedicated catheterization devices, and specialized cardiac nurses, technicians, and cardiologists. The performance of coronary artery bypass grafting (intensive open-heart surgery to restore blood flow to the heart) requires heart-lung bypass machines, nurses with training for cardiac operations and cardiac intensive care, and specialized cardiologists and cardiac surgeons. David M. Cutler and Mark McClellan, "The Determinants of Technological Change in Heart Attack Treatment," NBER Working Paper no. 5751, Cambridge, Mass., 1996. Other heart disease technologies that require highly specialized labor and equipment include Swan-Ganz catheters to monitor heart performance quantitatively in intensive care, balloon pumps to assist the performance of the heart, and angioplasty to open up heart blood vessels. Mark McClellan and Haruko Noguchi, "Technology Change in Heart-Disease Treatment: Does High Tech Mean Low Value?" *American Economic Review* 88 (1998): 90–96.

23. Peter R. Kongstvedt, *Essentials of Managed Health Care* (Gaithersburg, Md.: Aspen Publishers, 1997).

24. *Modern Healthcare* (September 6, 1999): 55.

25. Telephone call, July 21, 1999, with Greg Lehman of the National Business Coalition on Health, the national organization for more than 100 health care purchasing coalitions of employers.

26. *Managed Care Week* (September 21, 1998): 6.

27. Moskowitz, "Outcomes-Based Buying Goes Direct," *Business and Health* 16 (1998): 48.

28. Telephone call, January 1999, with Patrick Casey, Executive Director of the Health Action Council of Northeast Ohio.

29. Jonathan B. Baker, "The Antitrust Analysis of Hospital Mergers and the Transformation of the Hospital Industry," *Law and Contemporary Problems* 51 (1988): 93–164.

30. Regina Herzlinger, *Market Driven Health Care: Who Wins, Who Loses in the Transformation of America's Largest Service Industry* (Reading, Mass.: Addison-Wesley, 1997).

31. Lisa Soroka, "Specialty Carve-outs: Shifting the Risks to Specialty Medical Groups," *Managed Care Week* 8 (1998): 6–7.

32. Dominic Hodgkin, Laurence Baker, and Jose J. Escarce, "HMO Penetration and Hospital Specialized Service Offerings in U.S. Metropolitan Areas," paper presented at the Sixth Northeast Regional Health Economics Symposium, Newport, R.I., August 3–4, 1998.

33. Likewise, the number of hospitals (as opposed to the proportion of hospitals) in each MSA offering 11 out of 17 specialized services increased between 1990 and 1994.

34. These results were discussed in the context of the medical arms race in Chapter 2, and thus will not be repeated here.

35. See Robert E. Bloch, "Analysis of Provider Networks Outside of the Safety Zones," paper presented at the National Health Lawyers Association Conference on Antitrust in the Healthcare Field, Washington, D.C., February 12–14, 1997.

36. Department of Justice Business Review Letter re: The proposed merger of

The Heritage Alliance and Lackawanna Physicians Organization, September 15, 1998.

37. One of the charges in this case was that the Marshfield Clinic, a physician-owned clinic that is vertically integrated with its HMO, had monopolized the market for physician services.

38. *Blue Cross and Blue Shield of Wisconsin et al. v. Marshfield Clinic et al.*, Nos. 95-1965, 95-2140 (7th Cir. 1995).

39. One of the charges in the Vicksburg case was that the proposed merger of the two largest physician groups in town would lessen competition in the market for physician services.

40. The court accepted the plaintiff's definitions of the product markets for general surgery, urology, and otolaryngology services, as there was no opposition from the defendant.

41. *HTI Health Services, Inc. v. Quorum Health Group, Inc., River Regional Medical Corp., and Vicksburg Clinic, P.A.*, U.S. District Court for the Southern District of Mississippi, Western Division (Civil Action No. 5:96-CV-108Br(S)).

42. Only a small subset of studies (specifically, studies based on data from the 1990s) is mentioned in the text. For a review of the studies based on data from the 1970s and 1980s, see Dennis P. Scanlon, Michael Chernew, and Judith R. Lave, "Consumer Health Plan Choice: Current Knowledge and Future Direction," *Annual Review of Public Health* 18 (1997): 507–528.

43. Thomas Buchmueller and Paul Feldstein, "Consumers' Sensitivity to Health Plan Premiums: Evidence from a Natural Experiment in California," *Health Affairs* 15 (1996).

44. David M. Cutler and Sarah J. Reber, "Paying for Health Insurance: The Trade-off between Competition and Adverse Selection," *Quarterly Journal of Economics* (May 1998): 433–466.

45. Anne B. Royalty and Neil Solomon, "Health Plan Choice: Price Elasticities in a Managed Competition Setting," *Journal of Human Resources* 34 (1999): 1–41.

46. However, the network HMOs offered a greater choice among primary care providers as compared with the group-practice HMO.

47. Center for Studying Health System Change, "Health Care Costs: Will They Start Rising Rapidly Again?" Issue Brief No. 10 (1997).

48. Gail A. Jensen and Michael A. Morrisey, "Managed Care and the Small-Group Market," in *Managed Care and Changing Health Care Markets*, ed. Michael A. Morrisey (Washington, D.C.: AEI Press, 1998).

49. Kaiser Family Foundation, *National Survey of Small Businesses: Highlights and Chartpack* (Menlo Park, Calif., April 2002).

50. Center for Studying Health System Change "Health Care Costs."

51. Karen S. Collins, Cathy Schoen, and David R. Sandman, *The Commonwealth Fund Survey of Physician Experiences with Managed Care* (New York: Commonwealth Fund, 1997).

52. Atlantic Information Services (4th Quarter 1998): 5.

53. Ibid.

54. *Managed Care Week* (May 11, 1998); and *Managed Care Week* (August 12, 1996).

55. American Association of Health Plans, *HMO and PPO Industry Profile, 1995–1996 Edition* (Washington, D.C.).

56. Ruth S. Given, "Ensuring Competition in the Market for HMO Services," in *Competitive Managed Care: The Emerging Health Care System*, ed. John D. Wilerson, Kelly J. Devers, and Ruth S. Given (San Francisco: Jossey-Bass, 1997); Cutler and Reber, "Paying for Health Insurance."

57. 64 U.S.L.W. 3624, March 18, 1996 (No. 95-1118).

58. 784 F.2d 1325 (7th Cir. 1986).

59. For a review of other relevant court decisions see Robert E. Bloch and Scott P. Perlman, "Analyzing and Defending HMO Mergers under the Antitrust Laws," paper presented at the American Association of Health Plans Annual Managed Care Law Conference, February 12–14, 1997; and Arthur N. Lerner, "Mergers of Managed Care Plans," paper presented at the National Health Lawyers Association Conference on Antitrust in the Healthcare Field, Washington, D.C., February 12–14, 1997.

60. *U.S. v. Aetna and Prudential*, U.S. District Court for the Northern District of Texas (Civil Action No. 3-99 CV 1398-H), June 21, 1999.

61. K. G. Elzinga and T. F. Hogarty, "The Problem of Geographic Market Delineation in Antimerger Suits," *Antitrust Bulletin* 18 (1973): 45–81.

62. Gregory J. Werden, "The Limited Relevance of Patient Migration Data in Market Delineation for Hospital Merger Cases," *Journal of Health Economics* 8 (1989): 363–376; Cory S. Capps, David Dranove, Shane Greenstein, and Mark Satterthwaite, "The Silent Majority Fallacy of the E-H Criteria: A Critique and New Approach to Analyzing Hospital Mergers," NBER Working Paper no. 8216, Cambridge, Mass., 2001.

63. William D. White and Michael A. Morrisey, "Are Patients Traveling Further?" *International Journal of Economics and Business* 5 (1998): 203–222.

64. Barry C. Harris and Joseph J. Simons, "Focusing Market Definition: How Much Substitution Is Necessary?" in *Research in Law and Economics*, ed. Richard O. Zerbe, Jr., pp. 207–226 (Jai Press, 1989).

65. See, for example, Frederick I. Johnson, "Two Approaches to Market Definition under the Merger Guidelines," in *Research in Law and Economics*, ed. Zerbe, pp. 227–234; and Kenneth L. Danger and H. E. Frech, "Critical Thinking about 'Critical Loss' in Antitrust," *The Antitrust Bulletin* 46 (2001): 339–355.

66. *Modern Healthcare* (December 3, 2001).

67. Frank Porell and E. Kathleen Adams, "Hospital Choice Models: A Review and Assessment of Their Utility for Policy Impact Analysis," *Medical Care Research and Review* 52 (1995): 158–195.

68. Even empirical evidence based on data from the 1980s suggests that consumers' perceptions of quality influence hospital choices. Using California data from 1983, one study found that medical school affiliation (an indirect but easily observable measure of hospital quality) was associated with increased probability of a hospital being chosen. Harold S. Luft, Deborah W. Garnick, David H. Mark, Deborah J. Peltzman, Ciaran S. Phibbs, Erik Lichtenberg, and Stephen J. McPhee, "Does Quality Influence Choice of Hospital?" *JAMA* 263 (1990): 2899–2906.

69. See Luft et al., "Does Quality Influence Choice of Hospital?" and Lawton R. Burns and Douglas R. Wholey, "The Impact of Physician Characteristics in Conditional Choice Models for Hospital Care," *Journal of Health Economics* 11 (1992): 43–62.

70. Lee R. Mobley and H. E. Frech III, "Managed Care, Distance Traveled, and Hospital Market Definition," *Inquiry* 37 (2000): 91–107.

71. White and Morrisey, "Are Patients Traveling Further?"

72. Peter J. Cunningham and Linda Kohn, "Health Plan Switching: Choice or Circumstance?" *Health Affairs* 19 (2000): 150–157.

73. Center for Studying Health System Change, Data Bulletin: Why People Change Their Health Care Providers (May 2000).

74. Karen Davis and Cathy Schoen, "Assuring Quality, Information, and Choice in Managed Care," *Inquiry* 35 (1998): 104–114.

75. Werden, "The Limited Relevance of Patient Migration Data."

76. *HTI Health Services v. Quorum Health Group*, U.S. District Court for the Southern District of Mississippi, Western Division No. 5:96-CV-108Br (S).

77. At 40.

78. *BC and BS of Wisconsin et al. v. Marshfield Clinic et al.* (7th Cir. 1995).

79. The only court to have taken a contrary view was the trial court in *Marshfield Clinic;* however, the ruling was overturned by the Seventh Circuit. Bloch and Perlman, "Analyzing and Defending HMO Mergers."

80. Only 5 percent of individuals with employer-sponsored benefits were enrolled in conventional indemnity insurance plans in 2002 (Gabel, Levitt, Holve, Pickreign, et al., *Health Affairs* 21 [2002]: 148).

81. *U.S. Healthcare, Inc. et al. v. Healthsource, Inc. et al.*, U.S. District Court for the District of New Hampshire No. 91-113-D (1992).

82. This is different from previous criticism. As discussed earlier in this chapter, patient flow statistics have been criticized in the past for presenting a static, rather than a dynamic, picture of hospital patients' willingness to travel to more distant hospitals.

## 5. Entry Barriers in Health Care Markets

1. *Ball Memorial Hospital Inc., et al. v. Mutual Hospital Insurance Inc., et al.*, 784 F.2d 1325 (7th Cir. 1986).

2. Joe S. Bain, *Barriers to New Competition* (Cambridge, Mass.: Harvard University Press, 1956).

3. George Stigler, *The Organization of Industry* (Homewood, Ill.: Richard D. Irwin, 1968).

4. Dennis W. Carlton and Jeffrey M. Perloff, *Modern Industrial Organization* (New York: HarperCollins College Publisher, 1994), p. 51.

5. Richard J. Gilbert, "Preemptive Competition," in Joseph Stiglitz and G. Franklin Mathewson, eds., *New Developments in the Analysis of Market Structure* (Cambridge, Mass.: MIT Press, 1986).

6. For example, Physician Partners Company and North American Medical Management, a subsidiary of PhyCor, develop physician networks. In 1998 the two firms formed a joint venture to create a network of physicians around the New York Presbyterian Hospital Network of 27 hospitals. *Modern Healthcare* (October 26, 1998).

7. For example, the national PPO network of Private Healthcare Systems of Waltham, Massachusetts, is rented to more than 70 customers. *Managed Care Week* (April 12, 1999): 4.

8. Richard Schmalensee, "Product Differentiation Advantages of Pioneering Brands," *American Economic Review* 72 (1982): 349–365.

9. These sorts of contracts are discussed in Chapter 7.

10. Information provided by Thomas R. Piper, past president and editor of the American Health Planning Association and director of the Missouri Certificate of Need Program.

11. Ibid.

12. Mark A. Satterthwaite, "Consumer Information, Equilibrium Industry Price, and the Number of Sellers," *Bell Journal of Economics* 10 (1979): 483–502.

13. See Joseph Newhouse, Albert Williams, Bruce Bennett, and William Schwartz, "Does the Geographical Distribution of Physicians Reflect Market Failure?" *Bell Journal of Economics* 13 (1982): 493–505; Thomas McCarthy, "The Competitive Nature of the Primary-Care Physician Services Market," *Journal of Health Economics* 4 (1985): 93–117; and Herbert Wong, "Market Structure and the Role of Consumer Information in the Physician Services Industry: An Empirical Test," *Journal of Health Economics* 15 (1996): 139–160.

14. Timothy Bresnahan and Peter Reiss, "Entry and Competition in Concentrated Markets," *Journal of Political Economy* 99 (1991): 977–1009.

15. Andrew N. Kleit and Malcolm B. Coate, "Are Judges Leading Economic Theory? Sunk Costs, the Threat of Entry and the Competitive Process," *Southern Economic Journal* 60 (1993): 103–118.

16. These potential opportunities for anticompetitive vertical foreclosure are discussed in Chapter 7.

17. The material in this paragraph is based on Clark C. Havighurst, "Doctors and Hospitals: An Antitrust Perspective on Traditional Relationships," *Duke Law Journal* (December 1984).

18. John D. Blum, "The Evolution of Physician Credentialing and Managed Care Selective Contracting," *American Journal of Law and Medicine* 22 (1996).

19. Havighurst, "Doctors and Hospitals."

20. 745 F.2d 786 (1984).

21. Both osteopathic physicians (D.O.s) and allopathic physicians (MDs) are equally qualified for state licensure to practice medicine and surgery in Pennsylvania. Osteopaths utilize generally accepted physical, medicinal, and surgical methods of diagnosis and therapy, while giving emphasis to normal body mechanics and manipulative methods of detecting and correcting faulty structure.

22. Evidence was presented that suggested York Hospital had a historical presumption in favor of admitting any MD who applied for staff privileges, regardless of the MD's medical ability or social graces. Evidence was also presented demonstrating that York Hospital engaged in "strict scrutiny" of D.O. applicants' medical qualifications and social acceptability and that the hospital denied a D.O.'s application if the D.O. was found lacking, even minimally, in either area or was found lacking, based purely on hearsay.

23. However, the court also clearly stated that York Hospital could not "willfully" maintain its monopoly position, in violation of Section 2 of the Sherman Act, in the market for hospital services by excluding D.O.s. In fact, York Hospital is likely to weaken its monopoly position by excluding D.O.s because rival hospitals may provide competing hospital services with the excluded D.O.s.

24. 486 U.S. 94 (1988).

25. This case ended up going all the way to the Supreme Court. The Court of Appeals reversed the District Court's decision on the grounds that conduct in hos-

pital peer-review proceedings falls within the state action exemption from antitrust, and thus is immune from antitrust scrutiny. The Supreme Court, however, reversed this decision because no state actor in Oregon actively supervises hospital peer-review proceedings, and therefore the state action doctrine does not protect peer-review decisions from application of the federal antitrust laws.

26. According to the *Hospital Accreditation Standards* of the Joint Commission on Accreditation of Healthcare Organizations, the hospital board "appoints and reappoints the medical staff and grants initial, renewed, or revised clinical privileges, based on medical staff recommendations, in accordance with the bylaws, rules and regulations, and policies of the medical staff and of the hospital."

27. Further, the hospital can be held liable for malpractice of the physicians rendering services at its facility, even if those physicians are not hospital employees.

28. *FTC v. Medical Staff of Broward General Medical Center,* 114 FTC 542 (September 10, 1991).

29. Christopher J. Conover and Frank A. Sloan, "Does Removing Certificate-of-Need Regulations Lead to a Surge in Health Care Spending?" *Journal of Health Politics, Policy and Law* 23 (1998): 455–481.

30. Ibid.

31. Ibid.

32. Ibid.

33. Ibid.

34. These potential opportunities for anticompetitive vertical foreclosure are discussed in Chapter 7.

35. U.S. Court of Appeals, 784 F.2d 1325 (7th Cir. 1986).

36. This sort of learning-by-doing is firm-specific. The benefits of experience are private and do not spill over to other competitors.

## 6. The Effects of Horizontal Consolidation

1. David Dranove, *The Economic Evolution of American Health Care* (Princeton, N.J.: Princeton University Press, 2000).

2. Center for Studying Health System Change (2001).

3. *Federal Trade Commission v. Butterworth Health Corp.*, 1996-2 Trade Case, (CCH) 71,571 (W.D. Mich. 1996).

4. There are only a few empirical studies that estimate differences in costs and qualities across consolidating and nonconsolidating health care firms, and those studies are limited to markets for hospital services. Fortunately, it is possible to infer some information about consolidation of physicians or health insurers from empirical studies comparing costs and quality across large and small health care firms.

5. *BNA's Health Law Reporter* (October 30, 1997): 1654.

6. *Blue Cross/Blue Shield United of Wisconsin and Compcare Health Services Insurance Corp. v. Marshfield Clinic and Security Health Plan of Wisconsin, Inc.*, Case No. 95-1965 (7th Cir. Slip op., September 18, 1995).

7. According to *Modern Healthcare's* annual survey of contract management companies, many hospitals outsource housekeeping, food service, clinical/diagnostic equipment maintenance, emergency, laundry, and pharmacy operations. *Modern Healthcare* (September 1, 1997): 51–56.

8. *Blue Cross and Blue Shield of Wisconsin et al. v. Marshfield Clinic et al.*, Nos. 95-1965, 95-2140 (7th Cir. 1995).

9. *Modern Healthcare* (July 28, 1997): 17.

10. Robert A. Connor, Roger D. Feldman, Bryan E. Dowd, and Tiffany A. Radcliff, "Which Types of Hospital Mergers Save Consumers Money?" *Health Affairs* 16 (1997): 62–74.

11. Jeffrey A. Alexander, Michael T. Halpern, and Shoou-Yih D. Lee, "The Short-Term Effects of Mergers on Hospital Operations," *Health Services Research* 30 (1996): 827–847.

12. Heather Radach Spang, Gloria J. Bazzoli, and Richard J. Arnould, "Hospital Mergers and Savings for Consumers: Exploring New Evidence," *Health Affairs* 20 (2001): 150–158.

13. There are also studies based on data from the early 1980s, for example, Stephen M. Shortell and Edward F. X. Hughes, "The Effects of Regulation, Competition, and Ownership on Mortality Rates among Hospital Inpatients," *New England Journal of Medicine* 318 (1988): 1100–1107. Using data on Medicare beneficiaries who received inpatient care for sixteen clinical conditions in 1983 and 1984, these researchers found that inpatient mortality rates were not associated with the competitiveness of markets for hospital services, measured as whether the hospital competed with more or fewer than two other hospitals.

14. Vivian Ho and Barton H. Hamilton, "Hospital Mergers and Acquisitions: Does Market Consolidation Harm Patients?" *Journal of Health Economics* 19 (2000): 767–791.

15. It should be noted that when a hospital system acquires an independent hospital, there may be no change in local market concentration. Thus, this study does not estimate the impact of increasing concentration on hospital quality.

16. Daniel P. Kessler and Mark B. McClellan, "Is Hospital Competition Socially Wasteful?" *Quarterly Journal of Economics* 115 (2000): 577–615.

17. The literature suggests at least three reasons for especially high transaction costs; see Ronald Coase, "The Nature of the Firm," *Economica* 4 (1937): 386–405, and Oliver Williamson, *Markets and Hierarchies: Analysis and Antitrust Implications* (New York: Free Press, 1975). First, significant uncertainty about future conditions, such as the number of health plan enrollees or the health status of those enrollees, may increase the costs of negotiating contracts with all possible contingencies. Second, in markets with few alternative suppliers (for example, few local hospitals) there may be opportunities for opportunist behavior. Third, transaction costs are higher when extensive coordination among the firms at the different stages of production (for example, among physicians and hospitals) is required.

18. Charles E. Phelps, *Health Economics* (New York: HarperCollins, 1992), p. 234.

19. David Dranove, "Economies of Scale in Non-Revenue Producing Cost Centers: Implications for Hospital Mergers," *Journal of Health Economics* 17 (1998): 69–83.

20. *Modern Healthcare* (February 10, 1997): 34–36.

21. A review of the older empirical literature concludes there is "strong and consistent evidence that physicians in groups are more productive than solo practitioners," and scale economies "from group practice appear to be maximized in mid-size groups." Gregory C. Pope and Russel T. Burge, "Inefficiencies in Physi-

cian Practices," in *Advances in Health Economics and Health Services Research* 13 (JAI Press, 1992): 159.

22. Jose J. Escarce and Mark V. Pauly, "Physician Opportunity Costs in Physician Cost Functions," *Journal of Health Economics* 17 (1998): 129–151.

23. Jose J. Escarce, "Using Physician Practice Cost Functions in Payment Policy: The Problem of Endogeneity Bias," *Inquiry* 33 (1996): 66–78.

24. Ruth S. Given, "Economies of Scale and Scope as an Explanation of Merger and Output Diversification Activities in the Health Maintenance Organization Industry," *Journal of Health Economics* 15 (1996): 685–714.

25. Douglas Wholey, Roger Feldman, Jon B. Christianson, and John Engberg, "Scale and Scope Economies among Health Maintenance Organizations," *Journal of Health Economics* 15 (1996): 657–684.

26. Robert Rosenman, Kris Siddharthan, and Melissa Ahern, "Output Efficiency of HMOs in Florida," *Health Economics* 6 (1997): 295–302.

27. Based on 1990 data from the American Hospital Association, one study found that the percentage of hospitals offering cardiac catheterization, angioplasty, neonatal ICU, and hemodialysis increases with hospital size. William J. Lynk, "Nonprofit Hospital Mergers and the Exercise of Market Power," *Journal of Law and Economics* 38 (1995): 437–461.

28. Martin Gaynor and Mark Pauly, "Compensation and Productivity in Partnerships: Evidence from Medical Group Practice," *Journal of Political Economy* 98 (1990): 544–573.

29. Lynk, "Nonprofit Hospital Mergers."

30. Mark V. Pauly, "Economics of Multispecialty Group Practice," *Journal of Ambulatory Care Management* 19 (1996): 26–33.

31. James C. Robinson, "Physician Organization in California: Crisis and Opportunity," *Health Affairs* 20 (2001): 92.

32. Richard J. Bogue, Stephen M. Shortell, Min-Wooing Sohn, Larry Manheim, Gloria Bazzoli, and Cheeling Chan, "Hospital Reorganization after Merger," *Medical Care* 33 (1995): 676–686.

33. *Maine Sunday Telegram*, January 19, 1996, 1A and 6A.

34. *Modern Healthcare* (May 19, 1997): 21.

35. Elliot K. Wicks, Jack A. Meyer, and Marcia Carlyn, *Assessing the Early Impact of Hospital Mergers: An Analysis of the St. Louis and Philadelphia Markets* (Washington, D.C.: Economic and Social Research Institute, 1998).

36. Ibid.

37. Center for Studying Health System Change, "Community Report: Cleveland, Ohio" (Fall 1998): 3.

38. *National Health Lawyers News Report* 24 (November 1996): 6.

39. Maria Hewitt, *Interpreting the Volume-Outcome Relationship in the Context of Health Care Quality: Workshop Summary* (Washington, D.C.: Institute of Medicine, 2000).

40. Robert G. Hughes, Deborah W. Garnick, Harold S. Luft, Stephen J. McPhee, and Sandra S. Hunt, "Hospital Volume and Patient Outcomes: The Case of Hip Fracture Patients," *Medical Care* 26 (1988): 1057–1067.

41. Edward Hannan, Harold Kilburn, Harvey Bernard, Joseph O'Donnell, Gary Lukacik, and Eileen P. Shields, "Coronary Artery Bypass Surgery: The Rela-

tionship between Inhospital Mortality Rate and Surgical Volume after Controlling for Clinical Risk Factors," *Medical Care* 29 (1991): 1094–1107.

42. Kathryn A. Phillips, Harold S. Luft, and James Ritchie, "The Association of Hospital Volumes of Percutaneous Transluminal Coronary Angioplasty with Adverse Outcomes, Length of Stay, and Charges in California," *Medical Care* 33 (1995): 502–513.

43. Dean E. Farley and Ronald J. Ozminkowski, "Volume-Outcome Relationships and Inhospital Mortality: The Effect of Changes in Volume over Time," *Medical Care* 30 (1992): 77–94.

44. All three of these types of cases are treated at most community hospitals. However, hernia repairs are increasingly treated on an outpatient basis, and neonates with acute respiratory distress syndrome are often transferred to hospitals with neonatal intensive care units.

45. John D. Birkmeyer, Andrea E. Siewers, Emily V. A. Rinlayson, et al., "Hospital Volume and Surgical Mortality in the United States," *New England Journal of Medicine* 346 (2002): 1128–1137.

46. *Data Strategies and Benchmarks: The Monthly Advisory for Health Care Executives* 2 (1998): 37–42.

47. Lucian L. Leape, Donald M. Berwick, and David W. Bates, "What Practices Will Most Improve Safety? Evidence-Based Medicine Meets Patient Safety," *JAMA* 288 (2002).

48. Robert H. Lee, "Monitoring Physicians: A Bargaining Model of Medical Group Practice," *Journal of Health Economics* 9 (1990): 463–481.

49. Eve A. Kerr, Brian S. Mittman, Ron D. Hays, Barbara Leake, and Robert Brook, "Quality Assurance in Capitated Physician Groups," *JAMA* 276 (1996): 1236–1239.

50. Kevin Grumbach, Janet Coffman, Karen Vranizan, Noelle Blick, and Edward H. O'Neil, "Independent Practice Association Physician Groups in California," *Health Affairs* 17 (1998): 227–237.

51. *Data Strategies and Benchmarks* 2 (1998): 37–42.

52. Price was measured as operating revenue per outpatient-adjusted admission.

53. Robert A. Connor and Roger D. Feldman, "Horizontal Hospital Mergers and Their Effects on Non-Merging Hospitals in the Same Market Area," in *Managed Care and Changing Health Care Markets*, ed. Michael Morrisey (Washington, D.C.: AEI Press, 1998).

54. Robert A. Connor, Roger D. Feldman, Bryan E. Dowd, and Tiffany A. Radcliff, "Which Types of Hospital Mergers Save Consumers Money?" *Health Affairs* 16 (1997): 62–74.

55. Mesa County Physicians IPA, D. 9284 (complaint issued May 13, 1997).

56. Three of these studies are mentioned in Chapter 3 in the discussion about nonprofit status and the exercise of monopoly power, and thus are not covered again here.

57. M. Staten, J. Umbeck, and W. Dunkelberg, "Market Share/Market Power Revisited: A New Test for an Old Theory," *Journal of Health Economics* 7 (1988): 73–83.

58. Glenn A. Melnick, Jack Zwanziger, Anil Bamezai, and Robert Pattison,

"The Effects of Market Structure and Bargaining Position on Hospital Prices," *Journal of Health Economics* 11 (1992): 217–233.

59. John M. Brooks, Avi Dor, and Herbert S. Wong, "Hospital-Insurer Bargaining: An Empirical Investigation of Appendectomy Pricing," *Journal of Health Economics* 16 (1997): 417–434.

60. David Dranove, Mark Shanley, and William White, "Price and Concentration in Hospital Markets: The Switch from Patient-Driven to Payer-Driven Competition," *Journal of Law and Economics* 36 (1993): 179–204.

61. Costs are measured as the Medicare RBRVS fee schedule.

62. Jack Zwanziger and Christi Davis, "Are Physician Fees Negotiated with Managed Care Plans Converging to RBRVS Values?" Paper presented at the Sixth Northeast Regional Health Economics Symposium, Newport, R.I., August 3–4, 1998.

63. For a review of this literature see chapter 6 of H. E. Frech, *Competition and Monopoly in Medical Care* (Washington, D.C.: AEI Press, 1996).

64. Douglas Wholey, Roger Feldman, and Jon Christianson, "The Effect of Market Structure on HMO Premiums," *Journal of Health Economics* 14 (1995): 81–105.

65. Roger Feldman, Douglas Wholey, and Jon Christianson, "Effects of Mergers on Health Maintenance Organization Premiums," *Health Care Financing Review* 17 (1996): 171–189.

## 7. The Effects of Vertical Consolidation

1. Michael H. Riordan, "Anticompetitive Vertical Integration by a Dominant Firm," *American Economic Review* 88 (1998): 1232–1248.

2. Alison E. Cuellar and Paul J. Gertler, "Strategic Integration of Hospitals and Physicians" (School of Public Health, Columbia University, May 1, 2002, photocopy). This study finds that PHOs have little impact on hospital costs, but a positive and significant impact on hospital prices.

3. U.S. Court of Appeals for the Fifth Circuit, 123 F.3d 301; decided September 25, 1997.

4. Federal Trade Commission and Department of Justice, "Statements of Antitrust Enforcement Policy in Health Care" (August 1996), pp. 80–81.

5. For a review of the economics literature on vertical integration, see Martin K. Perry, "Vertical Integration: Determinants and Effects," in *Handbook of Industrial Organization*, ed. Richard Schmalensee and Robert Willig (New York: North-Holland, 1989).

6. H. E. Frech and Kenneth L. Danger, "Exclusive Contracts between Hospitals and Physicians," *Health Economics* 7 (1998).

7. Michael A. Morrisey and Deal C. Brooks, "The Myth of the Closed Medical Staff," *Hospitals* 59 (1985): 75–77.

8. Bryan A. Liang, "An Overview and Analysis of Challenges to Medical Exclusive Contracts," *Journal of Legal Medicine* 18 (1997): 1–45.

9. John K. Iglehart, "The Federal Trade Commission In Action: The FTC's Robert F. Leibenluft," *Health Affairs* 17 (1998): 65–74.

10. Fred J. Hellinger, "The Expanding Scope of State Legislation," *JAMA* 276 (1996): 1065–1070.

11. *Managed Care Week* (August 11, 1997): 2.

12. The Supreme Court in its *Jefferson Parish* decision (*Jefferson Parish Hospital District No. 2 v. Hyde*, 466 U.S. 2 [1984]) said that the tying and tied products can be considered separate if there is "sufficient demand" for the tied product to allow the identification of a distinct product market in which it is efficient to sell the tied product separately from the tying product.

13. In the first-stage market physician services and inpatient hospital services are separate and distinct products. There is a separate consumer demand for hospital services and for physician services. Insurers creating their managed care networks often contract separately for hospital and physician services. Likewise, in the second-stage market individual patients often demand physician services without hospital services. However, in the second-stage market hospital services are not demanded separately from physician services. Without physicians to admit patients, order diagnostic tests, and perform surgical and medical therapies, a hospital can be thought of as just a hotel with a nursing staff and a collection of very expensive technologies.

14. The Supreme Court stated in its *Jefferson Parish* decision that "the essential characteristic of an invalid tying arrangement lies in the seller's exploitation of its control over the tying product to force the buyer into the purchase of a tied product that the buyer either did not want at all, or might have preferred to purchase elsewhere on different terms" (p. 12).

15. Michael D. Whinston, "Tying, Foreclosure, and Exclusion," *American Economic Review* 80 (1990): 837–859.

16. *Modern Healthcare* (December 3, 2001).

17. Under the agreement, the two systems are prohibited from negotiating separate deals with managed care plans. *Modern Healthcare* (September 21, 1998): 28.

18. Cuellar and Gertler, "Strategic Integration."

19. Anthony J. Dennis, "Antitrust Issues for Insurers in Establishing and Dealing with Provider Networks," paper presented at the National Health Lawyers Association Meeting on Antitrust in the Healthcare Field, Washington, D.C., February 21–23, 1996.

20. Others also argue that vertical associations among hospitals and physicians are an effective means to raise quality. See, for example, Stephen M. Shortell et al., *Remaking Health Care in America: Building Organized Delivery Systems* (San Francisco: Jossey-Bass, 1996).

21. See, for example, Robert H. Bork, *The Antitrust Paradox: A Policy at War with Itself* (New York: Basic Books, 1978).

22. To illustrate this point, consider the case of a monopoly hospital acquiring an insurer. The Chicago School argument is that the monopoly hospital has nothing to gain from acquiring the insurer, since the hospital is already earning monopoly profits in its sale of hospital services to all insurers.

23. Michael H. Riordan and Steven C. Salop, "Evaluating Vertical Mergers: A Post-Chicago Approach," *Antitrust Law Journal* 63 (1995): 513–568; Fred M. Westfield, "Vertical Integration: Does Product Price Rise or Fall?" *American Economic Review* 71 (1981); John M. Vernon and Daniel A. Graham, "Profitability of Monopolization by Vertical Integration," *Journal of Political Economy* 79 (1971).

24. Aaron Director and Edward H. Levi, "Law and the Future: Trade Regulation," *Northwestern University Law Review* 51 (1956): 281–296.

25. Hospital and physician services are complements, so an increase in the price of hospital services will reduce demand for physician services.

26. See Janusz A. Ordover, Garth Saloner, and Steven C. Salop, "Equilibrium Vertical Foreclosure," *American Economic Review* 80 (1990): 127–142; Oliver Hart and Jean Tirole, "Vertical Mergers and Market Foreclosure," *Brookings Papers on Economic Activity: Microeconomics* (1990): 205–276; Thomas G. Krattenmaker and Steven C. Salop, "Anticompetitive Exclusion: Raising Rivals' Costs to Achieve Power over Price," *Yale Law Journal* 96 (1986): 209–293; and Riordan and Salop, "Evaluating Vertical Mergers."

27. *U.S. and State of Connecticut v. Healthcare Partners et al.*, U.S. District Court for the District of Connecticut, Civil Action No. 3:95-CV-01946.

28. A. Douglas Melamed, "Exclusionary Vertical Agreements," address before the American Bar Association, Antitrust Section, Washington, D.C., April 2, 1998.

29. William J. Lynk and Michael A. Morrisey, "The Economic Basis of Hyde: Are Market Power and Hospital Exclusive Contracts Related?" *Journal of Law and Economics* 30 (1987): 403.

30. Frech and Danger, "Exclusive Contracts."

31. *U.S. v. Woman's Hospital Foundation and Woman's Physician Health Organization*, Civil Action No. 96-389-B-M2 (U.S. District Court for the Middle District of Louisiana). Complaint filed April 23, 1996.

32. The DOJ found clear evidence of Woman's Hospital's anticompetitive motives. For example, Woman's Hospital first attempted to keep General Health out of the market for inpatient obstetrical services by threatening not to contract with General Health's managed care plan. Immediately after General Health's announcement of its intent to build the new hospital, Woman's Hospital announced its intention to stop contracting with the local managed care plan owned by General Health. Then in private negotiations with General Health, Woman's Hospital offered to continue contracting with General Health's local managed care plan in return for General Health's agreement not to provide inpatient obstetrical services for the next 5 to 7 years. The DOJ also found evidence that the Strategic Planning Committee of Woman's Hospital's Board of Directors had explored various competitive responses that would avoid Woman's Hospital's "deep-discounting every delivery" to keep women from selecting the new hospital rather than Woman's Hospital.

33. U.S. District Court for the S.D. of Miss., Western Division, Civil Action No. 5:96-CV-108Br(S).

34. *Modern Healthcare* (January 4, 1999): 2–3 and 12.

35. Economists say that vertical foreclosure in the market for hospital services occurs when nonvertically-related hospitals' opportunities to deal with the vertically-related physicians are foreclosed.

36. The 1996 DOJ complaint mentioned at the beginning of this subsection did not address the issue of entry barriers into the market for OB/GYN physician services, and thus whether General Health Inc. could recruit physician-entrants (OB/GYNs) to practice at its new hospital. Without entry barriers into the market for OB/GYN physician services, Woman's Hospital's strategy could not be anticompetitive in the long run.

37. Nos. 95-1965, 95-2140 (7th Cir. 1995).

38. In addition, BC/BS charged that the use of MFN clauses in physicians' contracts reduced competition in the HMO market.

39. It is unclear what motivates provider$_y$ to sign an exclusive deal that enhances insurer$_y$'s market power and thus may result in lower profits for provider$_y$.

40. Economists say that vertical foreclosure in the market for insurance occurs when nonvertically-related insurers' opportunities to deal with the vertically-related providers are foreclosed.

41. William M. Sage, "Judge Posner's RFP: Antitrust Law and Managed Care," *Health Affairs* 16 (1997): 44–61.

42. *Modern Healthcare* (February 1, 1999): 44.

43. 986 F.2d 589 (1st Cir. 1993).

44. However, the opinion is of limited precedential value because the plaintiff had pursued the case solely on a *per se* theory of liability, and therefore did not offer evidence in support of a rule of reason challenge. Christine A. Varney, "Efficiency Justifications in Hospital Mergers and Vertical Integration Concerns," prepared remarks before the Health Care Antitrust Forum, Chicago, May 25, 1995.

45. In this case a hospital challenged BC/BS's proposed termination of its participating provider status under the BC/BS plan. The BC/BS termination of this hospital coincided with the hospital's integration with a competing health plan. Specifically, Hospital Corporation of America bought both the hospital and the health plan.

46. 663 F. Supp. 1360 (D. Kan. 1987).

47. Frances Miller, "Vertical Restraints and Powerful Health Insurers: Exclusionary Conduct Masquerading as Managed Care?" *Law and Contemporary Problems* 51 (1988): 195–236.

48. John D. Blum, "The Evolution of Physician Credentialing and Managed Care Selective Contracting," *American Journal of Law and Medicine* 22 (1996).

49. 996 F.2d 537 (2d Cir.), 791 F. Supp. 956 (N.D.N.Y. 1992), cert. denied, 510 U.S. 947 (1993).

50. According to economists, vertical foreclosure in the market for physician or hospital services occurs when nonvertically-related providers' opportunities to deal with the vertically-related insurer are foreclosed.

51. For a review of these cases see Anthony J. Dennis, "Most Favored Nation Contract Clauses under the Antitrust Laws," *University of Dayton Law Review* 20 (1995): 821–854.

52. Ibid.

53. Robert E. Bloch, Scott P. Perlman, and Luke Levasseur, "Most Favored Nation Clauses in Contracts between Health Care Networks and Providers: The Search for Practical Antitrust Guidance," *Antitrust Report* (September 1996): 5.

54. U.S. Court of Appeals, First Circuit, No. 88-1851 (August 21, 1989).

55. *Ocean State,* 692 F. Supp. at 71.

56. 65 F.3d 1406, 1415 (7th Cir. 1995).

57. At 1415.

58. The fees that Ocean State paid to physicians were comparable to the fees paid by BC/BS; however, Ocean State put physicians at risk with its 20 percent withhold contingent on the profitability of the HMO. In 1986 the HMO kept the 20 percent withhold of physician fees, effectively lowering physician reimbursement levels. For physicians participating in both the BC/BS and the Ocean State plans, under the MFN clause fees from BC/BS could also be reduced 20 percent. Lawrence G. Goldberg and Warren Greenberg, "The Response of the Dominant

Firm to Competition: The Ocean State Case," *Health Care Management Review* 20 (1995): 65–74.

59. Bloch, Perlman, and Levasseur, "Most Favored Nation Clauses."

60. For reviews of economists' thinking on MFN clauses, see Jonathan B. Baker, "Vertical Restraints with Horizontal Consequences: Competitive Effects of 'Most-Favored-Customer' Clauses," *Antitrust Law Journal* 64 (1996): 517–534, and Martin Gaynor and Deborah Haas-Wilson, "Vertical Relations in Health Care Markets," in *Managed Care and Changing Health Care Markets* ed. Michael A. Morrisey (Washington, D.C.: AEI Press, 1998).

61. Jonathan B. Baker, "Vertical Restraints among Hospitals, Physicians and Health Insurers That Raise Rivals' Costs: A Case Study of *Reazin v. BC/BS of Kansas and Ocean State Physicians Health Plan v. BC/BS of R.I.*," *American Journal of Law and Medicine* 14 (1989): 168.

62. Goldberg and Greenberg, "The Response of the Dominant Firm."

63. Carol Gentry, "R.I. Doctors Win Round over Fees," *Wall Street Journal*, September 2, 1998, NE1.

64. *U.S. v. Delta Dental of Rhode Island*, DC RI, CA 96 113 (filed February 29, 1996).

65. *U.S. v. Delta Dental Plan of Arizona*, 1995-1 Trade Cas. (CCH) 71,048 (D. Ariz. 1995).

66. *U.S. v. Oregon Dental Service*, 1995-2 Trade Cas. (CCH) 71,062 (N.D. Cal. 1995).

67. Kristen Hallam, "Ohio Insurer Signs Antitrust Decree," *Modern Healthcare* 28 (1998): 14.

## *Conclusion*

1. Almarin Phillips, "Antitrust Principles and Regulatory Needs," in *The Antitrust Impulse*, Vol. 2, ed. Theodore P. Kovaleff (New York: M. E. Sharpe, 1994).

2. On the other hand, there are few safeguards against overly lenient enforcement agencies. Private parties may pick up some of the slack.

3. A related study, specifically a study estimating the impact of the 1990 merger between two of the three hospitals in Santa Cruz county in California (a merger that would have been challenged by the FTC had the FTC received prior notification of the transaction), found a 30 percent higher post-merger price increase by the merged hospital, relative to other peer hospitals in California during the same time period. Michael G. Vita and Seth Sacher, "The Competitive Effects of Not-For Profit Hospital Mergers: A Case Study," *Federal Trade Commission Working Papers* no. 226, Washington, D.C., 1999.

4. Whether a particular market is characterized by natural monopoly conditions can change over time. Technological innovations can change firms' production methods and costs of production, and thus the extent to which a firm is a natural monopoly. Even without technological innovation, increases or decreases in consumer demand over time can change a natural monopoly to a competitive market.

5. See William Baumol, "On the Proper Cost Tests for Natural Monopoly in a Multiproduct Industry," *American Economic Review* 67 (1977): 809–822, and William Baumol, John Panzar, and Robert Willig, *Contestable Markets and the Theory of Industry Structure* (New York: Harcourt Brace Jovanovich, 1982).

6. American Hospital Association, *Hospital Statistics* 2001 (Chicago: Health-care Source), and *www.va.gov/About_VA/orgs/VHA/index.htm.*

7. Jean-Jacques Laffont and Jean Tirole, *A Theory of Incentives in Procurement and Regulation* (Cambridge, Mass.: MIT Press, 1993).

8. W. Kip Viscusi, John Vernon, and Joseph Harrington, *Economics of Regulation and Antitrust* (Cambridge, Mass.: MIT Press, 2000).

9. *Modern Healthcare* (August 20, 2001).

10. *Modern Healthcare* (September 4, 2000): 2 and 16; *Modern Healthcare* (April 30, 2001): 19.

11. Although the federal agencies may be taking a break from challenging hospital mergers, they are not neglecting their other enforcement duties in health care. Between 1997 and 2002 the FTC performed 16 enforcement actions and participated in 37 substantial investigations of health care providers, including hospitals, physician organizations, and medical equipment manufacturers. During the same time period the DOJ performed 13 enforcement actions and participated in 47 substantial investigations in the health care industry. However, only four of the FTC's actions and investigations since 1997 have involved hospitals. Mark Taylor, "Antitrust Cops May Get Backup," *Modern Healthcare* (May 6, 2002): 12–13.

# Index of Organizations

# Subject Index

235